LIONS 77

LIONS 77

On tour in New Zealand

Keith Quinn

EYRE METHUEN

First published in New Zealand 1977 by
Methuen New Zealand Ltd, 238 Wakefield Street, Wellington

Published simultaneously in Great Britain by
Eyre Methuen Ltd, 11 New Fetter Lane, London EC4P 4EE

© 1977 Methuen New Zealand Ltd

ISBN 0 413 38850 6

Printed in Great Britain by
Cox & Wyman Ltd, Fakenham, Norfolk

Contents

Acknowledgements

The author and publishers would like to thank the following for supplying photographs for use in this book:

Peter Bush (Plates 1-4, 6, 9, 12, 14, 16, 17, 19-25, 27-30)

Christchurch Press (Plates 5 and 11)

Ian Mackley (Plates 7, 8, 10)

Rugby News (Plate 13)

The Dominion (Plates 15 and 26)

New Zealand Herald (Plate 18)

THE 1977 BRITISH ISLES RUGBY TEAM
TO NEW ZEALAND AND FIJI

Manager: Mr George Burrell (Scotland)
Assistant Manager-Coach: Mr John Dawes (Wales)

Fullbacks
Andy Irvine (Scotland)
Bruce Hay (Scotland)

Wingers
John Williams (Wales)
Gareth Evans (Wales)
Peter Squires (England)
Elgan Rees (Wales)

Centres
Mike Gibson (Ireland)
Ian McGeechan (Scotland)
Steve Fenwick (Wales)
David Burcher (Wales)

Fly-halves
Phil Bennett (Wales—Captain)
John Bevan (Wales)

Halfbacks
Douglas Morgan (Scotland)
Brynmor Williams (Wales)
Alun Lewis (Wales)

Number Eight Forwards
Willie Duggan (Ireland)
Jeff Squire (Wales)

Flankers
Terry Cobner (Wales)
Derek Quinnell (Wales)
Tony Neary (England)
Trevor Evans (Wales)

Lock Forwards
Moss Keane (Ireland)
Gordon Brown (Scotland)
Nigel Horton (England)
Bill Beaumont (England)
Allan Martin (Wales)

Prop Forwards
Graham Price (Wales)
Phil Orr (Ireland)
Clive Williams (Wales)
Fran Cotton (England)
Charlie Faulkner (Wales)

Hookers
Bobby Windsor (Wales)
Peter Wheeler (England)

1
The Bennett & Dawes Rugby Company

It was no fun to be a touring rugby player in New Zealand between the months of May and August 1977.

In that time, unaccustomed and depressingly high rates of rainfall tumbled from the Kiwi skies, falling invariably in the towns and cities where the 1977 British Isles rugby team were playing their twenty-five tour matches. The weather played a big part in the nature of this tour and the development of the group character of the thirty-three players, manager and coach who made up the British Lions party.

As the rain fell, especially in the second half of the tour, so did the standards of play. From a lively start in the first match and an unbeaten run of eight games, the level of performance rarely peaked again.

The team became depressed by the weather and their self-imposed isolation, and were despondent when they left New Zealand, beaten 3-1 in a closely-fought test series with the All Blacks. This was, and will be judged, I am sure, one of rugby history's tragedies.

In the team, captained by Phil Bennett of Wales, managed by George Burrell of Scotland, and coached by John Dawes of Wales, were some of the most exciting rugby players in the world today. Men like Bennett himself, Andy Irvine, John J. Williams, Mike Gibson, Bobby Windsor, Gordon Brown, Derek Quinnell and others were widely-known and respected stars before they arrived in New Zealand, to show their merits on a full scale tour. Television replays of Home Internationals had brought these individuals and their

brilliance into the living-rooms of every New Zealand rugby sup-
porter.
Why then was the tour, in playing and social terms, not rated a
success? Why were these Lions, so brimful of brilliance, eventually
judged as just another team — to rest somewhere in history between
the high standards set by the Lions of 1971 in New Zealand and
1974 in South Africa, who were vastly honoured, and the low standing of the 1966 team in New Zealand, who almost lost as many
matches as they won?

On Sunday 14 August 1977, Air New Zealand flight 546 trundled
out to the end of the runway at Auckland International Airport. On
board among the 150 or so passengers bound for Suva were the
members of the 1977 British Isles rugby team, which had just completed its three month tour of New Zealand. During that time the
team played at eighteen different venues and met New Zealand's
national team, the All Blacks, in a four-test series.
The flight paused at the end of the runway. Seatbelts were already
fastened and cigarettes extinguished, everything checked and made
ready to go. Slowly the DC-8 moved into the first forward thrust that
would accelerate to lift-off.
In the passenger cabin the British Lions sat shoulder to shoulder,
taking up nearly six rows, sitting six across. They looked tired, worn,
battle-weary. It had been a long tour. Conversation stopped as the jet
engines increased their roar and drove the massive frame of the
plane into its high-speed charge down the runway.
The plane bumped and lurched, gained speed and lifted, and the
power of the engines in full thrust was lost behind a louder noise.
The thirty-five men of the British Lions gave, in unison, a massive
and prolonged cheer. Not the cheer of relief at making a successful
take-off, but a roar of approval and delight, one of total ecstasy at
being homeward bound at long, long last, out of the defeats and
dreariness of the New Zealand winter.
The depressing run of bad weather had made New Zealand a
dispiriting place. Repeated rainy days and soaked pitches meant that
men no longer relished outdoor activity. The indoor activity that was
the alternative, invariably built around their hotel life, proved no
substitute, only serving to depress the team even more.
But to suggest, as team manager George Burrell did at tour's end,
that the weather was the major influence for his team's lack of
popularity off the field and lack of success on it, was a judgement far
short of reality.

A harsh fact of modern day values is that a losing sporting team is not a successful team. No matter how close the test matches are, if your side is not ahead on the scoreboard at the end, then you have been beaten. 'Moral victories' do not apply in modern-day Rugby Union.

The Lions came within a smidgeon of winning the test series. The first test win, 16-12 to New Zealand, came from an opportunist breakaway score by the All Black winger, Grant Batty. The second test, won by the British Isles 13-9, could have swung New Zealand's way had Lyn Jaffray, their second five-eighth, held a bobbling late pass and scored beneath the posts. The third test, won by New Zealand 19-7, looks the clearest-cut victory of the series but was in fact a match where forward possession was so dominated by the Lions they *should* have won by a street. The fourth test, where the win went New Zealand's way by 10 to 9, could well have been a British victory had not a Lions forward, Willie Duggan by name, attempted at the end a solo try where a continuing scrum-shove by his team would have made victory a certainty.

For John Dawes to say at tour's end 'We only were beaten once but lost three times in the test matches', is a sentiment of old-world charm that has no place in modern sporting theory, where victory is the only winner and the only winner is victory. A moral victory, as the Lions could claim with some justification from the third and fourth tests, where they won so much ball but could not profit from it, does not count, as they themselves would say, as a 'W on the record card'.

Using Dawes' logic, the All Blacks beat the Springboks in 1976, and Hitler won the Second World War. Assumptions like these are naive in the extreme. For the right reasons or not, winning today is all-important. Historians and statisticians of the future will not see, as they view the cold hard facts, the mud or injuries or runaway tries or dominated possession. They will see only the results. And the 1977 Lions, because the results went New Zealand's way 3 to 1, will not be judged a successful team on the field.

Let it be said that this team had its days of glory during the course of its tour, days when the Lions gave every hope of sustaining the winning streak of British Rugby in the 1970s.

Their eight tries in the Masterton mud, in the 41-13 win over Wairarapa-Bush, were classically constructed wet-weather moves. Their brilliance at Taumarunui, in their 60 to 9 victory over King Country-Wanganui, did not result from easy tries against an easy team. The individual skills that day, particularly from Phil Bennett, the brilliant fullback Andy Irvine, and the speedy left winger J. J. Williams, were outstanding. Their determination to succeed in the second test was rugby worthy of the highest admiration, and their fightback to gain ascendency against the New Zealand Maoris was a sporting spectacle of high drama and great merit.

There were truly top-ranking features about the team's play. They possessed a forward division far stronger in scrummaging and mauling techniques than any combination of the best of their New Zealand opponents.

There were giant lessons for New Zealanders in goal-kicking techniques. On a rating basis only Auckland's Steve Watt, Southland's Brian McKechnie and Wellington's Richard Cleland, from all the New Zealand kicking talent seen, would make it into a Top Ten ranking list. The Lions would fill all the other places. Douglas Morgan, Phil Bennett, Andy Irvine, Mike Gibson, Steve Fenwick and Alan Martin all possessed easier, more relaxed and more successful kicking styles than most of the New Zealanders.

They also had individuals among their backs who were in the highest order of British traditions in running back play. To the team's eternal discredit will be their decline in ability to employ the shining talents of Andy Irvine and Phil Bennett. These two began the tour with a brilliant style that is seldom seen in New Zealand, or anywhere else in the rugby world; sadly the supporting back play did not sustain this brilliance. In the later matches Bennett, shackled by the captaincy and heavy-hearted through homesickness, was a hacker and a has-been compared with his normal self; Irvine, back at fullback, became neglected, forgotten and ignored.

The heavy inroads that the captaincy made on Bennett's playing qualities proved, in the end, that he was the wrong man for the job. A quiet, withdrawn person from a tiny Welsh town, Bennett had insufficient outward personality to be a hit with New Zealanders as, say Karl Mullen was with the 1950 team, or Dawie de Villiers was with the 1965 Springboks, or Willie-John McBride was with the 1974 British team in South Africa. Bennett's aftermatch speeches were mechanically pleasant, saying all the right things about 'my lads' and 'your lads' and the referees, but containing little that was memorable or witty.

A very human person who suffered the torments of losses and homesickness so much that it could be read on his face, and more with each passing day, Bennett might have got away with being a nominal social captain had his leadership on the field been better.

Unfortunate it was for the Lions that their captain was also, potentially, their top player. He had the reputation as a dazzler from the fly-half position, a wonderfully deft sidestepper and runner, and a goal kicker of world repute. Eventually the burden of leadership got to Bennett's game and no matter how well he may have led them in the dressing-room with team talks and the like, he fell seriously away from assurance on the field.

Terry Cobner, a driving hard-nosed flank forward, with a no-nonsense approach to rugby, would have been my choice as captain. He was typical of about a dozen members of this team's forward players, who scented victory at each game's kick-off and who were willing to die for the cause.

If Cobner had have been captain I believe that would have un-chained Bennett and allowed him to play with a free rein; accordingly the backline would have been freed to attack with true Lions flair, instead of their fruitless crabbing and crashing of the tests.

The lack of brilliance in many of the other backs lowered the tenor of performance in match after match towards the end. These British backs of 1977 could not possibly have been the natural descendants of the dashing striders who had worn the same colours to New Zealand in 1950, 1959, 1966 or 1971. Their mediocrity proved a major influence in the way New Zealand approached the tactical playing of the test matches.

As the coach of this team was John Dawes, it is at his door that the test-loss charge-sheet must be laid. At no stage in tactical rugby matters did he appear to implement a plan to beat the All Blacks that capitalised on the gains of his team's greatest strength, the forward pack.

Dawes' inclination at all times to play 'quality rugby' (his term), using backs and forwards equally, was an admirable attempt to allow his men to express themselves with flair on the playing-field. That he could not devise scoring attacks and counters for his non-penetrative test backline showed a lack of rugby resource on his part. The tactical blame, as coach, is his.

It was a fortuitous coincidence for the All Blacks that the decline in performance by the British backs occurred at precisely the same time as their New Zealand opposites were riding high. New Zealand had a backline in 1977 that was its most potent for many seasons. The benefits of painstakingly developing attacking talents and atti-tudes in young players — like the now-mature Robertson and Bryan Williams — paid off handsomely for Jack Gleeson, John Stewart and Eric Watson, the New Zealand selectors.

For once New Zealand was on top through the backs. Bruce Robertson was in such powerful form that had he played the second test the All Blacks could have won the series 4-nil; but a statement like that is only falling into supposition again.

What was not supposition was the determined commitment the New Zealand selectors made in this series to use their backline in a running manner. The shame was that a serious decline in New Zealand forward standards failed to win them much possession to exploit through the backs.

But on any rugby tour where the spotlight of attention from radio, television and newspapers focuses on the every activity of a touring team, there are other attainments that are needed to be won to call a tour a success. Off-the-field activity, undertaken with friendliness and politeness, is nearly as important to a team's image as winning. In that regard the disfavour this team fell into with New Zealand rugby people — players, officials and followers — may well be what some people remember them most for.

The high-handed manner with which well-meaning hospitality was avoided by the team must reflect on the management. George Burrell seemed unconcerned that his players were not mixing socially with New Zealanders. The reputation they soon won for not turning up to functions or for keeping to themselves when they did, could have been rectified with one word from the manager. If he ever advocated 'the natives are friendly' approach, it was certainly not acted upon by the players.

This lack of discipline and, may I say, good manners was never more evident than in the hours following the Lions' test victory at Christchurch. The Linwood Rugby Club laid on a dance for both teams at their clubrooms. The All Blacks, hardly in the mood for socialising after the bitterness of defeat, turned up en masse and within the restraints of their sad day's work, appeared to enjoy them-selves. A bus was sent to the Lions' hotel but it left later, completely empty. Even in their triumphant moments the Lions had no interest in the company of their opponents, nor obligation towards those who wished to honour and entertain them.

The shame was that, individually, separated from the team en-clave, the personnel of this Lions party were splendid examples of young British manhood. Who could forget such characters as Gordon Brown, a gentle Scot with a delightful sense of pleasantry? Or Brynmor Williams, seemingly so shy yet possessed of the warm friendliness of the Welsh valleys? Or Mike Gibson, the seasoned traveller, still keen to listen patiently to those who just wanted to pump his hand and say, 'thanks for coming again'. Or Peter Squires, the Englishman with the dashing good looks and winning smile! Aye, the 'lads' were great — good blokes, as we New Zealanders say.

But somehow, somewhere, this Lions team came adrift from the people of the country they were visiting. They set up social barriers, withdrew into themselves, and from their introspective aspect gazed out at New Zealanders and their ways. They were an impossible group to have fun with, as most of their opponents found at aftermatch functions. They simply preferred their own company. Reports of social misbehaviour spread quickly and the team's reputation as bad mixers grew.

This was a great shame. In those early days a stern word from Burrell could have prevented the later reference the team earned as 'louts' and 'animals' from two New Zealand newspapers. I am satisfied that they were not any of those things, except that stories of excessive hotel revelry could not be denied, and the irresponsibility of some reflected badly on the whole.

The Lions felt the pain of the press barbs directed at their behaviour and were soon aware they were not popular. Their withdrawal from social intermingling continued till they were not unlike the common seaside shellcrab; they came out to see what the environs offered outside, found they didn't like them and withdrew again into themselves.

Intertwined with these feelings toward New Zealanders and the dreadful weather, were the pangs of homesickness that came as a result of their isolation. The final straw was their on-the-field rugby which could have salvaged the tour had it been at all successful in terms of results.

Alas for the Lions, a final, determined bid for the fourth test was negated by acts of indiscipline late in the game. At that moment, the game, the series, and the tour were lost.

I feel that had this Lions team had better management, better coaching strategy, better captaincy and better team discipline and sociability, the tour would have been a success. But then am I not falling into the same plethora of hypothetical theory by which John Dawes judged his team's test efforts? I think I am.

To get the true story of this tour one must go back to the results. New Zealand: three tests, the Lions: one. The scoreboard speaks for itself. The tour was not a success for the Lions because they did not win and because they did not allow the public of New Zealand to like them.

2
The Lions Prepare

Even before the 1977 Lions left London, New Zealand fans and followers knew what they were in for, in anticipating a visit by a team of thirty individuals representing the best players available in England, Ireland, Scotland and Wales.

They knew it would be a lot harder to turn back the Lions' challenge than it had been in earlier times. In the old days local rugby folk used to watch British rugby teams play in New Zealand with an air of almost quaint amusement. Trying to beat the All Blacks was an impossibility for them, we Kiwis used to think. The British teams of 1930, 1950, 1959 and 1966 which toured New Zealand were laden with attractive backs and powerful forwards but the results were usually the same. The All Blacks won most of the tests, almost as of right. The Lions, in those early days, won little else. Except friends, that is.

But 1971 changed all that. In the winter of that year, the fourth Lions team to New Zealand, led by John Dawes, stormed New Zealand, and to the shock of all, perhaps including themselves, won the test series.

It was a defeat New Zealanders found devilishly hard to accept. It stuck in the craw, because it had been the Kiwi way to regard Lions teams as having little chance of winning against the All Black myth of giant forward packs and big-booted fullbacks. Those of us who watched, revelled in the reflected glory of continually beating the 'bloody poms'. (Welsh, Scots, English and Irish were usually lumped in together for this — the ultimate and kindly generalisation.)

With Dawes' captaincy, and shrewdly and brilliantly guided by subtle, expert managers, the 1971 Lions defeated, but more importantly, outsmarted the 1971 All Blacks.

Coming as it did for New Zealand rugby, straight after a three-one defeat in the 1970 tests in South Africa, and after fifteen All Blacks had retired, 1971 has assumed its place among one of the worst ever years for the game in New Zealand. No one, with perhaps the exception of Peter Whiting on his retirement, has had the courage to admit that the All Black test teams of 1971 were woefully weak and devoid of any great strength. 'Our backs that year,' Whiting told a radio audience in May, 'were very poor.'

He was right. The circumstances of facing such a strong Lions team that year, after the sobering results of 1970 and with the drop-out rate so high, makes that year a low-water point for New Zealand rugby. From there, thankfully the tide has risen again.

What lessons Dawes' team taught the rugby game in New Zealand! For a start, they were so solidly prepared, in terms of research, that they knew almost every trick New Zealand had before that trick was played. The team abounded with talent. Barry John, Mike Gibson, David Duckham, John Bevan, Gerald Davies, Mervyn Davies, Willie-John McBride, Ray McLoughlin and Ian McLauchlan are names now much revered in New Zealand. They were the most glittering of a team of stars.

Yet those individuals belied this team's greatest asset. They were, in the full meaning of the word, a team. They could be beaten — they lost the second test and drew the fourth — but they played their rugby with an ease and confidence that was a lesson to the All Blacks. The New Zealand approach, in its traditional way, was grimness and tightness. The other fourteen All Blacks were mood duplicates of their captain, Colin Meads. I do not mean that as a criticism of Meads, for his determination and talent meant much to the re-building New Zealand team. But the Lions showed New Zealanders that there were other modus operandi that could be used in a team's approach to a test match. The Lions were chockablock full of their own conviction. A confidence in themselves bred from a happy base. Their team spirit and their unity instilled within them the assurance that they were the better side. As they most definitely were. They relaxed their way through their matches, mostly always winning, but always preparing and playing the game at a far higher intellectual plane than the teams they met. The opposition in New Zealand relied mostly on the traditional rip, snort and bust tactics that had been so successful for All Blacks in the previous twenty years. The change of attitude that the Lions of 1971 showed New

Zealanders, was picked up by J. J. Stewart, Jack Gleeson and several others, and incorporated into the All Blacks' approach within the next four years. In that way, these men paid Carwyn James, John Dawes and Co. their greatest tribute.

In 1971 I was a 'cub' reporter, if you like, with the NZBC in Auckland and therefore not assigned to cover the tour, as has been my honour and privilege in 1977. However, clever manipulation of annual leave, an understanding wife and some film assignments for Northern Television meant I was able to see, in all, thirteen of that team's twenty-four matches. Who could forget the many thrill-packed moments of those three months. My personal memories are of Barry John's brilliance at Waikato; J. P. R. Williams falling on the ball, a courageous act, in the face of some thundering and well-directed North Auckland boots; Geoff Evans, the replacement lock, charging in for a try against Auckland; Gareth Edwards' bursting running in the third test at Wellington; Willie-John McBride carried off the field shoulder-high at Palmerston North; and the elation of J. P. R. Williams at dropping a goal in the final and vital stages of the fourth test. There are many more, of course. Those Lions were a great side. All of which meant that Phil Bennett's team of 1977 had the stamp of greatness on the previous team to match, or better, before they could create an image in their own right.

In that regard, Bennett's team had been burdened with disadvantage before the tour started.

The word that applies is circumstances. It was simply circumstances that forced two of the great players of the 1971 British team in New Zealand and of the 1974 British team to South Africa to declare themselves unavailable for the trip. J. P. R. Williams was, at 28, right at the peak of his powers as a fullback; his impending appointment as registrar at the University of Wales Hospital in Cardiff and his wife's pregnancy were the factors which he ruled as having higher priority than three and a half months playing football in New Zealand. Edwards' situation was much the same. He decided a career was more important than touring again, and who could blame him? For the last ten years he had played rugby almost twelve months a year. Both had achieved all they could from the game, except perhaps a higher heap of accolades had they toured New Zealand.

But their standards in two such vital positions, fullback and half-back, were of such magnitude that anyone else in those places would be regarded almost as a weakness, a player to be probed by New Zealand teams. The men with the task of trying to match the peerless standards set by J. P. R. Williams and Gareth Edwards were brave indeed. They were Bruce Hay and Andy Irvine at fullback, and Brynmor Williams and Douglas Morgan at halfback.

Hay and Irvine had been seen in New Zealand before. They had been the fullbacks for Scotland in 1975. Hay from Boroughmuir was not a regular international player. It was his lot to play second string to Irvine in Scotland, and on selection for the Lions, it was expected that that situation would remain the same. Irvine was to be the key man.

While Hay was known and respected in New Zealand for some courageous defensive play while here with the Scots, his attacking talents were nothing like those possessed by Irvine. Irvine was a flyer, Hay a rock, in their approach to playing the fullback's game. J. P. R. Williams was a rock and a flyer rolled into one, and then some.

Still, Hay deserved more than to be dubbed 'just a long stop' as he was on a TV2 programme just before the tour, by John Reason, reputedly one of Great Britain's best-informed rugby critics.

Certainly it was obvious early on in the tour that Andy Irvine was to be one of the major contributing factors in any success this Lions' team might aspire to in back play. On selection of the team in March *The Times* ran a personality piece by their expert, Peter West, headlined 'Filling the Boots of a Rugby Giant', which underlined how great a challenge Irvine faced in New Zealand. 'Whatever he achieves,' wrote West 'his performance will be compared with that of John P. R. Williams, the greatest player of that position in the modern era, who won such golden opinions on the 1971 tour. It will be difficult to follow a man whose forthright tackling, invulnerable catching and galloping surges, whether with ball in hand or in pursuit of his own kicks downfield, have made him something of a legend in his time and, not infrequently, an apparent candidate for a posthumous VC.'

West then added 'Rocklike consistency against the high or rolling ball is one of the prime requisites for a fullback in international rugby and never more so than in New Zealand. No one questions Irvine's courage, but the suspicion has persisted throughout his career at the top that this is the one area of his game from which opponents, sooner or later, may win a bonus.'

New Zealanders knew this. They had been most critical and sceptical viewers of Irvine during Scotland's tour of New Zealand in 1975. His play, whether he appeared at fullback or on the wing, was of the highest calibre. But the question was raised, in a country where courageous fullbacks in the Fergie McCormick mould were a dime a dozen, as to the size of Irvine's heart in rugby situations where big hearts were needed. It was in the watery, wet test match at Eden Park at the end of the Scottish tour that Irvine had been truly tested. Duncan Robertson, the All Black first five-eighth had, that day, hoisted the ball towards Irvine no matter where he stood. These were no ordinary kicks and it was no ordinary day for catching kicks of an extraordinary nature. Several inches of water covered the pitch and the ball was slippery and wet. Robertson, an expert in matters like these, sent the ball so high it must have been most difficult to see in the darkening skies and the low cloud. The altitude that these kicks reached gave the New Zealand forwards time to present a thundering presence to the Scotsman who stood underneath. And most of the time that day it was Irvine who was required to make the catch. He had originally been selected as a wing but when Bruce Hay had his arm broken, Irvine had shifted back to fullback.

The New Zealanders' tactic of punting a high ball to Irvine was clearly directed at a knowledge that had preceded him on tour. It was widely understood that his reputation was shakey under the high ball in circumstances where pressures were high. Irvine, on that slippery day, did not do well. The final score, a 24-nil against his team, was due in no small part to Irvine's unease under the All Black mortars.

No amount of brilliant running and solid catching, displayed to New Zealand fans via television replays of his later fine performances in Great Britain, would convince local people that he was of the same quality and quantity as J. P. R. Williams.

The halfback situation was simpler. Replacing Gareth Edwards was a difficult enough task but it was made easier for Brynmor Williams, at selection time the reported number one, because he had no previous form for New Zealanders to consider.

He was almost the complete unknown, outside of Great Britain. He had made the choice, years before, to stay faithful to the Cardiff Rugby Club, even though that meant spending many seasons playing in the shadow of Edwards himself.

Williams was a 24-year-old school-teacher from Cardigan in West Wales. Since 1972 he had been waiting to claim his rights when Edwards retired or lost form for Wales. But that never happened. Williams, in the end, achieved every honour in the game, except that of ousting Gareth Edwards. He played, with Edwards, for Cardiff. He also was a Wales 'B' International, a Barbarian and, in 1977, a Lion.

But no matter how good a reputation he brought with him, Williams and the Scotsman Douglas Morgan were in vulnerable positions in the Lions team. In the first few tour games and the early Test matches it was obvious that they were going to be put to the test by New Zealand teams. There was almost a sense of relief that Edwards was not in the team, as it meant that home teams would not need to be as vigilant near the scrums or as closely attentive to stopping his runs now that there were 'lesser' players as the Lions' halfback.

The third key player, at selection time and prior to the tour starting was obviously the captain, Phil Bennett.

At home in Felinfoel, a tiny west Wales village, where Bennett had been raised as a boy, there was obvious delight at his selection as the Lions leader. Throughout the rest of Great Britain his selection was accepted with general approval.

Bennett had been seen before in New Zealand — as had thirteen of the 1977 team — with either Lions, Scottish or Irish teams. He had come with Wales in 1969 but on that tour was an insignificant player. He appeared only once, against Taranaki, and after that sat in the stands acting as emergency in case the great Barry John should do himself a mischief.

I recall well Bennett's game with Taranaki. In the 9-all draw he had played exceptionally. It was his first full game for Wales, an honour that is not well known at Rugby Park, New Plymouth. He displayed the twinkling elusiveness that is his hall-mark today, and kicked adeptly. I can remember remarking how sad it was that such a good player had to stand so long in the wings because the man ahead of him was so good. History, of course, changed that. Barry John retired in 1972 and Bennett moved easily into the Welsh fly-half slot. There is a strong resemblance, in fact, between Bennett understudying Barry John and the situation of Brynmor Williams and Gareth Edwards.

While Britons were applauding the appointment of Bennett as captain there was more than a small degree of reservation in New Zealand. It was widely agreed that he was a brilliant runner, but before he got to run one yard in New Zealand there were many and varied theories as to how and why he would be prevented from doing that on the Lions tour.

While visiting with Jack Gleeson in Feilding, the All Black selector told me that flankers in the mould of Kevin Eveleigh, Ken Stewart, Dennis Thorn, Stuart Cron and Graham Mourie were abundant in almost every representative team in New Zealand. They were men intent solely on destroying opposition back moves at their point of inception, the fly-half. They were lightly and lithely built players, fast off the mark and sure in the tackle. 'Flankers in the United Kingdom,' Gleeson told me, 'do not work that way. There are no Eveleighs, Mouries or Stewarts over there.'

The inference was that the latitude Bennett customarily gained would not be allowed in New Zealand.

Bill Freeman, the New Zealand Rugby Union's executive director of coaching, and one of the country's best rugby judges, had a different theory on stopping Phil Bennett. In a discussion on 'Sportsnight' that was replayed on the BBC in Wales, Freeman told me: 'I would like to see Bennett involved more in trying to stop our players from doing something. Physically involve him in tackling charging forwards and therefore take the glamour out of what he is required to do on the field.'

On the same programme Tane Norton chipped in that his pet memory of Phil Bennett was his side-step out of the way of Ian Kirkpatrick as the big Poverty Bay farmer set sail for the goal-line at Cardiff's National Stadium in 1974.

The feeling of those men was that they would diminish the brilliance of Bennett, and of Irvine, by attacking their points of weakness. Such were the pressures that applied before the tour started, to the key players and their positions.

There were other imponderables, pre-tour ones that is. Much interest was placed upon the high percentage of Welshmen in the tour party. At selection time, there were sixteen. Questions were raised as to whether or not the Lions could be anything else but a Welsh team in stance and planning, as the coach, captain and fourteen other players were from that country. Even prominent Welshmen were critical. Carwyn James, coach of the Lions in New Zealand in 1971 and now a writer and commentator, wrote that, 'Wales hardly played well enough in their successful quest for the triple crown to warrant such a high number being picked. . . . The influence of John Dawes weighed heavily on the selection.'

The English writer, Chris Lánder, supported that; writing in the *New Zealand Truth* he said 'John Dawes clearly got the side he wanted and emerged as the strong man behind pre-tour policy;' while in *The Times* Peter West's story was head-lined 'Lions Party more Welsh than Ever.'

The collective concern of the critics was that the party might be split into nationalistic factions; the Welsh, having the biggest faction, would run the side. It had happened before with British Isles' teams and there had been times when team spirit and the will to do well on the field had been seriously impaired by these divisions. The 1966 team in New Zealand had been bad in that regard as, I am told, was the 1968 team which went to South Africa. No such problems had affected the Lions team which toured New Zealand in 1971. Outwardly, they looked a harmonious unit. In their case the wisdom of their manager, Dr Doug Smith, and the coach, Carwyn James, never allowed the problem, if indeed it existed, to manifest itself on the playing field. Harmony within Lions teams seemed to breed success.

In terms of man power for winning matches, reaction to those chosen to tour New Zealand in 1977 was generally favourable. Though men like J. P. R. Williams, Gareth Edwards, Mervyn Davies, Gerald Davies, Peter Dixon and Fergus Slattery may have all been included in the team had they been available, their absence was far more easily absorbed by Bennett's men than in previous Lions teams.

In the past six years the four British countries had achieved a broader spread of playing strengths to draw on at the highest levels. This had come about as the result of advanced thinking on the game at all levels by a type of planning not previously seen in Great Britain or anywhere else in the world.

Men like Carwyn James, Ray Williams and Syd Millar led the way. They introduced a far more effective tactical approach than has, for example, ever been seen in New Zealand.

The mood was carried on, in the years after the wheel of success in New Zealand in 1971, by coaches, both amateur and professional. The result was that all the advances in rugby techniques and planning that had proved successful in the nineteen-seventies were the product of either England, Ireland, Scotland or Wales. Their playing standards have gone ahead, their international records show that, and so too have the organisational aspects of coaching and drilling players and potential players.

The immediate result is, as I have already said, that the 1977 Lions team felt the loss of vital players less than Lions teams of twenty or even ten years ago.

At selection time in London John Dawes himself had said: 'The selectors have had a bonus this year in that there is an established pool of top players about, especially in tight forward positions. It means we are unlikely to pick any dummies to tour. That has happened in the past.'

Indeed it had. Perusal of the quality of the 1966 Lions team in

New Zealand showed that several were well below average New Zealand provincial standard. This did not happen in 1977. No dummies for Dawes.

No doubt there are some New Zealanders who would still say, even today, that in rugby matters 'we' have always been and will always be ahead of the British. I believe that is not so. International matches played in recent seasons in Great Britain have been of a much superior technical standard than was obtained in New Zealand provincial teams and the All Blacks. This applies mainly to back play, which had been retarded by New Zealand coaches for years. This is because, I feel, our backs have been coached to maintain a status quo situation, based on the years when they played a secondary, sometimes nearly sedentary, role to the forward power in front of them.

Only when the rewards are reaped from the new emphasis on ball skills implemented recently by Bill Freeman, in his coaching weeks, will back play in New Zealand generally match what has become the norm among British, French, South African and indeed Australian players.

Freeman told me during the season: 'No one wants to see brutality in our game any more . . . they want to see continuity in the backs and forwards, supporting play and skill to match skill.'

The All Blacks had been trying it in the J. J. Stewart era and with Jack Gleeson, but it was not yet a natural thing. Indeed, of the five test matches played by the All Blacks in 1976 (one against Ireland and four against South Africa) there was very little exceptional play evidenced by both sides. The games got by, for the spectator, by the seesawing on the scoreboard, the tenseness of the occasion and little else.

In the 'Sportsnight' rugby discussion mentioned earlier, Duncan Robertson agreed that there had been no back play in the 1976 New Zealand-South Africa test series that compared with the brilliance that had been seen on occasions in the 1976-77 Five Nations International championship.

It was Phil Bennett who climaxed that series in a brilliant manner, scoring a try that would have been inconceivable to any New Zealand team. It was in the match between Scotland and Wales at Murrayfield, which Wales needed to win to clinch the Triple Crown.

Late in the game, with the scores close, the Scots, playing way above their station, and wildly encouraged by their hoards on the terraces, sent wave upon wave of attacks at the Welsh line. All were turned back but the Scots still retained possession. Finally the ball popped loose to Steve Fenwick, the Welsh centre. In this instant a New Zealander would have kicked for touch, for it was within his own 22 metre line. Not so Steve Fenwick. He ran across the face of the 22, found that his fellow backs had dropped back in support of him and there, eighty metres from the Scots' goal-line a try was conceived. Fenwick, Gerald Davies and Bennett ran with spirit to halfway, sharing the ball among their sure hands. Perhaps Bennett's pass then to Burcher was marginally forward but who cares? In the momentum of the movement the ball was sent spinning 60 metres till Bennett himself received again from Burcher. A side-jerking twist of the body and the defence was shattered. Bennett cantered to the line for a try that rates with the best ever seen. Before 1977 that try could never have been scored by an All Black backline, but by season's end the current All Blacks were well on the way to matching that kind of prowess.

Wales won the match to clinch second place on the table. Their Triple Crown was not quite as good as France's Grand Slam.

In the television highlights of each game seen in New Zealand, Wales looked far and away the best British side, although England had a renewed appetite for winning. Forward play was of a high standard between England, Wales and France; Ireland and Scotland were less good.

Strangely, the impression of Welsh supremacy seen on television, did not seem to be a true reflection of what had actually happened. Some of the British Press contingent touring with the Lions, including Carwyn James, Chris Lander and Terry O'Connor, said that Wales had not been especially formidable. Perhaps the impression gained from television was false.

But that's of no matter. The home series was history as the Lions began their tour of New Zealand, the strengths of the Lions were well documented, the weaknesses much discussed. The only remaining question was: Was New Zealand ready for them?

3
Was New Zealand Ready?

When the 1977 Lions arrived in New Zealand they had good cause to approach the task of beating the All Blacks in a test series with some optimism. After all it was the Lions who had beaten the All Blacks in New Zealand in 1971. And if that had not surprised the doubters of world rugby, they had done the same to the Springboks in South Africa in 1974. Those two series wins ended for all time the myth that the so-called 'Rugby Crown' had permanent residency in South Africa or New Zealand. The wins also proved that the British Lions were capable of achieving a powerful team unity; no longer were they players from four nations masquerading uncomfortably in a common costume.

There was, undoubtedly, further encouragement for British rugby in the results they had read about, or seen on television, of the 1976 All Blacks in their 3-1 defeat by the Springboks in South Africa.

Chris Laidlaw, that great New Zealand halfback who has lived in France in recent years, sowed the first seeds of worry in New Zealanders' minds while in Wellington early in 1977. 'The Lions', said Laidlaw in a radio interview, 'used to come to New Zealand as underdogs, but after reading the results of the 1971, 1974 and 1976 tours again they will come to New Zealand in 1977 with the feeling of World Champions.'

Others echoed that opinion even though all had not been gloomy for All Black rugby since the Lions were winning the test series in New Zealand in 1971.

Sure, there had been changes made. Brian Lochore had given way to Colin Meads for the All Black test captaincy against John Dawes'

1971 Lions team. Ian Kirkpatrick was skipper in 1972 and 1973, and Andy Leslie had been named captain in 1974.

And there had been changes among those who aspired to coach the All Blacks. Those two stalwarts from the 'Old School', Ivan Vodanovich and Bob Duff, had controlled teams in 1971 and 1972-73. Jack Gleeson had coached and managed an All Black team that had toured New Zealand internally in 1972. But one year later came a change that was to herald the most significant development of the sport in New Zealand in the decade.

Introduced as convenor of the national selection panel, and to the coaching position that goes with the job, was John J. Stewart of Wanganui. The year was 1973, a quiet one by All Black standards. But it was Stewart, in a courageous act, who led the selection panel again in 1974 when Andy Leslie was boldly introduced as All Black captain for the tour to Australia: Stewart also picked fourteen other new caps in a team of twenty five. In terms of selection it was a sensational New Zealand touring team.

It was J. J. Stewart who inspired the confidence required by these newcomers to international play. They saw in him something more than the 'good bloke' image that previous coaches had offered. He was possessed of a dry manner, he was hard to approach and difficult to get to know (as I was to find out) but within his make-up he had the ability to draw players out of themselves. His manner, outwardly cold and colourless, possessed inner qualities which proved inspirational to Andy Leslie and the All Blacks teams from 1974 to 1976. Within those years we saw some of the most thrilling rugby ever played by the All Blacks.

Sadly, when New Zealand lost their four test series with South Africa in 1976, J. J. Stewart had to pay. He was summarily sacked as All Black coach, so that the 1977 Lions faced a new man, Jack Gleeson of Manawatu, as the planner and preparer of the New Zealand test teams.

In straight statistical terms New Zealand rugby had done well in the six years since the Lions were last in the country. The Australians of 1972 were easily beaten, their team being cruelly dubbed the 'awful Aussies'. In 1972-73 the All Blacks lost only one International out of five played in the United Kingdom and France. In 1974, the start of the Stewart-Leslie operation, Australia again took a licking — they get used to that. In the same year a most difficult assignment, a short tour of Ireland that included three effective international matches, became a triumph when the team returned home without being beaten. Scotland's short tour of New Zealand in 1975 ended swimmingly for New Zealand; the All Blacks won well on a memorably deluged and super-saturated Eden Park. The Irish of 1976 became another statistic on the All Blacks' winning ledger when their side lost out at Wellington.

That was the bright side. What was not so impressive was an alarming trend, verging upon irresponsibility and shoddiness, which sneaked into the All Blacks in 1972-73. The headgear and defiance which characterised this self-satisfaction were unpleasant and disruptive, but those who flaunted with the authority vested in the managers of the 1972-73 team were soon weeded out. Most of them returned to the All Blacks in later years, for they were all fine players. When they did they preferred to follow the traditions that go with the proud and humble wearing of one's national colours.

Had the so-called 'Mafia' of those years been permitted to retain and extend their negative attitudes to team unity, the situation may well have developed whereby future All Black teams were as unpleasant as some of the sneering, arrogant teams that Australia was sending into cricket and rugby league test matches about the same time.

Happily for our national game, J. J. Stewart's arrival on the scene begat a change of attitude that was apparent in the All Black teams of 1974-75-76. There were never better blokes. Well, mostly anyway.

Curiously, J. J. Stewart looked for all the world like one of the 'Mafia' himself. This had nothing to do with dress or deliberate intent. His bearing was gruff, his face grim and his humour grey; one never knew when to laugh. He was a difficult man to get close to but his personal mien warmed something in the hearts of the All Blacks that had not been warmed by his uninspiring predecessors. Suddenly they all wanted to play with pride again.

The first consequence was the tour of Australia in 1974, when an All Black team with fifteen new caps thrashed one team by 117 to 6 and deservedly took the test series.

That year was my first as touring television commentator. I joined the team for their last nine games in Australia. Coming from Auckland at that time and, before that, Wellington, and being a youngster, I had never really crossed paths with the great J. J. Stewart, let alone most of the touring players. Though Andy Leslie and his team were a fine touring unit and very friendly towards the small Press party, I never got through to John Stewart. Our first meeting was in his hotel room on the morning of the game with New South Wales. The NZBC radio man, Brian Russ, invited me to sit in on an interview with Stewart. I did, but on hearing the curt rejoinders to Russ's reasonable questions, I fled in horror. I remained on nodding acquaintance only with Mr Stewart for the rest of the tour. I marvelled at the qualities of the man yet I could not find it in myself to approach him to find out what made him tick.

I had interviewed him for radio and television several times and a photograph of one of these interviews taking place made an amusing front page in the *Auckland Star* and in T. P. McLean's *The All Blacks Come Back* in 1974.

He was approaching a crest of coaching and match-winning achievement, and deservedly so.

It was the same on the tour to Ireland, Wales and England that came at the end of 1974. Andy Leslie and his happy band of All Blacks swept through that journey, winning matches and friends. J. J. Stewart was now hailed as an international rugby figure, respected world-wide. People asked me what he was like. 'You must know, you've toured with him', they would say. I replied 'He's great, just great, he really is'. I said so on the air, too. I could not find it in myself to admit that I stood in awe of the man. I never really knew him.

Came 1976 and the All Blacks were ready for the Springboks, or so the fans said. What had happened in 1974 and 1975, the resurgence by the All Blacks after the troughs of 1972-73, produced a feeling of great optimism in New Zealanders' breasts. They could feel their dander rising. 'The Springboks must be beaten!' The cry went up.

But for what? There were many who thought the tour of South Africa should never go ahead, as a protest against apartheid, which applied racist policies to sport. The hue spread wide against the tour, the cry was for the New Zealanders not to go. The resurgence of New Zealand rugby was of short-term and secondary consequence compared with the positive act of not sending a team to South Africa, and thus affirming to Africa and the world that New Zealand valued human rights more highly than games of football.

The shock of seeing twenty-seven nations withdraw from the Olympic Games because of a government-endorsed New Zealand rugby tour to the Republic of South Africa forced many New Zealanders to regret the tour. No man is an island, no nation stands apart.

The profound irony is that time will show that a percentage of New Zealanders only wanted the All Blacks to tour South Africa because they were confident of a New Zealand victory. The traditional rivals would be squashed, the rugby balance of power would be righted.

Half-way through the tour, when it became clear to some that the tour was going sour in more ways than one, a large body of rugby supporters changed their minds about the rightness of it all.

In my television sporting work I am supposed to talk of sport alone. That was hard in 1976, for the issues of the tour to South Africa, its rights and its wrongs, overshadowed all else. Television One has never made it public but the audience viewing figures for the All Blacks' matches in South Africa were poor, very poor in fact. Even live telecasts of the test matches failed to get the great mass of New Zealanders involved in the tour and its rugby-above-all outcome. The African boycott at the Olympic Games overclouded the rugby. Simple as that. New Zealanders gained consciousness in 1976.

It takes an exceptional young man to refuse selection as an All Black because of his social or political convictions. Serious social responsibility is not normally active in them, partly because the game is so engrossing and its challenges so demanding.

'Leave the politics and other wrangling to the higher-ups. Let them sort it out. Our job's to play football.'

So it was an increasingly-disturbed band of young men — the All Blacks in South Africa — who came to realise that the whole of the Black World was allied against *them* and that, incredibly, the world's greatest sporting occasion had been shattered because of *them*.

The gloom that their tour had cast over the world affected their attitude towards the game, and towards the country and its white citizens who were hosting them. Sure, they were angry at losing the tests, and wild at some lousy refereeing but most of them, to use a Kiwi idiom, 'had had a gutsful' of South Africa and its ways before the tour came to an end.

I do not rate 1976 as a year in which New Zealand rugby, on the field, was set back. I prefer to rate the All Blacks' performances in South Africa in a void, to be neither considered with merit nor forgotten with scorn.

It was a 3-1 defeat for New Zealand in the series. Rugby officialdom in New Zealand obviously rated it a bad series to lose; the axing of J. J. Stewart as coach confirmed that.

Other points of issue took on major importance. Should we have been in South Africa in the first place, playing this game of rugby? Should we play them again under South Africa's freer basis of selection? Should the Springboks tour New Zealand again, or the All Blacks tour South Africa? Should we play them again in any sport?

I felt at the time a good number of the All Blacks were truly sickened by apartheid. Sickened enough perhaps to allow their feelings to be disturbed. The question could be asked: Did they lose one quarter of their tour games because, sub-consciously, they would have preferred to be somewhere else?

The fundamental conflict between race and rugby in South Africa was epitomised for me in the moments leading up to the playing of that dramatic match with the Quagga-Barbarians Club. It was my first visit to Ellis Park in Johannesburg. (I had come from working at the Olympic Games in Montreal and had missed the first ten games on tour.) A line of policemen marched around the ground, some with dogs on leashes, in much the same manner as in many sports stadia around the world. Imagine the delight of the huge crowd when one of the dogs stopped on the side-line, directly in front of the main stand, and proceeded to pay heed to nature's call. It really was funny. The first section of the line of policemen kept on marching, oblivious of the crowd's mirth. The men behind marked time, waiting for the dog to do his business.

In time, when doggy had finished, the policemen all marched on. The incident seemed finished, though it did cross my mind, somewhat whimsically, at what might happen if some big Quagga or All Black wound up having his nose rubbed in it, to coin a phrase.

What happened next summed up for me, in miniature, and emotively I admit, just what apartheid is.

In front of that crowd, near 55,000, a small black youth, surely not more than sixteen years old, slunk on to the ground. His embarrassment was total, for it was he, armed with a tiny shovel and brush, who had to clean up the mess. The crowd erupted again in wild hysteria. I can still see in my mind's eye fat-faced white men slapping their sides with laughter. Others pitched oranges at the lad while he stooped to scoop away the offending pile. The guffawing and chortling did not die away until the boy, head down and holding the shovel as far as he could from his body, had disappeared. All the patience and suffering of the black man in South Africa was, for me, epitomised in that boy. As of 1976 the only time that that boy would be allowed on that park, the most noble seat of South African rugby, would be to clean up the excrement of a dog.

O.K., O.K., I hear you say. An extreme example, a minor incident long since forgotten. But it's odd, some twelve months on, the things one recalls first when writing in summary of a rugby tour of South Africa.

I saw as much of South African people and life as I could, at all levels and with all races, although limited in some areas of opportunity by the all-white structure of the tour. I also listened carefully to the statements made by Mr Ron Don of the New Zealand Rugby Football Union when he returned from South Africa in April 1977 proclaiming, for all to hear, that equality in sport was fast becoming the norm in that country. Could you blame me for not believing the promises? After all, the changes which he reported had been made to the race-sport set-up would have been impossible of achievement in the seven months since I had seen the comprehensive nature of apartheid law on sports grounds and in sporting clubs. I must conclude by stating that my own attitude to rugby tours, and to the hoary sport-versus-politics issue, was reversed by what I saw in South Africa in 1976.

I will tell no more tales about apartheid. Except to reiterate that it was against the New Zealand politics-Black African politics-South African apartheid-Olympic debacle backdrop that the tour went on. Who's to say it did not affect, and indeed, upset some of the All Blacks? Who's to say their record might not have been better had it only been rugby they'd been involved in? For in rugby terms alone the New Zealanders and the South Africans were, in my view, equal in playing strengths.

I have written that a revival of New Zealand rugby came about through the agency of a gifted coach in J. J. Stewart. What manner of man was he?

In that regard 1976 had not started well. I had taken a camera crew to Athletic Park on the Thursday before the Ireland-New Zealand test match. The All Blacks were training on an empty ground, actors without an audience, as police security against possible anti-South African tour outbursts was strong. I asked the camera crew to inch a little closer to a practice line-out — 'but not too close'. Unhappily for us we moved several feet too close to 'Jay Jay', who was lambasting the troops. He turned. His message to the cameraman, the sound-girl, to me and the whole wide world was curt, cold and to the point! And both the words he used echoed around the empty Athletic Park, with its whispering memories of great players, great matches and — dare I say it — great coaches!

And yet, upon arrival in South Africa I was told again, from all quarters within the team, that they were playing their guts out for J. J. Stewart — 'because he's such a great guy'. Could one be blamed for being confused?

But one meeting between us on that tour changed my personal

opinion of the man. The tough exterior is just that, an outer shell only, for within lies a very human person, one who does not easily express warmth to outsiders.

I spoke with Stewart late in the night in Bloemfontein after the second test, which the All Blacks had won. It was around midnight. He was on his own in the midst of a joyous victory party, which most of his team had got bored with and left. The All Black supporters, always loud, surpassed themselves in decibel level around us. Stewart looked lonely. I ventured congratulations on the test win. He thanked me. Our conversation was halting in the noisy room.

Perhaps it was because I was a more familiar face than others in the crowd, but a discussion sprung up between us.

In that meeting I discovered some of the man's magnetism. His resources of power and persuasion are, in many circumstances, overlaid by reserve. He is an intensely devoted family man; he doted on his children whilst so far away. He could quote passages from their letters — 'Dad, even if you do lose over there, it'll still be a great day when you come home' — and he recalled them with obvious pleasure.

He does not, as they say, suffer fools gladly. He didn't that night. He spoke of the second test win in a totally modest and realistic manner, not glorying in the result, not diminishing the opposition. And he praised the manner of the men who had done the job on the field, and the support they had had from the remainder of the tour party as well.

From then on and to this day I hope I have enjoyed a good working relationship with John Stewart, which is noteworthy, considering he did not speak at all to several members of the New Zealand and South African press corps covering the 1976 tour.

That conversation was the breakthrough that provided insights to the most influential man in New Zealand rugby this decade. Stewart was, and is, grouchy, grey and grimfaced by nature. On television his speech is slow and close to a monotone and his visage is dead-pan except for a slightly moving lower lip, the only indication when he is actually speaking.

But listen to what he has to say and it's all solid sense and logic. This is the man who could motivate, inspire and enlighten adult males into playing the most spectacular kind of rugby, in defence of New Zealand's honour, and of achieving what other coaches had been unable to do, with substantially the same players and experience to work with.

J. J. Stewart was cast aside as national coach of the All Blacks in

1976 because he coached a losing team in South Africa (and voiced some strong opinions about South Africa and its ways). This was a rugby injustice of the most fearful nature. Not even the choice of his successor Jack Gleeson, a coach with the highest credentials, would dim the depth of loss that some of the 1974-76 New Zealand rugby representatives felt for J. J. Stewart. He had earned their total loyalty and respect.

All that meant that Jack Gleeson's job, in taking over in 1977, was to be much harder than usual. What then was the state of All Black rugby as the Stewart coaching era passed into history?

Firstly, it had become a running game, for that's the way the players wanted it. Every man of the All Black team on the field, in any match, contributed his ideas on the playing style — that was Stewart's way. And even though trumpets sounded loud and long in praise of the star players of the era — Grant Batty, Sid Going, Bryan Williams, Ian Kirkpatrick — the All Blacks in recent years were encouraged, at all times, to play together, as a fifteen man team. And equal efforts to the team cause came from those in the rugby districts where toughness and tightness are essential.

All Black rugby in the 1970s was not only a running game for backs. The forwards did their running and passing as well, while not slipping too far from their traditional power role.

On the 1972-73 tour of Great Britain the All Black team's scrummaging fell behind that in the Home Nations.

But Hamish MacDonald's dedicated pushing, Peter Whiting's strength, Frank Oliver's hardness, the pillars to push on that Kerry Tanner, Bill Bush, Kent Lambert and Tane Norton formed in the front row, gave New Zealand's front five the ideal solid platform needed at scrum-time.

At line-outs Whiting was a tapper not a catcher, but his talent in this department kept New Zealand up with the rest of the world in this untidy area of forward rugby.

In loose work, Ken Stewart and Kevin Eveleigh were dashers and dancers creating donner und blitzen amongst opposition backlines. Ian Kirkpatrick was, at best, a driving surger capable of initiating attacks on which the traditional All Black charges could be made.

Behind them always had been Andy Leslie. He had proved, with inspirational leadership based on his qualities as a man, that he was totally worthy of the highest regard from his team.

When Leslie was first picked as an All Black in 1974 there were many, especially some of my old Auckland friends, who had grave doubts as to whether he would command a place in the test team. He proved them all wrong, with intelligent play and calm control of his team.

In the back divisions New Zealand, in the years up to 1977, tended to stand or fall on whether Sid Going was on form, or not, at half-back.

He was an enigma of brilliance, the unpredictability of one blessed with so much genius. If Sid played well, so did the All Blacks. Most of the time he did play well, thank God, but on some exceptional occasions (against England at Eden Park in 1973, against South Africa, Third Test, 1976) his form was poor. He was out-played by lesser men. Was it coincidence that New Zealand lost on those days?

O.K., you may be saying. Don't blame Super Sid when we get licked. Unfair perhaps? But on the other hand let it be said that in any top level match when Going was 'on', the All Blacks were 'on' as well.

In the outside back positions New Zealand had wingers and centres possessed of more in skills, speed and know-how than any others in world rugby. Even though Grant Batty should never have toured South Africa in 1976 he was, on that tour, even with his rickety knee, capable of displaying enough to convince some South Africans of his greatness. In earlier seasons Batty's terrier-like adhesion to all that is aggressive in the winger's brief, plus his ability to skip away from would-be tacklers, made him one of our greatest wingers. Bill McLaren, the BBC TV commentator, who is, to my craft, like Shakespeare is to English literature, once described Batty as playing like 'a runaway bullet'. That description applied perfectly to Batty's pre-1976 form.

On the other side of the threequarter line was Bryan Williams, whose thighs defy description, so large are they. His reputation matched his thighs, if you know what I mean. The man was all-powerful and all-elusive and his bursting talent was the perfect foil for Batty's nimbleness and dexterity.

Though I have no real idea of what it is like, I imagine Bryan Williams is the most difficult player in the world to tackle head-on. With his massive legs pumping in a high-speed run, while still remaining light enough on his toes to unleash devastating side-steps, I have seen the runaway Williams stopped properly only twice.

I had felt Bryan Williams was, at the beginning of the 1977 season, still a great player; but like so many top sportsmen he was not seen at his best unless playing in situations that truly tested his abilities.

Bryan was always reliable at club and provincial level, and indeed for the All Blacks, but by his own high criterion he was not the player of old. It took test matches to lift Williams' performance. It was T. P. McLean who first used the word 'iconoclasm' in a rugby book. Its dictionary sense means 'breaking of images or attacking cherished beliefs' and McLean used the word in reference to a criticism he made of Sid Going's play in 1974. I use it with reference to Williams. He is a great player, with great mastery of his craft, greatness that sits lightly on his shoulders. But is he the player of old? Was he so good in his younger days that he set a yardstick in performance that was impossible even for him to match in later years? Or have we just grown too familiar with his greatness?

I realise that to criticise an idol of Williams' stature is to stand on very shaky ground. When the 1977 Lions tour began New Zealand rugby sorely needed good play from him to counter and gain ascendency over a Lions team which looked thin on experience on the wings. One of the first things I looked for in the series was whether Williams could dominate as well as he had done in the past.

But what of the other backline positions in the All Black team? In what state were they when Jack Gleeson took over as coach?

By and large, they were solid and sure; at second five-eighth Joe Morgan was unendingly courageous in South Africa; understudy Bill Osborne was promising. Duncan Robertson and Doug Bruce had been heady players, as the old timers used to call it. That is, not brilliant or flashy, in ways that other countries required of their fly-halves or stand-offs. Rather the New Zealanders reflected a kind of guardedness in their play that was a throw-back to the rugby played in New Zealand under the old laws. They could run the ball, these two, and kick effectively, but they were, at their roots, players built more for security purposes than attack.

What I'm talking about had been called 'safety first' rugby in the days when a five-eighth could kick out of play on the full. Only when they received the ball in perfect or near-perfect circumstances was it moved on by hand.

The laws were changed in the 1969 season in New Zealand and the right to kick directly over the touch line was banned forever, thank goodness. More running and passing were therefore encouraged but still, I believe, our five-eighths have retained their steady ways. It is something they have inherited from our rugby past. To this day if our rugby system throws up a back with inborn brilliance and flair he is usually told to play the game at centre or on the wings.

But Doug Bruce and Duncan Robertson had done well within the limitations of New Zealand inside back conventions. One player who was a centre and who reflected a mastership of that position was Bruce Robertson. He was the best back in South Africa in 1976. Fast, power-packed, strong, his freedom from injury on that tour uncorked from him his best-ever football. He had been among the first picked in any All Black team in recent years.

Which leaves just one position. Fullback.

By All Black standards and the great heritage New Zealanders place on their 'custodians' this position was in a sad state of neglect early in 1977. Kit Fawcett and Laurie Mains were disappointments in South Africa and this was likely to earn them life-time banishment from future All Black teams. So what was required was a new man. The lack of solid candidates was almost beyond the belief of most Kiwi fans. They had been used to seeing great players in that position and presumed there would be more in the various moulds of Wallace, Nepia, Scott, Clarke and McCormick. But in the 1970s great fullbacks were hard for New Zealand rugby selectors to find, develop and build upon. Joe Karam had done the job well until he cashed in in 1976 and went to Rugby League. The others who had played for the All Blacks since Fergie McCormick's release from national duty had all been 'oncers'.

Indeed, a popular pastime around my office this year was to name the 17 fullbacks who had played for the All Blacks since 1970. I admit that the 'oncers' I talk of include players playing out of position in mid-week provincial games. Yet the six-year list of New Zealand fullbacks is still long: McCormick, Kember, Milner, Furlong, Mains, Morris, Sid Going, Karam, Lendrum, Bruce, Ken Going, Robertson, Fawcett, Richard Wilson, Rowlands, Farrell, and Bevan Wilson.

Of course the list is not a true indication of the problem. Only ten of the fifteen had played in tests during the same period. Compare that with the requirement of only three players to play fullback for New Zealand over the 11 seasons from 1959 to 1969. Don Clarke, Fergie McCormick and Mick Williment shared 45 tests between them in that decade. It had been the same in the 1950s. Bob Scott, Pat Walsh and Clarke carried the burden and the continuity of selection over the best part of that 10 year period.

The problem in finding suitable fullback material takes us back again to the changed laws. In Don Clarke's era the accent in playing was on the big boot. The fullback was truly the 'last line of defence'. He was security personified, forever driving back attacking ball with huge touch finders. He also landed penalty kicks from the most prodigious of distances. Clarke's enormous success encouraged others to imitate his mode and manner on the field. Since then only Fergie McCormick has come near to what, ideally, is needed by fullbacks today. Without the kick out on the full as first priority it is now a position of real opportunity, a place where a runner rather than a robot is required.

And if new talent was to be needed in any position for the Lions' series, where was it to come from? In this respect Jack Gleeson (with J. J. Stewart and Eric Watson re-elected as fellow-selectors) had had a first hand role in choosing fifty-eight men to wear the All Black jersey in a five month period in 1976. Firstly, as a supporting selector, he had helped choose the 'A' All Blacks, who were sent, as I have said, with J. J. Stewart to South Africa. Then, remaining in New Zealand, Gleeson and Watson, on their own, had watched a domestic season. The climax to it was their pick of another All Black touring team. This 'other' band of travellers, led by the 24-year-old Taranaki flanker Graham Mourie, trail-blazed their way through South America playing mainly in Argentina.

Their results were so successful that it was they, and not the 'senior pros' who had toured South Africa, who returned with the flush of success.

It was reported that team manager Ron Don did not over-manage the team as I would have laid odds he would do. Away from the harsh glare of the media men who followed every mile and every move, on and off the field, of the All Blacks in South Africa, the 'Argentina All Blacks' moulded into a merry band, playing winning rugby and thoroughly enjoying themselves in a land where All Blacks were novelties.

Jack Gleeson was there too. As coach, he was able to watch first hand the development of new talent in the All Black nursery, plus the maturing in richness of some of the more seasoned members of the side.

Television coverage of the tour was scant so the folks back home could not, as they had done with the 'South African All Blacks', make their own pass/fail judgement on individual team members from the comfort of the fireside.

Jack Gleeson, on his return, was ecstatic. Even Ron Don was too. Murray Taylor of Waikato had been a major discovery at first five-eighth. The lock Andy Haden of Auckland had proved bigger in heart and talent than his height, which is more than considerable. Stuart Wilson of Wellington was rated by many to be as good a centre as Bruce Robertson. The individual excellence list though somewhat overstated made it obvious that the tour had been a whale of a success and the cleverness of many players much advanced.

Jack Gleeson told me what had happened. 'A player came to me in Argentina and said there was an attitude developing in the ranks that the team was just the 'third fifteen' of New Zealand rugby. To hell with that, I said, so I ripped into them at the next team meeting and told them that they might not have been picked for the South Africa tour but, by heck, if the All Blacks had have been picked late in the season a whole swag of my team would have got in.'

It did the trick. The players in Argentina took a new look at the worth of their All Black jerseys. 'From then on there was no stopping them', says Gleeson. Their happiness together was part of their new discovery.

The team came home unbeaten. They beat Argentina twice, and easily. Pretty well all reputations, both on and off the field, were improved.

After a few months came the 1977 season. And almost with the first breath of winter came the rumours. It was said, all over the country, with seemingly high authority, that Gleeson, having been voted convenor of national selectors in the off-season, was dead keen to take on the Lions with just his 'Argentina talent'. It was said he didn't care a hoot for those who had struggled but lost in South Africa. This gossip gained momentum around New Zealand and all sorts of ghastly fates were predicted for the senior citizens of Andy Leslie's 1976 New Zealand team.

All of which meant there were abundant riches on display when the 1977 New Zealand trials were played at Wanganui in May. Not only were there the usual man-to-man struggles that are the norm on trials day, but there was an undercurrent of rivalry between those who had toured South Africa and who were defending test places and those who had toured Argentina and who aspired to test places.

Jack Gleeson was a far too logical and sensible a man to have put about the whispers that led to this confrontation, but he was pleased that players from the two All Black touring teams were now inspired rivals for the test team of 1977. Seldom has so much blooded talent been available at one time.

I spent two days in his company before the Lions arrived in New Zealand. For the purposes of a television profile on Gleeson-the-Man, I asked him whether these rumours had been a deliberate ploy on his part to fire up the 'oldies'. He replied 'I wonder who started that rumour. I certainly didn't. But it's been good rumour-mongering just the same. Whoever started it has done a magnificent job for New Zealand rugby.'

I doubt whether Gleeson, who is a gentleman and a good bloke, would have entertained starting such a rumour. But, before the season and once it had started, some who could have been called oldies fell by the wayside. Firstly Graeme Crossman, then Kerry Tanner, then Andy Leslie himself, and finally Peter Whiting: all announced that they had retired from international rugby.

It is not credible that rumours of 'Argentina All Blacks take over' were a serious influence in these players' decisions. There were the demands of business and family, so much greater in an amateur sport than a professional one; the observable tactical preferences of the new chairman of selectors; and the reality that rugby was still but a game and not necessarily a way of life, even for some of its prime exponents.

But time passes. Gleeson's task in taking over the All Blacks after so popular and effective a man as Stewart was fraught with difficulty and ominous in its potential. At the first test of 1977 there were stories that he would not have the team wholly behind a commitment to play his 'rugby philosophy'. (Of which philosophy, more later.)

By the time the season had played its way out Gleeson had proved his sterling qualities — as man, leader, tactician and coach. He appeared to have most or all of the complex skills and strengths required for the position of convenor of the New Zealand selection panel. Including victory.

4
Six for Openers: Matches 1-6

1. Lions 41, Wairarapa-Bush 13. Snowballs. In May. In Masterton. It sounds like the title of some oddball romantic ballad, ridiculously destined to make its lilting way into the top ten; but Masterton was no place for songs on Wednesday, 18 May 1977.

It was there, on an afternoon that had been directly preceded by snow, hail and sleet, that Phil Bennett's fifth British Isles touring team dramatically began their rugby journey through New Zealand. The Lions won by 41 points to 13 over Wairarapa-Bush, and did it with style.

Everyone had been talking about the foul and ill-timed weather that had encompassed the hospitable Wairarapa plains, and most of New Zealand. But Bennett's boys warmed up the day, a miserable 7°C at kick-off, with an expression of the running rugby game. The match conditions were totally cheerless. The wind whipped its icy breath straight off the Tararua Ranges, thirty miles to the west, and rain swirled in gusty squalls. The slush underfoot, pointlessly stirred up by the playing of a college curtain-raiser, soon made the forward adversaries united in colour, if not intent.

The Lions had arrived in New Zealand six days before, quietly slipping into the country before the fans were awake. The early hour of their Auckland arrival was marked by a welcome from local officials (it is never too early for a speech) and several pressmen. The Lions said they were tired after such a long journey and first priority in Masterton would be bed, and lots of it.

Once the new day dawned the Lions bustled about their business.

First impressions were of the bulk of the bigger men. Nigel Horton, Moss Keane and Allan Martin all looked considerably larger than the heights and weights given in the pre-tour bumf. In the opening conference for the sixteen or so tour pressmen, Burrell and Dawes did most of the talking.

Dawes was quick to qualify a remark made to farewelling officials in London. There, it was reported, Dawes had vowed to go through New Zealand without a loss. In Masterton he adjusted his tour pledge to 'I just hope we can go through the twenty five games unbeaten'; adding the professional soccer manager's rider, 'we'll take each match as it comes'.

In their first training runs the Lions showed diligence beyond reasonable expectations after such a long trip. They packed down fifty-three scrums, with Nigel Horton's face rubbing raw against the tracksuit pants of the prop forward in front. The scrums looked low and tight, totally in keeping with British developments in this area in recent years.

Twenty-four hours before kick-off it rained hard and snowed steadily. It was a crying shame that one of Wairarapa's rare days of rugby glory should have been so badly affected by the weather. Temperatures dropped and the Lions left practice for their hotel. There was excited bar room chatter about snow, a rare sight in Masterton, and some was tossed about in the car parks. By high-spirited New Zealanders though. The Lions looked ho-hum about it all. Just like home perhaps?

The Wairarapa-Bush coach, Rod McKenzie, brought his team into the grandstand at Memorial Park to watch the curtain-raiser; clad mostly in pullovers and blazers, they must have got a damning chill, sitting as they did for about half an hour. Perhaps this move reflected McKenzie's hardline approach.

The game kicked off in front of a crowd of 9000, all of whom looked like delegates to a wet-weather-wear convention. Straight away it was obvious McKenzie's pre-match plan was to instill in his forward pack the most intractible of attitudes. They took on the Lions in a most encouraging manner, even though they conceded to J. J. Williams the first try of the tour after only two minutes. After half-time, the margin between the two teams widened quickly, but Wairarapa-Bush's forwards were never truly outclassed by the British pack. In the backs, the locals were poor.

Williams scored from a clever cross-kick by Phil Bennett. The ball skipped across the wet grass and the winger was there before the locals had time to consider retreating to it. The action of the next thirty minutes almost made those watching forget the coldness of the day. Neil Kjestrup, the home fullback, landed a straight penalty from 35 metres. Soon after, a great cry went up when Gary McGlashan, the hooker, charged down a clearance by the new Lions halfback Brynmor Williams. The ball deflected over the Lions' goal line. McGlashan, charging on, dived and hugged the ball in scoring the try.

Peter Squires on the Lions left wing was then on the receiving-end of a tidy set-up play by Phil Bennett and David Burcher. Squires ran in comfortably for a try to complete the move but must have regretted skidding into the corner for it. Covered in mud, he took little part in subsequent play and shivered with cold in his secluded spot on the wing.

Only the most violently parochial followers of Wairarapa rugby believed their side had a chance of a win when the half-time break came. The local team scored again when J. J. Williams was reminded of the difficulties of picking up a slippery-soaped rugby ball. Clive Paton, the winger, followed the kick and when it eluded Williams, was grateful to pounce on the ball for a try. Kjestrup's conversion made Wairarapa-Bush the half-time leaders.

Early in the second half Squires seemed sure to score again for the Lions but in the instant of diving for the line he lost the ball, whereupon Terry Cobner, an excellent worker, made it his. Cobner had scored in the first half too and the Lions' reserves, huddled in blankets in the stand, hooted at him in good-natured derision. Clearly the whole team was delighted with the quality of movement in the tour's opening game and on such a difficult surface.

There was more to come. Three back moves, as good as you would see on a dry day, all produced further tries, two to David Burcher and one to J. J. Williams. The portents were there in the clever handling and sure-footedness for some thrilling rugby on tour. The rhetorical question clearly was: 'If this was how they went in the wet, then . . . .?'

The scoring was climaxed in a spectacular and typically skilful British manner. As if not requiring their hands, the last try came from the combined efforts of Bennett, Burcher and J. J. Williams successively mud-kicking the ball seventy metres up field in soccer manner. Williams completed his third try by cleverly toeing the ball over the line and winning the race for the dive.

Apart from the tacky hands and good running there were other aspects of play which Dawes and Co. would have been delighted with. Bennett landed four goals, all from wide angles, with a ball heavy with clinging Wairarapa mud. The forwards competed gainfully at line-outs and scrums; Evans and Keane, in particular, were regular tigers. Keane looked a far more mobile lock than when he had toured with Ireland in 1976.

On the debit side were the injuries to Nigel Horton and Bruce Hay. Hay limped off in the second spell, with the appearance of a serious ankle injury. It was later found to be heavy bruising, with pain accentuated by the acuteness of the cold.

Horton was another case. He fell to his knees to a peach of a punch thrown by Ian Turley, the Wairarapa-Bush flanker, who spoilt his good showing in the match with his testiness in that moment. Horton, a tough policeman, took the count, actually sagging back to the ground after making it to his knees. He was destined to spend the night in Masterton hospital. In typical fashion, some aftermatch observers, New Zealanders, justified the punch by saying the big Englishman had asked for it.

When it was all over and the Lions had a winning scoreline of 41 to 13 the locals played their trump card, one that had the Lions completely beaten. *In that chilly place, made colder by the lateness of the day, the tourists discovered that there was no hot water for showering.* In the last line of my television commentary that day I had said to a close-up of a shivering Phil Bennett, 'He's heading for the hot showers. . .' but Freezing Phil did not get one. Nor did his teammates. The local team had hot water and showered. Theirs worked. Clever huh?

It was an odd sight, to say the least, to see a naked Willie Duggan, with towels strategically placed, making the short dash from the dressing-room to the coach. He and the rest of the side headed for the hotel several miles away. All this caused a lengthy delay to the start of the aftermatch function, a most serious crime.

While we waited I chatted to Brian Lochore, ex-All Black captain and a good judge of a touring team's play first-up. He had liked what he had seen. After one viewing, are they a threat in the test series? 'Hell, yes', said Lochore.

The teams:
Lions: Hay (replaced by Irvine); Squires, Burcher, McGeechan, J. J. Williams; Bennett (captain), Brynmor Williams; Quinnell; Trevor Evans, Keane, Horton (replaced by Duggan), Cobner; Price, Wheeler and Orr.
Wairarapa-Bush: Neil Kjestrup; Clive Paton, Bruce Patrick, Kerry England; Hona Huriwai, Alistair O'Neill; Bruce Herangi; Neville Taylor; Ian Turley, Phil Guscott, Brian Clarke (replaced by John

Darlington), Peter Mahoney; Bill Rowlands (captain), Gary
McGlashan and Nigel Sargent.
Scoring:
Lions (41). Tries by J. J. Williams (3), Burcher (2), Cobner (2) and
Squires (1); conversions (3) and penalty by Bennett.
Wairarapa-Bush (13). Tries by Clive Paton and Gary McGlashan;
conversion and penalty by Neil Kjestrup.
Referee: Alan Taylor (Canterbury) Wednesday, 18 May 1977.

2. Lions 13, Hawke's Bay 11. It has been said before and still remains a truism that the fortunes of a touring rugby team can rise or
fall with the playing of each match, as surely as the tide rushes up
and back on a stoney beach. So it was with Phil Bennett's Lions
team. By virtue of their commanding and convincing performance at
Masterton they arrived in Napier brimful of the joys of being young,
alive and successful, and looking forward to reaping further rewards
and plaudits from match number two on tour.

But in eighty minutes of physical rugby excellence, as demonstrated by Hawke's Bay and not the tourists, the side's stocks
fell to all square in the ledger. Quite simply, the Lions scored thirteen
points to Hawke's Bay's eleven. So the ledger read: played two, won
two. Though the Lions scored more points than Hawke's Bay they
could not, by any stretch of credibility, claim to have beaten this
Hawke's Bay team. The British left the field at McLean Park with
their backsides in a sling, so severe was the beating they took by the
locals in several decisive areas of the play.

Things had not shaped up well for the Lions before the game. For
a start, upon arrival in Napier, they found themselves minus their
touring flag, which some enterprising character had uplifted from the
grandstand at Masterton. Then came the information from London,
received with much sadness, that the England number eight forward
Roger Uttley, who had been left behind to recover from a back injury, would not be able to make the trip.

Uttley had stayed behind, originally to rest the injury for a
fortnight. The problem, called a disc lesion, did not respond and it
was a twenty-five year old Welshman, Jeff Squire, waiting to sit a
university exam paper in South Devon, who received a phone call
naming him as Uttley's replacement.

Annoying too, in their preparation for playing Hawke's Bay, was
the injury to the winger, Elgan Rees, for it was hoped every man
would have had at least one appearance after the first two games. He

stood down, so as not to risk a delicate leg problem, and J. J. Williams played again.

After watching the Lions first tour match, as exposed on television, some well-informed locals, mindful that Hawke's Bay rugby had lost ground since the halcyon days of 1967, 1968 and 1969, were making all kinds of predictions as to the Lions' winning margin. Twenty, thirty and as much as forty points were wagered. Such, we were told, was the down-at-heel quality of Hawke's Bay rugby in the 1970s.

I asked Blair Furlong, a star of the three years' tenure of the Ranfurly Shield, whether 'The Bay' had a chance against the Lions. He pursed his lips, thought for a moment, and shook his head slowly. Kel Tremain, the greatest individual in Hawke's Bay's rugby history, was said to have stated that he could find a team of old-timers, train them up for a month and beat the Hawke's Bay team — no sweat.

On match day and under a greying sky, the bullet-like speed, the darting-diving elusiveness that is symbolised by their mascot, the magpie, and confidence that began like a whisper and ended soaring upwards like a jumbo jet, all these turned the chosen fifteen of Hawke's Bay into a unit that George Burrell said afterwards played 'absolutely out of their skins'.

The pack simply wiped the Lions out at the line-outs. The count, in Hawke's Bay's favour, was something like 27 to 15. Their leapers, Robbie Stuart and Mike McCool, mere 'battlers' on the New Zealand rugby scene, actually toyed with the much-praised Lions locks Allan Martin and Gordon Brown. In the front row, Ian Grant, once forecast as an All Black captain, ripped and tore in the mauls as to the manner born. Burly Bruce Dunstan and John O'Connor were props who scrummed well, then ran in splendid forward rushes with all the agility of some toey fly-half.

The loose men, Junior Pareha, Tim Carter and Pat Ryan, worked up an interlocking loose forward scheme that, close to the scrums, embarrassed the tourists and exposed a weakness in their defensive screen.

In the backs Hawke's Bay had the usual New Zealand dependability in Ricky Allen, Peter Durham and Roger Bremner (until he was in heavy collision with Gareth Evans and was rushed from the field). There were others who produced performances that must have raised the interest of the New Zealand selectors, Jack Gleeson and Eric Watson, who were present.

Murray Tocker, at fullback, was a splendid runner, quite elusive and therefore ruinous to the Lions defence divisions. Ken Taylor was a winger in his first game of first-class rugby and made a startling debut by tackling furiously and scoring a try with such skill that he looked all the world like a seasoned campaigner.

At first five-eighth the veteran Hepa Paewai, playing only his second Hawke's Bay game in six years, kicked high to test Andy Irvine, as we knew sooner or later New Zealand teams would. Paewai was given enough encouragement by Irvine's percentage of blunders to ensure that every five-eighth and halfback in future games would try the same.

The less said about the Lions the better. Their form was so bad that George Burrell and John Dawes re-selected ten of the team for the very next game, thus switching them from Saturday stars to second-rating mid-weekers.

Lock Gordon Brown gave the impression of being physically weak for the demands of his position; his partner Allan Martin confirmed some British press opinions that, as hard locks go, he was in the 'cream puff' mould. Bobby Windsor, the hooker, did not live up to the words of praise he had earned in South Africa in 1974; while Mike Gibson, the great Mike Gibson, looked for once in his life like a man of 34. Which he is.

Ironically, the game began encouragingly for the Lions. Three of the backs, John Bevan, Mike Gibson and J. J. Williams, manu-factured a try after eleven minutes. Bevan acted alertly by tapping a penalty kick to himself and running away from the tide of the play to link with Gibson and Williams. The run had Hawke's Bay baffled, so quickly had it happened. When Irvine took the last pass from Williams and scored, we in the media seats nodded sagely. The locals had been right. Twenty, thirty, as much as forty points.

Steve Fenwick then kicked three penalty goals, two of which were the result of punches thrown in anger by Tim Carter and O'Connor. There the Lions' scoring stopped.

Hawke's Bay's bid for the match reached its maximum pitch in the first twenty minutes of the second half. Their forwards ram-paged, simply that. The Lions looked woeful as they stumbled and fumbled their blocking of the charges but the breaks had to come the home team's way.

Robbie Stuart it was, who caught one ball in a line-out close to the Lions scoring zone. He was then bolstered with the extra weight of his pack and heaved his way over the line. A vigilant Bill Adlam, the referee, pointed deep into the crush to award the try to Stuart, later awarded the Man of the Match award.

As the seconds ticked away and the Lions led by 13 to 7 (Tocker having earlier landed a penalty) came Ken Taylor's moment. From a maul 25 metres out from the Lions' line, Bruce Dunstan, as fiery a prop as his red hair indicated, came charging loose with the ball. His progress in a 20 metre run was mostly sideways but his release pass to Ricky Allen straightened the move perfectly so that Taylor, like quicksilver, could be positioned for a spring in for the try at the corner. The crowd shrieked in delight and as the close-up television camera zeroed in on Taylor he beamed in ecstasy. He was, as young people say, rapt.

Again Tocker could not make the conversion successful and the scoreline read 13 to 11, where it was to stay. Tocker missed four penalties from handy angles and seven kicks in all. Just one more over the bar and Hawke's Bay's day would have been made.

As it was, in those last moments the Lions gathered up enough togetherness and applied a tourniquet to the momentum which stopped any further breach of their line.

However Hawke's Bay had done New Zealand rugby a great turn this day. In defeat they had mortalised the 1977 Lions. No longer was Bennett's team one to be feared. After Hawke's Bay had finished with them they definitely looked beatable.

The teams
Lions: Irvine; Gareth Evans, Gibson, Fenwick, J. J. Williams; Bevan, Morgan; Duggan; Quinnell, Martin, Brown, Neary; Cotton (captain), Windsor and Clive Williams.
Hawke's Bay: Murray Tocker; Ken Taylor, Ricky Allen, Peter Durham; Roger Bremner (replaced by Wayne Nixon), Hepa Paewai; Jock McCaroll; Pat Ryan; Tim Carter, Mike McCool, Robbie Stuart (captain), Junior Pareha; Bruce Dunstan, Ian Grant and John O'Connor.
Scoring:
Lions (13). Try by Irvine; penalties (3) by Fenwick.
Hawke's Bay (11). Tries by Stuart and Taylor; penalty by Tocker.
Referee: Bill Adlam (Wanganui).   Saturday, 21 May 1977.

3. Lions 25, Poverty Bay-East Coast 6. 'Never in doubt', John Dawes had offered, with a smile admittedly, as his first comment to the press after Hawke's Bay's relentless bid to beat the Lions. There was no denying Dawes' genuine concern, however, about his team's play. 'There was a lack of co-ordination between individuals', he said (another way of saying the calling for catches had been shoddy and the linkage between two runners bad). 'There was a lack of con-

1. 'The Lads' — The 1977 Lions in New Zealand and Fiji.
Back row (left to right): Elgan Rees, Peter Squires, Brynmor Williams, Bruce Hay, Gareth Evans, Phil Orr, David Burcher, Steve Fenwick, Douglas Morgan and John Bevan.
Second row: Bobby Windsor, Peter Wheeler, Terry Cobner, Trevor Evans, Nigel Horton, Allan Martin, Moss Keane, Willie Duggan, Tony Neary, Clive Williams, and Graham Price.
Front row: Derek Quinnell, John J. Williams, Ian McGeechan, Mike Gibson, George Burrell (Manager), Phil Bennett (Captain), John Dawes (Coach), Gordon Brown, Fran Cotton and Andy Irvine.
Absent are the replacements: Jeff Squire, Bill Beaumont, Charlie Faulkner and Alun Lewis.

2. Swooping in like a swallow — Lions style! Tony Neary tries to catch Hawkes Bay's fullback Murray Tocker at McLean Park. And guess what? There's no mud in sight. Unbelievable!

3. 'Aw gee, fellas, can we have our Andy back?' Andy Irvine's under there somewhere against Taranaki. But even when it was six men onto one Andy came up smiling — and usually with the ball!

4. Phil Bennett was 'mighty' on this tour — but only for some of the time. Here he tries to bypass Taranaki's Graham Mourie (left) at Rugby Park, New Plymouth. Bennett got away from his man here but in the third and fourth tests it was 'Mighty Mourie' who won the day. No. 6 is Ross Fraser.

5. A six year unbeaten run goes down the drain! Paul Macfie's big moment. He scores the clinching try for the New Zealand Universities in their 21-9 victory over the Lions in Christchurch. The Lion pulling the funny face is Elgan Rees. Other British Isles players are Keane, Burcher and Wheeler. The New Zealand captain Doug Rollerson (left), and winger Russell Hawkins (right) are witness to the winning dive.

6. A twelve point try coming up in the first test! That's what the Lions called it as Bruce Robertson's tackle forced Trevor Evans to pass upwards. Grant Batty, the All Black winger, reaches for the intercept but the try line is still 60 metres away . . .

7. . . . He must have been bats to think he could get away with it! But he did, in a runaway try at Athletic Park. The crowd noise for Batty's last major act in test rugby could be heard in Cuba Street, six miles away. Ian Kirkpatrick and Moss Keane can only chase and watch.

centration at kick-offs', added Dawes (Allan Martin, for one, had overstepped four kick-offs). 'And the ball-winning capacity of the team was disappointing', concluded the coach, surely the understatement of the hour.

So it was a much-chastened tour party which travelled on to Gisborne for the third tour game against Poverty Bay-East Coast. One rather got the feeling that already the Lions had reached their first Rubicon. For to play as consistently badly again would surely mean that there would be heaps of defeats for them in the upcoming tougher games.

George Burrell, not sounding too confident, said 'It was gratifying to get the bad one out of our system', but we television, radio and newspaper critics asked ourselves whether this was the thin end of the wedge. In more than one newspaper, for instance, the Hawke's Bay game was reviewed and then comparisons immediately drawn between what the 1977 Lions had just shown and the miserable journey of the 1966 Lions, with their twelve losses out of thirty-five matches.

The Poverty Bay-East Coast game proved only a little more helpful in making an accurate assessment of the quality of talent in this British team. The tourists won 25 to 6 but afterwards, as darkness spread across the North Island and I was flying home in a six-seater charter plane with the videotape of the game on my lap, I had to admit that the side was still a mystery. It was not yet possible to gauge accurately their true depth of talent and their true worth as a team.

We had seen them at their wet-weather best in Masterton, at their worst, surely, in Napier, and in Gisborne, a mix-up of those two contrasts, neither good nor bad.

Their team for the Poverty Bay-East Coast game had ten of those who had played against Hawke's Bay. At Gisborne most of them confirmed, for me at least, that they would be continuing members of the mid-week fifteen.

A cloudy day, and 15,000 spectators watched the Poverty Bay-East Coast team roar into action against the Lions. The ground was firm. The locals had been described by their captain Ian Kirkpatrick as being a 'well-balanced' fifteen — which doubtless covered the reality that there were several in the team who were deficient in terms of a good representative standard. They were robust enough, however, and maintained more than their share of the territorial percentage in the first twenty minutes.

But this game never came to life in a visual sense. What was happening in the mauls and rucks which seemed to occupy most of the match's duration might have been pleasing to the eye of those in the crowd who like their rugby bruising and tough but to those of us who enjoy a spectacle it became, especially in the second half, dead dull.

The Combined team were not helped by some backs who were clearly lacking in imagination and talent. The halfback, Stuart Donald, for instance, had a curious manner of positioning himself at the line-out, wide out and near the back. That was because he could only make his pass one way and not the other. Donald's combination with Graeme Thompson and the replacement Lance Rickard was not good, and Rickard, just a lad, kicked almost every ball he received as high as he could, but without much consideration as to where it would land.

In the pack, Colin Kirkpatrick, Ian's younger brother, and an eighteen-year old, Bruce Cameron, locked the scrum. But at six feet two inches tall they were too short to combat their lineout opposites, Moss Keane and Allan Martin. Martin in particular won bunches of lineout ball in the middle, though at the front and back Robbie Newlands, Lawrie Knight and Ian Kirkpatrick did rather better for the home boys.

Kirkpatrick had a grand game, making much ball available in the rucks and mauls. Was it because he was playing in lesser company or was his work-rate higher than usual on this day? Knight, his clubmate, was all industry too, although his performance went without notice from the national selection panel, all of whom were elsewhere.

The Lions did a whole heap better in this match than they had done at Napier. George Burrell, a worried man about his troops, went about with almost an air of lightheadedness after the game, such was his relief at winning. The principal point of improvement in the Lions play was at the lineouts. Much better too was the presentation of ball from ruck and maul to the day's halfback, Douglas Morgan. Scrummaging was sound.

In the backs confusion was still the operative word. Too many times the moves that Ian McGeechan and Mike Gibson conceived for their wingers were not completed because of a slip, a stray pass or a man adrift. Gibson, still lacking real form, was rather put off, if that's the phrase, by the attentions of the East Coast flanker Ray Falcon, who seemed intent on visiting Gibson even when the Irishman was not in possession of the ball. Gibson, however, still showed that in support of the ball carrier he was better than any youngster.

Poor Bruce Hay again left the field, suffering from a continuing ankle injury. His replacement was Andy Irvine who, a matter of seconds after receiving the referee's clearance to play, had to stand under a high kick sent his way by Lance Rickard. He caught it but dropped two out of a further three sent in his direction.

All this is supplementary to the running pattern of play in the game. Most of the time it was kick and chase and maul and ruck, and from the Lions we saw none of the winning flow that had been the overriding factor at Masterton.

All the tries came in the opening half of the match. The first was the best. It came in the Lions' most potent manner when Squires fielded a cross-kick back in defence, only metres from his own line. The approaching men in blue came too quickly and he was able to slip their tackles. Then he made a keen burst across his own ten metre line, dragging the cover defence of Poverty Bay-East Coast with him. As always, Gibson supported the runner and received from Squires an in-pass which opened up the way ahead. McGeechan, captain for the day, joined in and when he received the ball at half-way all he had to do was run on. This he did despite the desperate chasing of Graeme Torrie, Combined's left winger. From under the bar, Morgan converted the try.

Next, the Lions ran the ball among their backs at a set movement. As if knowing that McGeechan would be watched closely, Gibson left him out of the move and passed across him to Gareth Evans on the left wing. The ball dipped at the end of its flight and dropped to Evans' toe. His kick, on the fly, went across the line and Evans was able to get to it first unimpeded by the home team's fullback, Wilson Isaacs, stumbling in the grass as he turned.

The third, and as it turned out, the final one was perhaps the best-constructed move. Three mauls were won in succession by the British team and three waves of attack charged at Poverty Bay-East Coast's line. Their defence was, as they say, all over the place like a mad woman's washing and when Morgan moved to the narrow side after the third maul he slipped a pass to magical McGeechan, who twinkled lightly on his toes to beat the defence.

Encouraging were the signs at that point for the Lions. Alas there was no more delightful stuff. The half-time score was 16-0, three tries and two conversions. The second half scoring all came from penalties, two to the home team.

Most of the play in the second half was muddling in the extreme. The home backs, like most of their counterparts in New Zealand, had little to offer in terms of attacking ploys. The Lions were never really under siege and, in effect, coasted out to the final whistle.

At the end Willie Duggan donged Kirkpatrick a beauty and received one (or two) in return, which jolted all of us back into the game. What it was all about was unclear but that champion broadcaster Winston McCarthy hit the nail on the head afterwards when he said: 'If they'd had that little set-to in the first minute instead of the last it might've warmed things up and made a better game.' Right again Winston.

Another disappointing game? Maybe I was being super-critical and asking that all games be visually rich for the betterment of the spectacle on the television replays. None of the main newspaper journalists rubbished this performance. Rather it was seen as a tightly-controlled game by the tourists, an ideal type of attitude to take after a previous close shave.

So the Lions had won again. The first Rubicon had been reached and crossed without loss. Any comparisons that had been drawn between this Lions team and their 1966 counterparts were silenced for the present. The only similarity was in name.

The teams
Lions: Hay (replaced by Irvine); Gareth Evans, McGeechan (captain), Gibson, Squires; Bevan, Morgan; Duggan; Trevor Evans, Martin, Keane, Neary; Cotton, Windsor, Clive Williams.
Poverty Bay-East Coast: Wilson Isaacs; Graeme Torrie, Brett Sherriff (replaced by Lance Rickard), Jody Walters; Mike Parkinson, Graeme Thompson; Stuart Donald; Lawrie Knight; Ian Kirkpatrick (captain), Bruce Cameron, Colin Kirkpatrick, Ray Falcon; Robbie Newlands, Grant Allen, and Wilton McFarlane.

Scoring
Lions (25). Tries by McGeechan (2) and Gareth Evans; conversions (2) and penalties (3) by Morgan.
Poverty Bay-East Coast (6). Penalties (2) by Wilson Isaacs.
Referee: Mike Farnworth (Auckland).Wednesday, 25 May 1977.

4. Lions 21, Taranaki 13. I suppose when you get told by a man of high authority that the Lions are going to be beaten then you have to sit up and listen. It happened to me at the aftermatch function for the All Black trials at Wanganui. I had been chatting with Ian Eliason, the Taranaki lock forward and dairy farmer, about the trials and the upcoming British Isles tour. 'Don't make a big thing of it', he said, 'in fact we'd appreciate it if you didn't, but Taranaki is ready for the Lions, we're going to beat them, don't worry about that.'

Ian Eliason is a 31-year old. An ex-All Black. A thoroughly nice bloke. He has pushed in more Taranaki scrums, in fact he has played more games for Taranaki, than any other man. If anyone has reached a position to judge the merits of a Taranaki forward pack and the strengths of the team in general then it's Ian Eliason, true soldier for the amber and black.

His logic in making his assessment was sound, even if his kind of aggressive confidence is typical of Taranaki rugby folk. The Taranaki forward pack had laid the basis for a fifteen match winning streak that stretched back to 1975. They were led by Graham Mourie, a quiet man yet a pied piper on the rugby field, possessed of qualities that enticed men to follow his call. In the pack there were six who had been good enough to travel to the 1977 New Zealand trials. They had identical kauri trees as their solid props, the McEldowneys — Bryce and his lookalike brother John. ('Thank God Bryce has a moustache', said John Howson, of Radio New Zealand.)

Ross Fraser, a New Zealand surf-lifesaving representative, was with Mourie on the side of the scrum, with Mike Carey in the back. John Thwaites was Eliason's partner at lock and Felix O'Carroll, a 1976 Maori All Black, was hooker.

I had seen Taranaki in action in a representative match early in 1977 against Wanganui and had been impressed by their hard-nosed, earnest attitude. They were a unit playing with a purposeful togetherness, and looked capable of testing any pack.

The Lions had got wind of the kind of confidence that Ian Eliason exuded and the team travelled across from Gisborne to New Plymouth with their minds set on playing a 'fifth' test match.

Their approach was mirrored at the game's kick-off. As was their tradition they grouped together in a tight circle at half-way while the National Anthem played. This they had done at each game, a last moment to look into each other's eyes and pledge individual commitment to the common cause of the next eighty minutes.

The close-up TV camera, which can show blood-shot eyes at fifty metres, strayed across the backs of the players huddled in a tight group. For an instant, a gap appeared in the circle, and there, his mouth contorted with emotion, was Phil Bennett. Gone was his boyish look, gone were his quiet ways. The playing of his eyes across each face and the strong words we could not hear told us exactly what sort of dedication the Lions were committed to in this game.

The difference between the two teams at the final whistle was eight points, 21 to 13 in favour of the touring team.

Wider still was the margin in skilful rugby played, for this was the most convincing performance by the Lions to date. The manner in which the win was moulded was not, as one might have expected, by fleet-footed backs and tries galore, but instead by the forwards, who took on redoubtable opponents and bettered them in most aspects of a hard encounter.

What went wrong with Ian Eliason's prediction of a Taranaki victory? While his forwards were mighty good value and competitive from start to finish, the backs, Dave Loveridge excepted, were again typically New Zealandish — devoid of ideas, slow, sluggish and predictable.

It was obvious to everyone of the 30,000 at Rugby Park on this grey Saturday that one of Taranaki's great favourites, Paul Martin, the first five-eighth, would (a) kick high to Andy Irvine at every reasonable opportunity, and (b) attempt, when scrum and range were right, drop kicks for goal. These he did almost on cue.

Just as predictably the Lions had practised to perfection the art of catching high balls and while they conceded two drop goals they were also practised at keeping Taranaki back from positions where drop-kicks could be attempted. This successfully eliminated Taranaki from having a winning chance as they had no other ideas designed to force scoring plays.

For the third game in a row there were three tries in the match. The two that were scored by the Lions were splendid. For the first, Andy Irvine made an intrusion into the back-line from fullback, running splendidly and timing to a nicety his pass to J. J. Williams, who swiftly completed the move in the corner. Irvine calmly kicked the goal from the sideline, which added to a 51 metre penalty he had earlier landed.

As the game developed, it was extremely interesting to consider the mental capacity of Andrew Robertson Irvine. He had not kicked at goal in any of the first three tour matches, so it was several months since he had kicked competitively. Yet these first two boomers, plus another 50 metre success early in the second half, were kicked with such ease he looked as though he had been in the kicking groove for weeks.

Add to that the mental anxieties he must have had about the persistence of New Zealand teams to kick skyscraper punts to him, and the knowledge that he carried the burden of J. P. R. Williams' absence on the tour, and his man of the match performance at New Plymouth was made all the more illustrious.

Irvine, in fact, scored the second try himself. The forwards, with Terry Cobner in the van, had made a strong surge up the left, forcing Taranaki to back pedal. The ball came out via a Cobner pass to David Burcher. He slipped over but passed to Irvine, who had again ranged into the backline. Irvine sent J. J. Williams away but rather than stay back and admire the handiwork which had given Williams space to move, he stayed with the Welsh flyer. In the end Irvine received a return pass from which he scored. Fine support play and thoughtful rugby endeavour from Irvine.

He also had cause to gaze skywards on many occasions to catch kicks, knowing that they were so well sent upwards they would arrive at the same time as the thundering hoardes of Taranaki's best.

But in this match Andy Irvine was safe and secure. His security, in fact, left us all wondering whether or not any New Zealand provincial team would find or use an alternative way to cross the gain line through the backs.

Taranaki offered an excellent forward pack but they were outgunned by the Lions in a mean mood. Nigel Horton was a very good lock forward, almost of Colin Meads proportions. Cobner, Derek Quinnell, Phil Orr and Gordon Brown gave excellent support in the solid performance.

Of course some other things happened in the game. John O'Sullivan, the Taranaki left winger, scored a neat try at the end, picking up a bouncing cross-kick and diving over in the corner; and Paul Martin, in the tradition of Taranaki five-eighths, landed his two dropkicks. In similar positions the Lions would have run for tries and the chance of six points. The Taranaki forwards did their illustrious forefathers proud. And Eliason proved his prediction was not just shallow words by showing the way in the exchanges up front. But in the end Taranaki was well beaten.

A point to consider was that, time and time again, Phil Bennett denied his outsides the chance to run with the ball even though the Lions' captain surely knew that the home backs were much inferior to his own. Repeatedly Bennett, his scrumhalf Brynmor Williams, and Irvine kicked back to touch when instinct called them to open play up. They were playing to their forwards, testing them time and again against a good local pack.

'We wanted to play it tight till we'd put out their fire', said Bennett afterwards. A stunning point this. A British team beating one of New Zealand's best forward divisions by using New Zealand tactics! What next, we wondered?

The teams

Lions: Irvine; J. J. Williams, Fenwick, Burcher, Gareth Evans; Bennett (captain), Brynmor Williams; Quinnell; Trevor Evans, Horton, Brown, Cobner; Price, Wheeler and Orr.

Taranaki: Stephen Davidson; Tony Brown, Paul Wharehoka, John O'Sullivan; Barry Gladding, Paul Martin; Dave Loveridge (replaced by Peter Fleming); Mike Carey; Graham Mourie (captain), Ian Eliason, John Thwaites, Ross Fraser; Bryce McEldowney, Felix O'Carroll and John McEldowney.

Scoring
Lions (21). Tries by J. J. Williams and Irvine; penalties (2) and conversion by Irvine, penalty and conversion by Bennett.
Taranaki (13). Try by John O'Sullivan; dropped goals (2) and penalty by Paul Martin.
Referee: Peter McDavitt (Wellington).   Saturday, 28 May 1977.

5. Lions 60, Wanganui-King Country 9. There have to be drawbacks when an international touring team enters a hinterland of rugby. Back of beyond Taumarunui certainly is, but you would have heard few complaints from the British Isles when they stayed there for their match against Wanganui-King Country. True, the closeness everybody and everything is to the main trunk line meant those of us who are unused to the rattle and clang of railway traffic spent some sleepness nights there. And honestly, it is way out in the backblocks isn't it? I mean, they looked at me, kind of strange, in the Post Office, when I posted an air mail letter. I mean, gee mister, no airport here. Just an airstrip.

But let me tell you. Taumarunui was just great. King Country people made certain of that. What also helped our stay there was a delightful display of rugby turned on, not only by the British Lions, but by the Wanganui-King Country team as well.

Forget about the score of 60 points to 9 in favour of the Lions. That was supplementary to the fact that everyone at the Taumarunui Domain that day had a damn good time.

'We improved on our showing against Hawke's Bay by making a little head-way at Gisborne', John Dawes said before the game, 'we made further advances against Taranaki and now we look to further improvements here.'

Coach of the home team was 41-year old Colin Meads, of Waitete. The local boy (Te Kuiti-born like I am, I'm proud to say) who went on to become the grim-faced, slab-jawed giant who made the King Country known world wide as the place where 'Pinetree' Meads — the All Black — lives.

Meads the player we all knew, remembered, and loved well. Meads the coach was a mystery. His All Black attitude and bearing were always grimness and grit. As a coach might we expect the same hardlined approach?

Not on your nelly, Kelly. Meads' boys when they took the field were far from dour and dull. In fact they were quite the reverse, for when play kicked off, whistled by Jeff Walker of Otago, the 12,000 crowd at the Taumarunui Domain gave first roar for enterprise to the locals. In the second minute of play flick-flick went the ball along the Combined team's backline to a bloke named Barry Donovan on the wing. And heck, as they are wont to often exclaim in Taumarunui, could he go! All sorts of Lions, running like the clappers, had to gather quickly to stop their line being breached.

The Lions weathered Combined's initial promise — built on enthusiasm for the occasion and determination to do well — and when their storm had subsided, when their 'fire had been put out', the tourists took charge and turned the day into a truly memorable one for King Country rugby.

There were four British tries in the first half, three of them in the fifteen minutes before half time, two of them scored by Andy Irvine.

In the second half, there were seven further tries by the Lions, three more to Andy Irvine. There were eight conversions. Sixty points. Wow!

Irvine's continuation of top flight form had the sportswriters hoping that there would be enough superlatives to spread over three months of watching him play in his current mood. His tally of five tries was a record for a fullback in an International match. The man was unstoppable.

Combined had started solidly enough, holding the Lions, as I have said, by being the first New Zealand team to run the ball with any consistency. There was only one try in 25 minutes. Then the flood gates opened.

Wanganui-King Country began their scoring with a penalty in the second half and finished the match by adding a converted try.

The try did not diminish in value because it was scored when the opposition had sixty points on the board. Robert Snowden, a replacement for Bruce Middleton, paid Colin Meads a fine tribute by scoring it, for Snowden is a member of Meads' club, Waitete.

For the All Black selectors, Jack Gleeson and J. J. Stewart, who had made the long journey to watch the game, the day could not have been all champagne and caviar. They saw a Lions performance which was more than a threat to New Zealand's chances in the test series. The Lions were now, with the style of their win over Wanganui-King Country, series favourites. No New Zealand side that I could see, including the All Blacks, could counter the tourists' backs, especially with Bennett and Irvine so much on top of their form. Sobering too, was the memory, only five days' old, of the Lions pack outplaying Taranaki's forwards.

In the All Blacks' favour, at this point of the tour, was the suspicion about the defensive strengths of some of their backs, injuries robbing them of key players at key times, and the knowledge (perhaps hope?) that British forward play might not yet be up to the class of the All Blacks traditional frontal power.

In the match Bennett and Irvine were the stars. Irvine's assisting play to the man with the ball played a large part in his five tries, all completed with his usual superb running. Bennett scored one try and made breaks which led to others.

Irvine planted one of his tries down then ran into the crowd clustered behind the dead-ball line. The enthusiasm with which they greeted him was as warming as the winter sun which shone on the Lions for the first time in a match on the tour. And it was not until I watched a slow motion replay later that I noticed another piece of trivia concerning an Andy Irvine scoring move. For his fourth try, born seventy metres further back from two expansive sidesteps by Bennett, Irvine had joined in for a long run down the touch line. When the defence grouped in a threesome and the way looked blocked, the sensible thing for Irvine to do would have been to pass to Ian McGeechan, who was also there. But Irvine began a slight movement of body-feet co-ordination on the spot, what boxers might call 'bobbing and weaving', and the defence became all hither and yon. What amused me was that McGeechan, too, became confused by Irvine's jinking and ended up in his own tangle. When Irvine scooted off in the direction of the try-line, McGeechan had his back to his team-mate. He did not turn to watch. Above all it seemed McGeechan, who had played so much in Irvine's company, knew where the flying Scotsman was heading, and why he was heading there, so did not need to look and see the result. The rest of us saw it, a brilliant try.

Bennett again played superbly, though I can report that he was tackled in this match, something that had not happened in his other tour games. The Lions' captain was able to demonstrate another string to his bow with his handling of a high ball at top speed. Peter Squires made the pass, like a basketballer's hook shot. Bennett reached up, and not quite in control, bounced the ball off his hand. It dropped and was caught at his waist, and he dashed in for his first try of the tour. Dare I remind you that he also landed eight conversions, to tie with Irvine as the top points scorer of the day. Twenty each.

Wanganui-King Country got some consolation out of the match when they dominated the last ten minutes, during which time they scored their try. Bill Osborne played very strongly at second five-eight, something which Messrs Stewart and Gleeson would have noted. Murray Kidd was a lively and thrustful centre and Graeme Coleman looked a distinct All Black lock forward of the future.

At the final whistle the British press corps shuffled forward towards the great Meads, eager for quotes they could blow into headlines. Meads looked them up and down. They craned forward, pencils ready.

'The Lions?' said Meads, 'oh, they were terribly good.'

Terribly good? I'll say, Pinetree.

The teams

Lions: Irvine; Squires, McGeechan (replaced by Gareth Evans), Fenwick, J. J. Williams; Bennett (captain), Morgan (replaced by Brynmor Williams); Quinnell; Squire, Martin, Keane, Neary; Orr, Wheeler and Cotton.

Wanganui-King Country: Francis Hill (Wanganui); Barry Donovan (King Country), Murray Kidd (K.C.), Richard Murray (W); Bill Osborne (W), Colin Howard (W); Sammy Pye (K.C.); Jim Tarrant (K.C.); Ray Stafford (W captain), Graeme Coleman (W), Grant Mitchinson (W), Bruce Middleton (W) (replaced by Robert Snowden (K.C.); Brent Dallinson (W), Graeme Poteka (K.C.) and Grant Lethborg (K.C.).

Scoring

Lions (60). Tries by Irvine (5), J. J. Williams (2), Quinnell, Brynmor Williams, Squire and Bennett; conversions (8) by Bennett.

Wanganui-King Country (9). Try by Robert Snowden; conversion and penalty by Francis Hill.

Referee: Jeff Walker (Otago).   Wednesday, 1 June 1977.

6. Lions 18, Manawatu-Horowhenua 12. The first test loomed, as the month of May passed into June. For following the Palmerston North game would come a natural geographical division in the itinerary where the team would leave the north, after their six match swing and head for tougher things (we New Zealanders hoped) in the south of the South Island. Palmerston North then, and the Manawatu-Horowhenua match, was the end of the beginning for the Lions and a return to reality after the exhilaration of Taumarunui.

Upon arrival by train in Ranfurly Shield country, the tourists were first thrown into a scare about the condition of their halfback,

Douglas Morgan, injured about the rib cage in the Wanganui-King Country game and in considerable discomfort. But a Palmerston North doctor announced that the detached muscles around the ribs would, with physiotherapy, diminish in pain within several days. The pronouncement that he could therefore play within a week was greeted, I may say, with a measure of disappointment by several in the British press party. There were some who had hoped that Morgan, only an average performer on tour to date, might manage to be replaced by someone more lively, the name of Gareth Edwards being whispered about hopefully.

The Lions team was duly announced to play the combined Manawatu-Horowhenua team amid fears that John Dawes had underestimated the strengths of the home fifteen, twelve of whom hailed from Manawatu, the holder of the fabled Ranfurly Shield. Included in the Lions team line-up for this game was a fair smattering of those players who had already been dismissed by some, myself included, as just being sturdy mid-weekers, incapable of forcing their way into the top fifteen. But as things turned out, Bruce Hay, John Bevan, Willie Duggan, Moss Keane and Clive Williams, hitherto foundation members of the second fifteen, all proved great value, as Manawatu-Horowhenua toiled mightily but could not maintain their early lead and were beaten 18 to 12.

A boggy, muddy pitch was not helped by a heavy shower soon after the match kicked off, nor by the decision to play two full curtain-raisers. The Showgrounds Oval, Palmerston North, is the ugliest venue for top rugby in New Zealand, with its alternately dusty (on dry days) and muddy (on wet days) speedway track around the perimeter of the grass. On this day it was slushy, treacherous and a severe embarrassment to Palmerston North, especially as the Governor-General was in attendance and had to be persuaded to tramp his way through the mire to meet the teams.

About the match, let's be honest. Though Manawatu-Horowhenua held the lead for fifty-four minutes and during some of that time had moments of great encouragement, they never looked like winning. The Lions were greatly pleased afterwards to triumph 'with tries over kicks', as George Burrell remarked, for they had scored four times from touch-downs while Combined could manage only a dropped goal and three penalties.

The tall hometown five-eighth, Brian Morris, drop-kicked Manawatu into the lead after eight minutes. Thereafter their captain, Doug Rollerson, added three penalties, which had us all nodding our heads vigorously in approval. After all, whoever heard of a New Zealander kicking goals in this season of historical turnaround?

While Rollerson, with a relaxed chipping style, landed the goals which had his side in the lead by 9 to nil and then by 12 to 4, Steve Fenwick was in all sorts of bother trying to do the same for the Lions. He missed five kicks in the first half and seven in the second but, in cricketing parlance, they had to keep him on as the British selection panel had boobed and had left the other top kickers, Bennett, Irvine, Martin and Morgan, out of the team for that match.

'Who was the reserve kicker?' we asked afterwards. 'Mossie Keane', said Dawes, and we all smiled, though Dawes insisted the big Kerryman, who had a vastly improved game, would have been able to land them all right. That Manawatu-Horowhenua could not score a try cost them the game. They came close on several occasions, once when the halfback Mark Donaldson made a strong bid, only to land short of the line and concede a penalty for playing the ball off the ground.

The Lions scored just once in the first half, from the high kick ploy that had bothered the Lions themselves in the early tour games. Hay sent one down to Morris, who muffed the catch, and the bouncing ball fell into the hands of the advancing Clive Williams. He it was who crossed for the try, his first in international rugby.

After trailing 12 to 4 at half-time the gap was quickly closed by the Lions. Bobby Windsor, securing tightheads with ease against a weak opposite, won one in a good running position. Brynmor Williams sent John Bevan away, Burcher handled next, and the Combined team's backline defence was not secure enough to prevent Steve Fenwick being sent into a gap to score.

Bruce Hay joined in an attack from fullback and, like Andy Irvine, stayed in support to receive a return pass in a scoring position The fourth and final effort, and the best in a solo sense, went to Brynmor Williams. From another Windsor tighthead, Williams saw the opportunity to make a surging blind-side burst. The opposition were slow to react and the holes opened for Williams to make a direct run to the line. In his walk back to half-way, the close-up camera caught young Williams clenching and re-clenching his fists in triumph, as if it was some great relief to be playing well, in this, the most encouraging performance by a Lions halfback on tour to date.

Dawes had been impressed too. 'Today was good for Brynmor', he told me afterwards, though I detected a great sense of relief that a halfback had at last 'come right' for him on tour, especially Brynmor Williams, who had been one of the tour gambles.

For the Combined team Kevin Eveleigh, with no Bennett to

chase, chased everything else and committed his person to the fray in much the same manner as he had done so courageously in South Africa in 1976. John Calleson was good and strong at lock and winger Murray Watts was a terror all afternoon, making several runs through the tourists which caused great embarrassment, so deficient was their tackling. Tackling was one area in which this Lions team let itself down badly; true lack of application was apparent.

Again the action was marred by injuries, some serious, some caused by legitimate means, others not. Brian Morris, who had looked a useful colt, was carried off unconscious, maintaining the horrific record of the tour to date, of having at least one major injury per match. John Loveday stumbled off, not knowing where he was, and Terry Cobner, the Lions captain for the day, lasted just ten minutes before running into his own man's boot and departing to get eight stitches in the wound.

It was a stirring match. Not great, but kept exciting for the 25,000 crowd by the closeness of the scores. Afterwards the Lions were 'delighted to have beaten the Ranfurly Shield holders'; the victory must have been all the sweeter because they had been in arrears for much of the way.

Which leaves just one aspect of the match to report, and I do it with heavy heart. After fifteen minutes of play the forwards of both teams piled into a ruck, near half-way, tumbling over each other in the usual way, seeking the ball. Willie Duggan found himself at the bottom, lying helplessly with his hands placed about his ears in the traditional safety position. He was trapped and held between the ball and the Combined halfback Mark Donaldson. As the ruck played itself out above him, Duggan was in receipt of a clean kick to the lower regions of his back. I saw the offender to be Donaldson who had played so well, but who in this flash-point deserved to be sent from the field in disgrace. Duggan suffered in the incident from other boots as well (Rollerson having rushed in mad-headedly from second five-eighth to trample all over him as well) but the un-provoked kicking of a man's unprotected spinal area was a far worse crime. The referee, Tom Doocey of Christchurch, told me he did not see the incident though it appeared to happen right before his eyes. I accept his word, of course, for had he seen it he must surely have sent Donaldson off.

It is a rugby union realism that a man who goes down in a ruck or maul must be prepared to be trampled on to some extent. At the same time he has the secure knowledge that kicking a man is not tolerated at any level. Those who pursue this kind of action as a means of clearing opposition players from the ball deserve and require to be made an example of.

My vision of the incident was no better than anyone else's. I reported in my commentary what I observed and felt. Radio New Zealand's tour commentator, John Howson, did the same. For each of us it had to be an instantaneous decision.

In the first press reports the clearly-observed act of a New Zealander kicking a prone and unprotected opponent did not rate space. It was staggering to me, this reaction of New Zealand's sporting press. There they were, following the Lions tour in droves, each looking for an angle and each reporting minuscule details of teams and players. How could their match reports disregard what was so obvious to so many?

I think and hope my reaction would be the same if it had been the All Black captain or some other well-known player involved or, if you like, someone from the Lions camp. Brutally kicking a man on the ground where he can do nothing to help himself has no place in rugby, or in any sport.

In view of the newspaper uproar that had surrounded Moaner van Heerden's stamping of Peter Whiting's head in the third test in South Africa in 1976 and an incident, also widely reported, where a Welsh rugby league player, Jim Mills, had scraped the face of a New Zealand opponent during a World Cup match, the Donaldson affair did not show up the courage of the New Zealand sporting press in a good light.

I wonder if their timidity would have remained had it been Willie Duggan who had kicked Mark Donaldson?

The teams
Lions: Hay; Gareth Evans, Fenwick, Burcher, Squires; Bevan, Brynmor Williams; Duggan; Cobner (captain — replaced by Quinnell), Horton, Keane, Squire; Price, Windsor and Clive Williams.

Manawatu-Horowhenua: Alan Innes (Manawatu); Ken Granger (M), Mike Nutting (Horowhenua), Murray Watts (M); Doug Rollerson (M), Brian Morris (M) (replaced by Paul Broederlow (M), Mark Donaldson (M); Geoff Old (M); Kevin Eveleigh (M), John Loveday (M) — replaced by Gary Knight (M), John Calleson (M), Lindsay Robinson (H); Kent Lambert (M), Doug Easton (H) and Perry Harris (M).

Scoring
Lions (18). Tries by Clive Williams, Steve Fenwick, Bruce Hay and Brynmor Williams; conversion by Fenwick.

Manawatu-Horowhenua (12). Dropped goal by Brian Morris; penalties (3) by Doug Rollerson.
Referee: Tom Doocey (Canterbury).   Saturday, 4 June 1977.

5
Three in the South: Matches 7-9

7. Lions 12, Otago 7. As one who has had the pleasure to travel New Zealand from tip to tail in recent years to report rugby matches in all their distinctive and memorable variety, I have to record my opinion that it is in the South Island, and more particularly in the south of the South Island, that rugby is played in the manner that is nearest to my concept of the game at its best.

Some deep instinct is stirred when I see a Southland forward division driving and churning from a line-out; or when an Otago pack hears the frenzied call of its supporters and sees ahead a ball that is 'ruckable'; or when a Canterbury team charges upfield, driven by a momentum built on toughness, determination and grit. For South Island rugby is just that. Grit personified.

Not for them the knee-high socks and city-slicker hair styles of an Auckland team. Not for them the planned efficiency that is typical of Wellington's game. Not for them the cockiness and confidence of other North Island centres. South Island rugby is based on principles of commonsense, courage and a complete disregard for anything that is ostentatious. South Island rugby is grit.

It is, to be honest, a little old-fashioned in this world of counter-attacks, proficiency skills, second-phase plays and all those other terms that have become part of the modern approach. Good old-fashioned commonsense remains one of South Island rugby's greatest attributes. For it is still a winning style. Hard forwards, efficient backs, sound defences. On these cornerstones have risen a brand of rugby that has become easily recognised and attributable to only one part of New Zealand.

When Phil Bennett's lads flew to the South Island they knew it would be hard to play well and win well against Otago and Southland. These two matches, plus New Zealand Universities, were the final lead-up to the First Test in Wellington. Otago and Southland had a history of great success against the British style of play and, naturally enough, were determined in 1977 that it should continue.

The Lions came through their test, to turn back these two gritty combinations, if not with flying colours then at least with heads held high. Their wins might have been shaky, but wins they were.

Otago prepared for their match, at their vastly-improved and tidied venue of Carisbrook, with all their usual hardness. Their dedication, once the game had started, was as though they had condensed their lifetimes into eighty minutes. They gave themselves to an unspoken pact, a commitment to struggle and never concede. In terms of the playing of the match Otago succeeded in attaining and satisfying all their pre-match dedication and determination. They only missed one thing, to score more points than the Lions.

Otago did play mightily, as though their very lives depended on it, and knocked the Lions about as though they were empty trashcans in a high wind. But it was not enough. Phil Bennett, by game's end, had kicked four penalties for twelve points, while Otago had scored a try and kicked one penalty, for just seven points. The Lions won.

What the scoreboard did not show was a moral victory for Otago. They out-pointed their more illustrious opposition in those areas of the game which are most-revered in the South — rucking, tackling, gutsiness and effort. Therefore, the big, boisterous and occasionally boorish crowd went home satisfied at the end. They were unenvious of the Lions victory because it had been their own team which had outplayed the highly-regarded opposition in those areas of play that were nearest and dearest to their understanding of the game.

It was a moral victory for Otago, but more than that, a moral victory for the South Island style of play and, even in defeat, a great encouragement to the All Blacks for the series ahead.

Otago's effort was summed up beforehand by Mervyn Jaffray, their excellent captain 'We're going to get stuck in', he said. And they did.

All this happened even though the home team were without Duncan Robertson, their much-loved All Black, who was injured with a slightly-crushed nerve at the back of his knee. Neil Purvis, another proud Otago stalwart, had also withdrawn with a shoulder injury and the Otago team had also lost, for varying reasons, two of their other 1976 All Blacks, Laurie Mains and Paul Sapsford. Even without them the spirit was there. Rex Smith, the flanker, was an outstanding example of courage, playing fearlessly even though he was outweighed by every other forward on the field; he took some fearful punishment from the Lions, both foul and fair. In fact, in the match the British did little that they, in all truth, could call good. They were annoying to watch every time Otago had a scrum put-in, for they twisted and turned and crabbed away from the mark to prevent a quick delivery. That they were allowed to do this all game was a black mark against Brian Duffy, the referee.

The Lions back play was stodgy. Mike Gibson's form at centre was poor, his reactions slow. Elgan Rees, making his first tour appearance, looked a player of promise, though he had little or no chance to prove it, so poor was the combination of players inside.

The Lions forwards learnt, at their own expense, a solid rucking lesson. Their strength at the mauls was proved to be ineffective against a team that could ruck well.

The Lions had picked a strong team for the game, with the three undoubted back stars — Bennett, Irvine and J. J. Williams — all in the lineup. The pitch was softish but reasonable, considering the recent heavy rain.

There was concern early on when Nigel Horton left the field holding his hand tenderly. His broken thumb meant the call went out for England's Billy Beaumont to fly to New Zealand as a replacement. Horton would be missed,

Phil Bennett by this stage was rapidly heading towards the kingly status that had been accorded Barry John in the 1971 team. He was also, in the end, the only difference between the two teams. He landed a penalty after six minutes and another straight after the Otago fullback Bevan Wilson had scored the day's only try. The Lions led by 6 to 4 at half-time.

Wilson played soundly enough but I could not accept the after-match praise that was heaped upon him. The seven goal-kick attempts he missed were all hooked to the left; they cost his team the match, as some were from handy places. He did succeed with one so close he could have thrown it over, after Mike Gibson had strayed across the offside line. Otago were then ahead by 7 to 6 but two more of Bennett's penalties completed the scoring. 12-7 to the British Isles. So ended a rousing and thoroughly enjoyable spectacle.

Wilson, touted by many as the All Black test fullback, looked a good player but only at representative level, for he did not indicate to me any more tangible attributes than solidity and safety. Ideal characteristics these, but more suited to Otago rugby than for anything higher. What was more believable, though it could have been just talk, was the story that Jack Gleeson had told Rex Smith to 'Stay fit, we might need you'. That quote swept Dunedin like wildfire that night.

The teams

Lions: Irvine; Rees, Burcher, Gibson, J. J. Williams; Bennett (captain), Brynmor Williams; Duggan; Evans, Martin, Horton (replaced by Keane), Squire; Price, Wheeler, Cotton.

Otago: Bevan Wilson; Robert Gibson, Gary Bennetts (replaced by Simon Thompson), John Colling; Don Colling, Lyn Jaffray; Tim Burcher; Mervyn Jaffray (captain); Rex Smith, Wayne Graham, Gary Seear, Rob Roy; Lindsay Clark, Ken Bloxham, Ray O'Connell.

Scoring

Lions (12). Penalties (4) by Bennett.

Otago (7). One try and one penalty by Bevan Wilson.

Referee: Brian Duffy

Carisbrook, Dunedin.   Wednesday, 8 June 1977.

8. Lions 20, Southland 12. 'We're happy just to get another "W" on our record card', Phil Bennett told New Zealand television viewers as the darkness closed in on Carisbrook after the Lions tight match against Otago. At Palmerston North four days earlier George Burrell had said he was pleased that the Lions should have beaten Manawatu-Horowhenua by 'tries over kicks', but when he told the aftermatch crowd at Dunedin that it was nice to have won here 'with kicks over tries', he was not just playing with words to amuse those of us who had been at both functions. He was making obvious reference to that famous — or was it infamous? — day in 1959 when Don Clarke had made an All Black victory over the Lions by precisely the same means — the landing of penalty goals. What a bleating there was at that New Zealand test win! The 1977 Lions now smiled smugly. They knew what it was like to have won without scoring a try and New Zealanders who remembered the 1959 hoo-ha now knew what it was like to be on the receiving end of an all-boot loss.

So that was a score evened. Next it was Southland. 'Here we are in Invercargill', Nigel Starmer-Smith told his BBC viewers before the match, 'where the next stop going south is Antarctica.' It *was* cold.

The sun cast a pale warmth on the Lions preparation. The team had something to prove in this game. Was the Otago effort just a bad day? Or were there more horrendous experiences in store for 'Syd', 'Dod', 'Benny' and the boys.

Their Southland opposition was rated 'only a solid lot'. Just a typical New Zealand representative side. Frank Oliver, the skipper, was obviously their king-pin.

Oliver had been an outstanding figure in Southland rugby for years. In a province that bred big, tough forwards, Frank was in the top league. He had been a 1969 Junior All Black while still a youngster and missed several seasons with injury problems. But Frank Oliver is not the kind of man to fade away. His rugby in 1976 was of such a calibre that his selection in the All Blacks was a shot's eye certainty in Southland and widely expected in the rest of the country.

But even Frank Oliver and his ability to lift those around him could not stop the Lions beating Southland. The final scoreline of 20 points to 12 was much like the Otago game, another 'W' on the record card.

The game exhibited no greatness. Instead it was an absorbing struggle. Again, the Lions had to come from behind to secure their victory. Oliver played a handy role in his lively forward pack, with special mention for Ash McGregor, the number 8 forward.

Once more the Lions had to thank Andy Irvine. He again came on for the hapless Bruce Hay. There followed a fourteen minute scoring burst — three tries by the threequarters, two of them with Irvine involved. There was more to the win than that, of course. The second-half forward play was most satisfying to John Dawes after the 'lesson learned' at Dunedin. Allan Martin played his most significant role on tour, jumping high, and making two-handed clasps of the ball on many occasions.

'The come-back in the second forty minutes typifies the excellent spirit in this team', said Burrell afterwards.

Southland made a rattling good beginning to the game, with a brilliant passing rush from the kick-off, and going into the lead when Brian McKechnie landed a penalty after sixty seconds. They surged strongly on many other occasions and for a time the Lions' unbeatable record looked insecure.

The first Lions' try was from a break by Brynmor Williams, the ball then passing through Irvine's hands in a swinging movement to Elgan Rees, who made haste to the corner.

Irvine came in to the line two minutes later, and Gareth Evans enjoyed the extra space created for him to run thirty metres for the try.

The third, and last, went to Gibson. A five metre scrum. Squire, playing his fourth game in a row, peeled away to link up with the backs. Gibson scored the try after the ball moved along the chain and his grin (from our close-up camera again) was the happiest on tour.

Irvine added one conversion and Allan Martin, exhibiting his goal-kicking talents for the first time on tour, landed two big penalties after Bennett had missed two early on.

For Southland, Brian McKechnie, better known as a New Zealand cricket player, kicked four penalties out of four attempts, prompting every third person I met in Invercargill that night to advise me that he should be taking the kicks for New Zealand. McKechnie's general play from the first five-eighth position was very good, handling well and directing smoothly. But outside him was the star of the day.

Stephen Pokere is a frizzy-haired youngster, aged only 18. He came into the match with a reputation of brilliance that we outsiders decided he could not possibly live up to. He was called 'the greatest back Southland has ever produced'. He was called 'the best young Maori back since Mac Herewini'. He was called 'terrific', 'tremendous', 'super'. Poor Pokere, what a state he must have been in when he went on the field. But he showed not a trace of nervousness once the whistle had gone and the match started.

Pokere is like Sid Going, a Mormon. Educated at Southland Boys' High School, he possessed a natural flair at all ball games. Shortly after he was chosen to play in the 1975 South Island Under-16 soccer team, he gave up the round ball game and switched to rugby. In 1977 he made an instant impression by playing well in the Freezing Workers' Tournament, which is called 'the hardest rugby in the world'.

After just eight senior club matches, he was introduced to the Southland rep side. In his first-class debut, against North Otago, he drop-kicked two goals — a grand beginning for a youngster. Apparently his back was to the goal posts on each occasion; he had to turn, reposition his feet and let fly. This he did naturally, the movements of body perfectly integrated with his thought patterns — one kick off the left foot, one off the right!

In this match against the Lions, Stephen Pokere was every bit as good as his rave previews. Twice in the first spell when Southland was going so well, he cut through between Phil Bennett and Ian McGeechan. Perhaps he ran on too long on each occasion for no points were scored as a direct result, but that was due to his newness and enthusiasm. One could just imagine him saying to himself, 'Heck, I got through this far, I might make it all the way.' Pokere defended stoutly. As well as being strong in the tackle for such a young chap, he several times raced backwards, fielded kicks, and returned them to touch when the slightest falter would have put the Lions over.

So the tourists went on to victory. Once again they did not score a try in the first half but their victory was sound — not thrilling, not dazzling, just sound.

The referee was Auckland's John Pring, who had not changed one iota in physical appearance since controlling the four tests between the Lions and the All Blacks in 1971. Pring did a good job in this match and I, not usually one for compliments, told him so. 'Did the Lions like you?' I ventured. 'Not this time', he replied, 'They didn't say so, but you usually can tell.'

At the Invercargill airport that morning, waiting in the cold for the same plane, was the Associate Minister of Finance, Hugh Templeton. In his capacity as Minister of Broadcasting he had doubtless come to know who I was. We nodded and started chatting. 'Come and have a cup of coffee, Keith', he said 'and I'll tell you how the All Blacks can do these blokes.' So we did, and he did. His logic was sound, his rugby opinions well-judged. His forecast of a New Zealand win was based on his Southland background of winning through the forwards first and foremost and then opening up with the backs. Very pleasant it was. I thank you, Sir. What a change to hear such sound sporting logic from a National Party man!

The teams
Lions: Hay (replaced by Irvine); Rees, Gibson, McGeechan, Gareth Evans; Bennett (captain), Brynmor Williams; Duggan; Trevor Evans, Martin Brown, Squire; Orr, Windsor, Price.
Southland: Jeff Gardiner; Evan McLellan, Wayne Boynton, Shane O'Donnell; Stephen Pokere, Brian McKechnie; Dave Shanks; Ashley McGregor; Lester Rutledge, Frank Oliver (captain), Murray Leach, Sam Anderson; Dave Saunders, Bruce Lamb, Philip Butt.

Scoring
Lions (20). Tries by Rees, Gibson and Gareth Evans; conversion by Irvine; penalties (2) by Martin.
Southland (12). Penalties (4) by Brian McKechnie.
Referee: John Pring (Auckland)
Rugby Park, Invercargill.   Saturday, 11 June 1977.

9. Lions 9, Universities 21. There was no doubt about the great relief in the touring team's camp after turning back the challenges of two of the Lions' historical bogeys in New Zealand. The Otago victory was hollow, by virtue of the goal-kicks and some ineptitude in the face of vigorous rucking. The Southland win, though solid enough, was not nearly as convincing as a touring team wanted one week before a test match.

There was, at this stage of the tour, more than a matching comparison between Bennett's team and the 1974 Lions in South Africa. There, great store was placed, by Willie-John McBride and his team, on coming at the opposition late in the game. After Dunedin and Invercargill, not to mention Hawke's Bay, the 1977 Lions had shown they could do the same, that is play moderately well, even badly, and still be the victors.

The next on the list was New Zealand Universities. It was generally accepted that this match would be light relief before the rigours of successive Saturdays against the All Blacks in the first test, then Canterbury, Wellington (a much improved team this year) and the All Blacks again, in the second test. So there was little murmur when the Lions announced a side that contained most of those players recovering from injury.

No matter how much the team's management had insisted that they were 'taking each match as it comes' and 'treating each game as a separate entity' there was now a growing impression that this side was going from match to match with the confidence that no matter what kind of rugby New Zealand teams threw at them, the Lions were ready. After all, had they not turned back Hawke's Bay's fiery rampages? Had they not 'put out Taranaki's fire'? Had they not won by brilliant running at Taumarunui and by dour forward endeavour at Invercargill? And did they not win at Dunedin, in the manner of some of the 1974 matches, when they should not have? It was all falling into place. The side was growing up, developing maturity and security. The tour was setting up very nicely for them.

But the line between confidence and over-confidence is narrow and the difference between satisfaction and smugness is of the same dimension. You can teeter on it and topple either way. Could it have been that after repelling all boarders in their first eight matches the Lions were just too sure of themselves when it came to gauging the New Zealand University team which lay in wait on a dank, dark, smoggy Christchurch afternoon?

Starmer-Smith, interviewing Dawes in Invercargill for the BBC, had asked, 'So now you've got over this "fifth test", how do you feel?' Dawes replied with a smile and a shrug, 'Oh these New Zealanders, they're always telling us the next match will be our fifth test. I suppose now they'll be telling us we'll be in trouble against New Zealand Universities'.

What happened was this. A bunch of get-together no-names, dressed in black and called New Zealand Universities, with form that any sensible punter would call 'rough', re-wrote the dictionary meaning of the term 'intestinal fortitude' and gave it a new look.

'We set out', said their breathless captain, Doug Rollerson, afterwards to a silent British Press corps, 'to punch them up the guts'. He did not allude to any malicious forethought in this team tactic, for his was a New Zealand rugby phrase from the old school. It means, as Mervyn Jaffray had said in Dunedin, 'to get stuck in'. It also means 'to give them hell', 'to make life tough', 'to steam up', etc. And that is what New Zealand Universities did. They did all those things I have mentioned plus playing commonsense rugby without distraction or detraction. This match plan, to play the Lions 'up the guts' was the ideal ploy to use on this day.

The Lions hated it. They fumbled and fizzed about all match and never looked like maintaining the unbeaten record they had held since 1971. In this match there was only one winner, and it was not the British Isles.

The New Zealand Universities team had a flanker, Dennis Thorn, an Auckland player of some standing who had never been noticed or nominated for higher honours. It was Thorn, in brimming and bursting form, who ran among an inept British backline, cutting down attacks and building new ones for his team. A pace or two behind Thorn were Ray Scott and Graeme Elvin, ready to turn the breakdowns into on-going forward thrusts. At halfback Canterbury's Mark Romans, a schoolboy star several seasons before and an ex-Hawke's Bay and Otago player, spun out passes of such accuracy and velocity that he looked as though he could substitute the NZU jersey monogram for a silver fern any day.

In the outer backs there was Rollerson, who chipped over three penalties and hit the post with two others. His general play was built on enthusiasm rather than innate skill but his guidance and authority were important in his team's boundless effort. Paul Macfie, the first five-eighth, was sharp and reliable and fullback Doug Heffernan reached heights I had not expected him to attain.

In the first minute of the first half the Lions conceded, for the second match in a row, a kickable penalty. Once again, they failed to score a try in the first forty minutes. By the interval they were down by 3 to 9, all penalties.

An improvement by the Lions was indicated for a time in the second half. When Tony Neary snaffled up a loose University scrum heel, the former basketball player sent over a perfect hook-shot pass to Gordon Brown. Brown thundered on and passed to Derek Quinnell, who crashed over for a try. Good stuff. Douglas Morgan's sideline conversion squared the scores at 9-all and everybody nodded knowingly. 'Here's where the Students get it', was the forecast.

But the University team, whipped into a frenzy, were back in the game straight away. Rollerson told me afterwards he asked his team to 'die for the man next to you'. This they did, but they were all still standing at the end.

When the score was 12-9 to Universities the Lions missed a penalty, kicked by Douglas Morgan. On our TV replay it appeared to go over but the touch-judges, after hesitating, ruled it under. There was a school of thought that the equalising three points would have brought the Lions right back into the game, but for me the incident was of no consequence compared with the dominance Universities exerted over their illustrious opponents.

The second half was as dramatic a performance as I could recall from an underdog lineup against a touring team. The University men drove into tackles (Thorn was so good he rates another mention here, as well as centre Dan Fouhy), they out-mauled the Lions (Denholm and Paul Oliver, take a bow), and they played with a spirit that Doug Rollerson said was the best he had ever known.

There were only two tries in the match, one to each team. The University effort was scored by Macfie after good work in the build-up by Dave Syms. The referee, Kevin Lynch of Poverty Bay, did not see two knock-ons by Romans in the move but, no matter, the Lions were completely outplayed, completely outclassed.

Heffernan sealed the victory with a booming 50 metre penalty out of the Lancaster Park mud and at the final whistle, the New Zealand Universities team danced like demented dons in their moment of elation.

The hard facts for the Lions to bite on in the days leading up to the first test were these; they had taken the Universities far too easily; their team contained several players who were newly recovered from injury and accordingly they played rustily; Moss Keane and Gordon Brown both left the field at Christchurch, making big problems in selecting locks, as Nigel Horton was heading home.

Of major worry to John Dawes was the lack of fire from his team. This was a shoddy performance by the Lions, their first defeat in New Zealand since 1971, when they were beaten by the All Blacks on the same ground.

The last word must go to Doug Rollerson, the Universities' aggressive and well-spoken leader. Said Rollerson, 'When I'm an old man and dying and they start to shovel the dirt in on me, I'll still be able to say, WE were FIRST to beat the '77 Lions!'

The teams

Lions: Hay; Rees, McGeechan (captain), Burcher, Squires; Bevan, Morgan; Quinnell; Squire, Brown (replaced by Martin), Keane (replaced by Orr), Neary; Cotton, Wheeler, Clive Williams.

New Zealand Universities: Doug Heffernan (Canterbury); Randall Scott (Canterbury), Dan Fouhy (Victoria), Russell Hawkins (Massey); Doug Rollerson (Massey — captain), Paul Macfie (Lincoln); Mark Romans (Canterbury); Graeme Elvin (Otago); Dennis Thorn (Auckland), Garry Brown (Canterbury), Wayne Graham (Otago), Ray Scott (Canterbury); Greg Denholm (Auckland), Dave Syms (Auckland), Paul Oliver (Canterbury).

Scoring

New Zealand Universities (21). Try by Paul Macfie; penalties (3) and conversion by Doug Rollerson; penalties (2) by Doug Heffernan.

Lions (9). Try by Quinnell; conversion and penalty by Morgan.

Referee: Kevin Lynch (Poverty Bay).

Lancaster Park, Christchurch.   Tuesday, 14 June 1977.

6
The First Test: Wellington

10. British Isles 12, New Zealand 16. It takes a test played in Wellington's winter to show off the hardiness of New Zealand rugby folk. 42,500 brave souls huddled together in a strong, strong southerly to watch the playing of the first 1977 test match between New Zealand and the British Isles.

It was a muddling game, not played convincingly by either side. New Zealand won by 16 points to 12, the same score that the All Blacks had won by in the second test against the Lions, on the same ground, eleven years previously. Before the game it was widely felt that though the 1977 Lions had been beaten in their most recent match, and beaten badly, they would still start the Wellington test more favoured to win.

The All Black team seemed up against it before they walked on to the softish test pitch. Their preparation had been insufficient and they had to better a team that had lived as a unit for nearly five weeks. But this New Zealand team quickly warmed to the tasks set by their new coach, Jack Gleeson. In the end, the New Zealanders were thoroughly deserving of victory.

The All Blacks won so much possession from set starts that their opposition was denied the chance to unleash the attacking power of their superior back division, but the winning performance of the New Zealand team was far from complete. The All Black back play was as disjointed as it had been in the good old days when our backs stood behind the pack as though they were in an unemployment bureau.

As an exercise in encouragement, however, this match served as great value for the All Blacks. It gave them courage to take the battle to their adversaries rather than wait to let it come to them.

The Lions, suddenly a beaten team, were forced to recognise for the second time in four days the reality of meeting New Zealanders who were deeply determined to correct some of the disasters of recent years.

Athletic Park has many personal memories for me. From the TV commentary platform, high on the mountainous Millard Stand, I could look out across the neighbourhood where I had spent much of my childhood. Berhampore School, not two hundred yards from the park, was where I had been head prefect twenty years before. Behind the main grandstand was the South Wellington Intermediate School where, in 1959, the young Quinn had been given the highest honour known then to man — at least in my eyes — being appointed ball boy for the season at Athletic Park.

That was the year of Ronnie Dawson's British team. They played three matches at Athletic Park with Young Quinn running the balls back and forth to the wingers for all three. What dizzy days they were for a young boy! Over the years I came to love that ground with its brooding western bank, its dingy, dusty main grandstand and its chamber-like dressing rooms.

The ground has changed much over the years. For its 1977 test match it was for the first time an all-ticket affair. The embankments at the north and south end, previously allocated to those who prefer to stand and watch, were now covered with freshly-painted, brand-new, numbered, pre-sold seats. Underneath the main stand it is still dingy and dusty, and that familiar smell of liniment still hangs about, but Athletic Park has lost character as well as capacity, and lost the spontaneity of its standing-room-only terrace crowd.

The New Zealand selectors, Jack Gleeson, John Stewart and Eric Watson, had met in Dunedin after the playing of the Lions-Otago match, to consider and announce the All Black team for the test to be played on Athletic Park. They were housed in a tiny caravan away from the milling crush of the aftermatch function. When they emerged from the cold quarters, warmed only by a bottle of whisky, they released a side that contained three new test players, Colin Farrell of Auckland, Lawrie Knight of Poverty Bay, and Andy Haden of Auckland.

The selection of Colin Farrell at fullback was one that verged on the sensational. He had not played in the trials at Wanganui, six men being used ahead of him. He was obviously included for his running ability, which was an ambitious idea, but when the wind blew and the rain came and the conditions were against running, Farrell's solid play was below All Black standard.

Grant Batty had played six games of rugby in the Tauranga club competition, and no others, since the All Blacks had been in South Africa last year. 'How's the knee, Batts?' I asked, for this was the reason he had played so little in the new season. 'As good as it'll ever be', he replied. Before the test kicked off, however, a story came to my ears that the Batty knee was far from good. One hard knock, it was said, and his rugby career would be over.

It was typical of this pugnacious little combatant that he had made himself available, knowing that the risks involved were of hair-line breadth. This was part of the greatness of Grant Bernard Batty.

Interesting was the decision not to play Derek Quinnell. Moss Keane and Willie Duggan, the two Irishmen, were preferred as the second lock (with Martin, Gordon Brown and Nigel Horton being injured) and the number eight. The hardness of the Welshman at ruck and maul, where his bodily involvement was direct and intense, seemed a necessary part of the Lions forward drive. To leave him out was an error.

The All Black team came out to TV1 on the Friday night to watch again the film of their 1974 triumph in Cardiff. That was the day the All Blacks played Phil Bennett at the Arms Park and beat the 'Welsh XV' by 12 to 3. Ten of the team who had won so well on that occasion were to play Bennett again next day. Contain him, the next day at Athletic Park, force him to tackle and be tackled, and the All Blacks knew they had more than just a chance of winning.

As it was, when the wind whipped into Athletic Park in gusts of thirty knots and the temperature dropped to seven degrees, and the test match kicked off, it was the Lions themselves who made the error that forced Bennett's frontal weakness to be tested for the first time on tour. It came in the fourth minute of play. Earlier Andy Irvine had stretched the coincidence of first-minute penalties to three matches in a row; he kicked a goal from over sixty metres.

In the fourth minute Sid Going came to have the ball in his hands, some ten metres from the Lions' line. He looked left and then right, his opponents moved left and right in cover defence, for they were well aware of the New Zealander's brilliance at times like this. In doing so they left the space immediately ahead wide open. Going breezed in, passing seven or eight Lions in the process and ploughing through Phil Bennett for the try.

My reaction on seeing Bennett on the ground immediately afterwards was that he had collided heavily with Going. On watching the TV replay we saw that Willie Duggan, the big Kilken-nyman, had started late in an attempt to catch Going, had missed and fallen on Bennett. Duggan is over sixteen stone, Bennett is somewhere around eleven stone. The blow to Bennett's left shoulder left him weak and dazed. Surprisingly, for all the courage and strength attributed to him, Bennett did not bounce back into the fray. His injury cost the Lions a vital playing factor in the game.

The rest of the first half was exciting rugby action, with the crowd swept along in the high drama. Bennett recovered sufficiently to take over the goal-kicking and was successful three times, making four penalties in all. They were assisted, of course, by the wind. But as the Lions kicked goals the All Blacks scored tries. First there was Going's. The second went to Brad Johnstone, the big prop, who was rewarded for fast following-up of a Bryan Williams penalty attempt; as the ball tumbled out of Bennett's hands under the posts John-stone clutched it to his chest and scored.

The third brought the house down. Brynmor Williams, playing way above his previous tour form, made a running break at halfway, scattering the New Zealanders. He linked up with Trevor Evans who went looking for the backline. And there they were, stretched out to his right, four strong. A try was a certainty, allowing for all passes to be held, for the only All Black in the five to one situation was Batty.

Instinctively he dashed forward. Bruce Robertson, in one of his rare involvements in the game, tackled Evans in an enveloping motion, forcing him to lift his pass to Phil Bennett. Batty nipped for-ward, made the intercept, and ran. He ran and ran. Andy Irvine, who was up in the movement, told me later he turned and saw Batty disappearing into the gloom. 'I gave him about twelve metres start. I was gaining on him all the way but I thought Graham Price might get there first!' Batty laughed when recalling the incident. 'Fancy nearly being caught by a prop!' But there was no catching the most popular man in New Zealand. Batty went in by the posts, Williams converted and as there was no further scoring in the game, Batty became the match-winner.

There was more to New Zealand's winning margin than points on the board. The All Black superiority in general play was marked. Kevin Eveleigh and Lawrie Knight were splendid loose men, Eveleigh being the crusher of many potential Lions attacks.

Knight in his test debut forsook his usual emphasis on line-out play and became a driving tight-loose man. Without decrying the talents of Andy Leslie, who had occupied that position for the previous ten test matches, Knight gave the All Blacks forward surge more power. The team benefitted from the different style of play.

At line-outs the winning advantage to the All Blacks became almost laughable. Allan Martin and Moss Keane were completely beaten by Frank Oliver and Andy Haden. Aucklander Haden, the biggest man ever to pull on a New Zealand jersey, played the game of his life, leaping high for well-controlled taps, and at other times getting the ball in two hands as though Martin, his opposite, was not there at all. Oliver was a typical South Island forward, intent not on the showy side of rugby but working at overtime rates in those areas of the game which are hard, physical and brutal.

With the thrown ball being won principally by Haden, Oliver and Kirkpatrick and Johnstone and Knight getting some as well, the All Blacks won the line-out count on one score by 31 to 11. After the match Clem Thomas, the former Welsh International, Nigel Starmer-Smith of the BBC, Andy Lesie and myself marked Haden as 'Man of the Match' for a Lion Breweries promotion. It was just reward.

Bennett stayed on the field despite his pain, a gallant act, though many felt he might have served his team better by leaving the field to let a fresh man on.

Denied possession of any quality the Lions backs, already shackled by Bennett's injury, could not take their talents to their opposites. Instead they were forced into a defensive role. Steve Fenwick came into his own here, tackling grimly and allowing no man to pass. But the rest of the British backs, McGeechan and J. J. Williams in particular, were disappointments. Williams, in fact, might not have been there at all so little did he contribute to his team's cause.

Only in the front row did the Lions operate with equality. Afterwards there were many who said the Orr, Windsor, Price front rankers — in tussle with Johnstone, the new All Black captain Tane Norton, and Ken Lambert — created higher standards of scrummaging than had been seen in South Africa in 1976.

Though the All Blacks won by a more impressive physical margin than the scoreline of four points indicated, there was not a lot to enthuse about in the New Zealand's backs. Sid Going had a confusing match. His passing, when he got around to it, was shoddy. The man was obviously over the hill in this department. He missed Duncan Robertson time and time again, and as a consequence the Otago player was made to look in bad form. Bill Osborne, the second five-eighth, was thus left with a clean-up role, which meant he often

8. One of Andy Irvine's rare backline entry runs in the first test. He came in twice, was well tackled twice and was then withdrawn behind everything to watch. The New Zealand team was delighted. Peter Squires is in the foreground.

9. A significant date for your calendar — 18 June 1977. Sid Going has just scored one of his cheekiest, most brilliant tries for the All Blacks. The day was significant for the Lions too. With Willie Duggan's sixteen stone weight on top of him Phil Bennett suffered a most hurtful shoulder ailment. His form on tour took a decline from this moment.

10. With the All Black captain Tane Norton and Willie Duggan looking on, one of the great men of New Zealand rugby, Sid Going, makes a burst in the first test: hands firmly on the ball, body leaning forward into the run, eyes looking keenly for the next move. There will only ever be one 'super Sid'.

11. Never look back as you leave the battle they say in the B Grade movies. Well, you kind of have to, don't you, if the Lions have just scored? Alex Wyllie, Canterbury's captain, suffering from a knee injury has only been off the field for a few seconds, accompanied by his chief coach, S. F. ('Tiny') Hill. They look back to see that J.J. Williams has scored going through a gap where Wyllie would have been.

12. Four tests to nil in the series to the All Blacks if this pass had been caught? Who knows? Lyn Jaffray juggles the ball on the way to the goal line in the last seconds of the second test. Phil Bennett desperately tries to save the tour with his tackle. In the next second the ball had bobbed away from Jaffray, was forced by the Lions and the series was saved.

13. Fun and games in the second test at Lancaster Park. The crowd shows mixed reactions as (from left) Quinnell, Fenwick, Duggan, J. J. Williams (14), Haden, Johnstone (1), Wheeler (2) and Going (9) slug it out. But what really catches the eye is the little session of social chit-chat going on between Phil Bennett and referee Brian Duffy.

14. It's all worthwhile. Who cares about those teeth I lost some years back? Who cares about the scratch-marks and the dirty gear and the biggest beer-pot in the team? We won, didn't we? Peter Wheeler's delightful reaction after the Lions 13 - 9 victory in the second test. He has the ball, tucked up his jersey, and this photograph as a personal souvenir of a great day for the Lions.

had to gather a loose pass and run it back towards the forwards.

That, in turn, meant Bruce Robertson saw little play, a great pity, for the New Zealanders would have made him a linch-pin in their pre-match attacking plans.

Bryan Williams played with the aggression he had discovered in recent years. It was pleasing to see him, like a big brother, encourage and cover Colin Farrell in general play, for being a new test fullback on a windy Athletic Park is as difficult a rugby task as there is. Williams did all the goal-kicking, as had been expected. He was hardly a success, landing only two easy conversions from eight attempts at goal. But Jack Gleeson told me afterwards that he was happy enough, as twice Williams' kicks 'gained results' — reference no doubt to the Johnstone try scored from a missed penalty attempt and the time when Bruce Robertson nearly scored in a similar manner from a bouncing ball behind the line.

At fullback Farrell looked such a lovable boy, in his new All Black uniform. Everybody wanted him to do well. But he did not have a happy day. He missed his first high ball, plus several others, dropped a scoring pass in the second half, missed a fly-kick at the ball, and muddled about at other times. Again Jack Gleeson refused to be gloomy. 'It was no place, out there today, for a new fullback. I think he'll develop into a good New Zealand player.'

Which leaves Batty. As aggressive as usual, as busy as ever, it was great for him to play so well again. His speed had dropped considerably, though he said that was only because the severity of his injury had prevented any speedwork in training. After his runaway try the crowd gave him the Wellington cheer previously reserved for such Athletic Park favourites as Ron Jarden, Tom Katene and Bob Scott. Typically, Batty acknowledged nothing. His mind, obviously intent on taking the struggle straight back to the Lions, shut out the applause. No frills in the Batty make-up.

There was not a lot for the Lions to salvage out of this game. They were beaten soundly. Their forward effort was found wanting, their backs were weak in several areas, they failed to put pressure on a nervous new fullback, and more seriously failed to incorporate their star player Andy Irvine in much play, relinquishing him to a defensive kicking role.

In the press conference immediately afterwards it was disappointing to note the frivolous and patronising manner with which John Dawes answered questions about his team's performance. One pressman asked, in a serious manner, 'Where does the team go from here?' plainly directing his question to the state of the team's morale.

Dawes replied blandly, 'We go to the West Coast-Buller from here'. (In fact the next match was at Timaru, not Westport.) 'That's their business', was all he could say when asked how he thought the New Zealanders went.

Gleeson came in later to speak to much the same gathering. His attitude was entirely the opposite. He considered each question in his quiet way and made his replies simply and honestly.

'Why don't they change the bloody coaches', said one English journo.

So that was the test. 'A twelve point try', as Dawes called it, had swayed the pendulum New Zealand's way, for had not Batty scored the Lions must have, to make the score 18-10 their way instead of 16-12 to the All Blacks.

The All Blacks gave a performance of great forward dominance, tempered by incoordination in the back play, despite strength and potential. Considerable improvement would be looked for from Sid Going in the games ahead, or else he must go.

The Lions, judging by their aftermatch merriment, were not totally discouraged at losing the first test. They knew that if their forwards could win more parity in the line-outs in future games the winning or losing of the test series could revolve around the scoring potential of Andy Irvine and Phil Bennett.

I made mention of the similar score in the 1966 and 1977 Wellington tests. A comparison between Bennett's team and that of 1966, a divided and mediocre gang led by Mike Campbell-Lamerton, was too hasty after two defeats in a row. But the little signs were there that indicated, after Christchurch and Wellington, that a severe strain was being put on the heart of this British team. Someone would have to toughen this team at its core, in the forwards, or the excellence of what had been achieved in the early tour victories would slither, boots and all, into that land of mediocrity where the 1966 Lions team now lives.

After the first test at Wellington things looked ominous for the Lions. They had not learned about 'grit' and 'guts', the two ingredients that had been effectively demonstrated to them in their three South Island matches. To put it bluntly, they folded in the test.

For the All Blacks that night life was rosy. 'There's a good feeling in my team', said Tane Norton.

The teams
British Isles: Irvine; J. J. Williams, Fenwick, McGeechan, Squires; Bennett (captain), Brynmor Williams; Duggan; Cobner, Keane, Martin, Evans; Orr, Windsor, Price.

New Zealand: Colin Farrell (Auckland); Bryan Williams (Auckland), Bruce Robertson (Counties), Grant Batty (Bay of Plenty); Bill Osborne (Wanganui), Duncan Robertson (Otago); Sid Going (North Auckland); Lawrie Knight (Poverty Bay); Ian Kirkpatrick (Poverty Bay), Andy Haden (Auckland), Frank Oliver (Southland), Kevin Eveleigh (Manawatu); Kent Lambert (Manawatu), Tane Norton (Canterbury) (captain), Brad Johnstone (Auckland).

Scoring

New Zealand (16). Tries by Grant Batty, Brad Johnstone and Sid Going. Conversions (2) by Bryan Williams.

British Isles (12). Penalty by Irvine, penalties (3) by Bennett.

Referee: Peter McDavitt (Wellington)

Athletic Park, Wellington.   Saturday, 18 June 1977.

7
Five of the Best:
Matches 11-15

11. Lions 45, South Canterbury-Mid Canterbury-North Otago 6.
Who would have thought the Lions would arrive in Timaru, before
playing South and Mid-Canterbury and North Otago, so badly
needing a good win that the tour would hang in ribbons if a good win
was not achieved?

Judging by the singing that Sunday night in Timaru and the
powerful nature of Moss Keane's hangover at training the next
morning, the Lions party were in surprisingly high spirits, despite the
results of the previous two matches.

But questions were being asked. A 'win-them-all' team that suddenly loses two games in a row is a covey of sitting ducks for the
hunters of the press corps. Perhaps, some papers said, the partying
had been excessive. Perhaps the team lacked discipline. Perhaps aftermatch quotes about refereeing had been too kind. There were
shocks in store for the Lions in Timaru regarding all these matters.

Firstly, in assessing the reasons why the team's winning streak
had ended, Tony Bodley of the *Daily Express* told his British readers
the Lions should adopt a more disciplined approach to their social
life. This was obvious reference to the big party the team had apparently had after the New Zealand Universities match in Christchurch and to reports of merrymaking in Wellington after the test
loss.

I have to say that at this point on the tour I, personally, had not
seen any partying out of the ordinary although the stories of things
going bump in the night were too well documented to be entirely off
the mark.

Indeed, for me, the most shocking feature of the story was having to explain to my wife that my hotel room in Christchurch had not been hosed out by members of the Lions team. The assertion was put to her over the phone by an *Evening Post* reporter who had heard Young Quinn had been involved. Alas, no.

In refereeing matters the Lions had, in the first ten games of the tour, always been reluctant to criticise. Timaru changed all that. They were upset by the man who controlled the match, Barry Williams of Greymouth, and made a strong attack on him.

John Dawes hit out: 'The incompetence of the referee nearly spoilt the match,' he said, adding, 'he did not know the law concerning offside play in the mauls.'

Whether Williams did or did not know the laws is irrelevant, I feel, for in matters like these, one can say, with a high degree of safety, that disputes about refereeing are usually boiled down to confusion about interpretation.

That may sound naive, it's not. It is a fact of life.

Barry Williams I had seen several months earlier at the New Zealand trials in Wanganui, where he had earned my praise on television for a very fair refereeing display in a free-flowing match. He was obviously highly-ranked by the NZRFU's referees appointments committee to warrant a Lions match.

It was in Timaru at the normal press gathering straight after the game that Williams earned the wrath of Dawes and Burrell. Yet, if the management were upset, and they did seem to be, it was my impression that they had asked for it. Dawes was asked if this was the first time on tour he had been concerned about refereeing decisions. 'It's the first time I've said anything about it,' he said. If that was the case and he and others had needed to say things elsewhere about referees, then why did they not do so? A simple inquiry of official people and similar situations might well have been avoided.

The Lions are not the only team in recent times to say nice things about local referees while all the time they harboured bitterness about them. Andy Leslie's team in South Africa was the same. 'Thank you, sir, for your control of the game, we have no complaints at all,' was dragged out at each aftermatch. Privately, however, and 'off the record' they were disgusted at the treatment some South African referees had meted out to the All Blacks. When the team came home their bleating about referees was nothing short of whining.

In terms of discipline the Lions displayed very little in the first half of their match with the all-green South Canterbury-Mid Canterbury-

North Otago. They lacked pattern and leadership, continuation of the misery they had suffered at Christchurch and Wellington. Of course they had to weather the vigorous determination which local teams launch against touring teams.

Even allowing for that, the Lions played poorly. In the first half all they could score, against one of the weakest teams they would meet, were two penalty kicks by Andy Irvine — while conceding one to Doug Nicol, the local fullback.

The Timaru team even looked as though they could dominate the match, so vigorous were their forays into Lion country. Paul Williams continued the line of good halfbacks the Lions had met. The first five-eighth, Tony Goddard, a son of the late Morrie Goddard, a 1949 All Black, played extremely cleverly from behind his bay window stomach. Alan Grieve was a centre who ran so strongly and tackled so well that higher things could come his way. Only Quinnell and Cobner of the Lions looked anything like Internationals.

So half-time arrived with the Lions ahead by only 6 to 3, the fifth game in a row in which they had wasted the first spell as a try-scoring opportunity.

After the change-round came a transformation. Terry Cobner, who seemed to talk to the heart of the Lions team and call on them not only to save this match but save the tour, was seen banging his fist into his hand and declaiming the facts of rugby life in the strongest and most direct terms. It was the first time I had seen this from the team. Their normal captain Phil Bennett led them with more subtle ways.

Cobner's urging got home to every man of the Lions and the second half at Timaru was a complete turnaround in form. They scored six tries, all converted, plus another penalty, which put their score up to 45. The Combined added just another penalty, to put their score up to 6.

Some of the British tries were very good. One of them might, in time, be remembered as a classic. Andy Irvine, who had had a quiet first half, fielded a kick by left-winger Bill Cooper near half-way. The ball bounced high on the hard ground. Irvine, in his gentle way, completed the story later. 'I was worried about the bounce and had to reach up for it. When I clasped it above my head my first thought was to beat the advancing winger. This I did about half-way. Then I kept on going and the gaps opened right up.'

This, of course, was the usual Irvine understatement. For what he was talking about was a try resulting from a carving, swerving run at high speed through a completely bewildered home team. In this fifty metre play Irvine's heels were clipped momentarily by diving flanker Peter Grant. No other hands were laid on him, even though he had picked up the ball near the touchline and the whole combined team lay directly ahead. 'We thought he'd gone the wrong way,' said Fran Cotton when Irvine chose not to run to the open field, staying instead close to the touchline. Bill Anderson, Combined's captain, laughed afterwards. 'That Irvine try, we enjoyed watching that.' So did we all, Bill.

Elgan Rees scored, then J. J. Williams from one of his kick-ahead moves. Doug Nicol kicked off and Bill Beaumont, in his first tour match and playing well, caught it. A maul developed on the British ten-metre line. Cobner peeled away, in-passed to Quinnell at halfway. By then the speed was up. Quinnell passed to Wheeler, who got to the 22-metre line. His pass was actually directed to Douglas Morgan, but this was not a move for backs, only for forwards impersonating them. Instead Neary took it, made a classic break between two defenders, found Wheeler still handy, passed, and the hooker scored the try. Seventy metres of forward inspiration. Why had we not seen it before?

Gareth Evans, joining for this match an increasingly long list of weak Lions centres, had some compensation with a try. Elgan Rees got a second for himself, to make six in all for the team.

Irvine completed his day's work by converting the six tries and kicking three good penalties; a total, with the try added in, of 25 points, equalling the match record for a Lion in New Zealand. Things, then, were pretty rosy at the end for the tourists. Their wide winning margin meant they could look Canterbury right in the eye for the next match. What had happened in the second half at Fraser Park had not been perfect rugby by any means, but it was a zillion times better than the first half. There were more purpose and leadership on display than had been seen, certainly in the two previous matches, if not on the whole tour.

The teams
Lions: Irvine; J. J. Williams, Gareth Evans, Gibson, Rees; McGeechan, Morgan; Quinnell; Cobner (captain), Beaumont, Martin, Neary; Cotton, Wheeler, Clive Williams.
South Canterbury-Mid Canterbury-North Otago: Doug Nicol (South Canterbury) (replaced by Peter Keenan—MC); Bill Cooper (North Otago), Alan Grieve (Mid-Canterbury), Ian Palmer (SC); Alan McLaren (SC), Tony Goddard (SC); Paul Williams (MC); Harvey King (SC); Peter Grant (SC), Bill Anderson (SC) (captain), Jock

Ross (MC), Noel Glass (SC); Bryan Higginson (MC), Greg Prendergast (MC), Dave Sloper (MC).
Scoring
Lions (45). Tries by Rees (2), Irvine, J. J. Williams, Gareth Evans, and Wheeler; conversions (6) and penalties (3) by Irvine.
South Canterbury-Mid-Canterbury-North Otago (6). Penalties (2) by Doug Nicol.
Referee: Barry Williams (West Coast). Wednesday, 22 June 1977.

12. Lions 14, Canterbury 13. Maybe Phil Bennett did not get the story from his managers correctly. Was I hearing right? There he was, standing up at the aftermatch function in Timaru, telling us all in his usual perfunctory manner that he congratulated the referee Barry Williams on his display in the match. This came straight after Burrell and Dawes had got stuck in, for completely the opposite reasons, to the press. Bennett had not been at the conference, as it was team policy to have only Burrell and Dawes talk to the media after the games. We all had a chuckle at the trio's expense.

Bennett also made a quip with regard to the *Daily Express* report about late-night drinking-parties after mid-week games. 'Come on lads, drink up,' he said from the speaker's platform, 'we've got to get back to the hotel. The Salvation Army meeting begins at seven o'clock.' There were more chuckles, but not from the Lions, who had been greatly angered by the story. Several wives had rung up from home expressing concern. Tony Bodley, the writer, lay low for several days.

There was more controversy to come. Bill Mayston, Sports Editor of the *Christchurch Star,* obviously looking for a local reaction to the criticism of Barry Williams at Timaru, sought an opinion from Len Kirk, a former president of the New Zealand Rugby Referees Association and a Christchurch man. Kirk's allegations made front-page headlines the evening the Lions arrived at their Christchurch hotel.

Kirk claimed the Lions were deliberately breaking the laws, especially in offside play, lying on the ball and illegal movement in the lineouts. Not to mention deliberately collapsing the scrums. For Mayston, it was a good story. For George Burrell it was 'ridiculous and irresponsible' comment. The Lions would say no more.

Burrell sprang a surprise as well. After announcing the team to play Canterbury he added, for spice, a statement concerning the team's off-the-field behaviour. It seems, said George, there had been some 'horse-play' in the Christchurch hotel the night of the Universities game. Three players had been involved. Each had apologised to the hotel management voluntarily for any disturbance caused and damage done. This, my sources told me, was where a hose was played into a hotel room, one which someone at the *Evening Post* had thought was mine. Having got that little confession off their chest, and having been let off extremely lightly by the touring press, the Lions began their build-up to the match at Lancaster Park.

Obvious comparisons were drawn by the media between the 1977 match and the 1971 blood-bath where Ray McLoughlin and Sandy Carmichael had fallen to the fire of the Canterbury pack. In a match that contained a high degree of violence the Lions had won by 14 to 3, and the levelling of blame against individuals in Canterbury's team had persisted for years.

The British press, in particular, had used the game as the measuring-stick for everything that is bad in rugby. To me their stories were grossly exaggerated. 'It takes two to tango,' I had always felt.

'Will 15 man rugby beat 15 round rugby?' said one ridiculous radio commercial on the day of the game. Most other press previews reminded everyone about the fisticuffs of 1971, and also of 1966, making dark predictions about more such rough stuff. So it was with particular relish that George Burrell stood up at the aftermatch function, his 1977 team having beaten Canterbury by 14 to 13, to chide those of us, in the media and elsewhere, who had tried to stir the issue along some more.

'The knockers of rugby,' thundered Burrell, 'tried to relate this game with what happened in 1971. What a lot of bloody nonsense! It was the cleanest game on tour.'

The assembled mass 'Here-here'd' in solemn approval. But it was true. The game was clean. In fact I had a feeling it was a little too clean for Canterbury's good. The Canterbury forwards, capable of giving as good as they got, in a physical sense, played the game so virtuously that their usual hardness did not have its sharpest edge. Maybe, just maybe, if the odd punch had been thrown, as I am sure the Lions expected, Canterbury's effort would have become more entrenched, more determined, more aggressive, and they could have won.

As it was, both teams deserved commendation for their restraint for all the way this was a tremendously exciting match. The first twenty minutes were bitingly hard. A series of solid scrums from both packs and little or no running. Before we knew it the game was a quarter old.

The only light relief came from Andy Irvine, playing his tenth appearance in twelve games, and Doug Heffernan, his opposite, swapping early penalties. Then the Lions scored the day's first try. John Bevan backed up a move that was in danger of breaking down and he sent Gareth Evans away.

7-3 to the Lions at half-time with their forwards, again superbly led by Terry Cobner, at least holding parity with a Canterbury eight, with Alex Wyllie at the head of its surges.

After the hardness of the first spell the second contained much more spectacle for the 40,000 crowd. Canterbury had Lyn Davis in great touch at halfback and Doug Bruce looking good at first five-eighth. They controlled Canterbury's fortunes admirably. For the Lions Willie Duggan was great value, his best form yet on tour, and Gordon Brown gave a hint that, quite soon, he would shake off the effects of the heavy cold, bronchitis and flu that had affected his rugby.

Again Cobner was the man. His tackling was a joy to behold and his leadership lifted his team-mates. The announcement by Dawes, several days before, that Cobner would lead the forwards every time he played and captain them when Bennett was not available was, to me, the first admission that the Lions had, indeed, picked the wrong man to lead this team.

Canterbury scored the next try. From a scrum near the Lions tryline Doug Bruce ran wide. Heffernan and Murray McEwan cut back inside in a decoy ploy. Bruce swung a long ball right across them to Andy Jefferd, the centre, who carved through a gap as wide as Hagley Park to score. Doug Bruce said later the move, called 'Scotland', had been worked out by their 1975 coach Derek Arnold, for Canterbury's winning performance against the Scottish tourists. It was cleanly executed. Heffernan's goal made Canterbury the leaders 9 to 7.

Followed the sad sight of Canterbury's indomitable captain and ex-All Black, Alex Wyllie, leaving the field. He limped away with a painful knee injury and earned a sympathetic roll of applause. Before he reached the dressing-room the Lions had scored.

Willie Duggan, with a keenness of mind, anticipated that Canterbury would be at odds with Wyllie off the field. Duggan simply moved right from a scrum and fed J. J. Williams, who scooted over. There was not a hand laid on either of them. Apparently when John Phillips, the flanker, had tried to make a saving tackle of Duggan, he could not move as his prop, pushed back by the Lions shove, had trapped his foot.

That put the Lions ahead by 11 to 9 but Canterbury bounced back soon after. Allan Martin, in a defensive line-out made a bad tap to Morgan, who had played a 'shocker' at halfback. Between the two of them came John Ashworth, Canterbury's prop, to pick up and score. So Canterbury got the lead back again and the big crowd reached new heights of excitement.

It seemed to me that only a touch of brilliance by the Lions, Andy Irvine in particular, would save this match for the tourists. If this game was lost the tour would be beyond repair.

So with typical courage Terry Cobner called up Irvine. From a tap penalty John Bevan broke and Irvine raced up in a move that travelled fully seventy metres. The defence of the local team rallied to keep the try from being scored. From the resultant line-out the British peeled away. As they did referee Dave Millar of Otago gestured to mid-field but let play run on. When the advantage was lost Millar ran to the centre of the field and penalised Scott Cartwright for being up over the offside line. Irvine, the match-winner every game it seemed, planted the easy shot between the posts for 14-13.

Doug Heffernan, who had had a miserable goal-kicking day, had a late hour chance to win the game from a penalty but again missed.

The game ended. Exciting stuff and not a punch or semblance of a punch thrown. The game was a great credit to both teams and all that. Someone once said to me that you cannot write a rugby book in New Zealand without including the catch phrase 'rugby was the winner', because it's in everybody else's book. Well I refuse to use the expression 'rugby was the winner' to sum up that day in Christchurch.

Except that it was.

The teams
Lions: Irvine; J. J. Williams, Burcher, Fenwick, Gareth Evans; Bevan, Morgan, Duggan; Trevor Evans (replaced by Squire), Brown, Martin, Cobner (captain); Orr, Windsor, Cotton.
Canterbury: Doug Heffernan; Randall Scott, Andy Jefferd, Scott Cartwright; Murray McEwan, Doug Bruce; Lyn Davis, Alex Wyllie (captain, replaced by Stu Purdon); Dave Thompson, Vance Stewart, Graeme Higginson, John Phillips; Bill Bush, Tane Norton, John Ashworth.

Scoring
Lions (14). Tries by Gareth Evans and J. J. Williams; penalties (2) by Irvine.
Canterbury (13). Tries by Andy Jefferd and John Ashworth; conversion and penalty by Doug Heffernan.
Referee: Dave Millar (Otago).   Saturday, 25 June 1977.

13. Lions 45, West Coast-Buller 0. Our film crew's first task at Westport, 'capital' of the tiny Buller region, was to interview for the BBC several members of the Lions team, for replay five days later in Britain. Dewi Griffiths, the BBC's top sporting producer and a bubble of Welsh fun, lined up about ten Lions to be interviewed by Nigel Starmer-Smith. As they stepped up to answer friendly queries about 'How are you enjoying the tour', and so on, each one, and I mean every one, said they were 'looking forward to getting home'.

Westport was the half-way mark of the three-month journey. Three exciting test matches were to come, there was the challenge of fighting back from one test down and doing well, plus other delights offered by a hospitable New Zealand — and here they were all wanting to go home!

The interview session ended hilariously with water being poured over the interviewer and his subject from the hotel block above, and the giant lock Allan Martin, complete with monkey mask, creeping up from behind to startle Derek Quinnell, who was having his say at the time. Barry Lissette, the cameraman, was alert to Martin's approach and the result on film made a very amusing item for a 'Sports Extra' programme.

The fun came to an abrupt end with the appearance of George Burrell, to remind us that interviewing players on match day was strictly 'out'. He did not seem interested that only those who were not playing that day had been approached to appear. The BBC therefore withdrew.

At Victoria Square, the headquarters of Buller rugby, rain, solid and continuous, made the pitch almost as wet as Masterton had been. This quaint little ground has a tiny grandstand positioned towards one end, so small that the allocation of seats to the Lions non-players left room for only about one hundred other people. The team arrived at the ground by bus all changed and ready to go. They got out, warmed up thoroughly, then promptly got on the bus again, to avoid a heavy shower and wait until kick-off time.

Buller people love their rugby and are most gracious hosts, but

Westport was inadequate to the occasion. The town simply is not big enough and well-equipped enough to look after such a visitation. The local officials, headed by Bill Craddock Jr., worked bravely and hard, but housing the press on the back of a truck, having to send both teams away from the ground by bus to shower and change, and being too far-flung and awkward for television to provide its customary service, these were just three reasons why the local facilities were not up to scratch. Add to that the understrength capacity of the combined West Coast-Buller team, and the exercise was substantially a waste of time for the Lions.

It's no longer reasonable for the NZRFU to ask touring teams to carry the flag to each and every corner of the country. These areas are not isolated as they once were. Supporters of the game are not without means. For West Coasters keen enough, a trip to Nelson or Blenheim is no great problem, nor is the air fare to Wellington or Christchurch, if they wish to see a test match. And there is always television as a means of keeping up with the play.

If, as seems highly probable, future rugby tours have to pass by towns of the size of Westport, then so be it.

When the game kicked off rain was falling solidly. There had been a few problems with the Westport team, two of whom declined to play for 'personal reasons', one allegedly because he disagreed with the selections made. So the local lineup was further weakened. How stupid.

And politics reared its ugly head in another petty way. Whereas all the official forms and itineraries called the Lions opposition for this match 'West Coast-Buller', the programme and Westport advertising referred to 'Buller-West Coast'. A subtle difference which the local people enjoyed, no doubt.

There were three thousand stalwarts at the ground. All were in parkas, raincoats and supplementary rainwear. The Westport side, eight from the West Coast, seven from Buller, was outweighed by two stone a man in the forwards and outclassed in every other respect.

The game, simply, was a points-scoring exercise by the touring team. It was rather like a big boy playing cricket against his young brother. He knew he was going to win before he started, but he thought he would string it out for a while to give the youngster some encouragement to continue.

True, there were times when Combined booted the ball ahead, led usually by Jon Sullivan or John Gilbert, and its slipperyness confused the Lions. Generally though, the Lions just toyed with the opposition.

Of most significance for the tourists was the blanket-like efficiency its forward pack showed and the encouraging signs exhibited by Douglas Morgan at halfback. At long last he evidenced enough to convince us that he was not a complete bumbler and fumbler, as he had tried very hard to prove at Christchurch.

At one point he nipped around the blindside to score a try while referee Graeme Harrison of Wellington was still peering into the gloomy depths of a ruck several metres away. Harrison had to look up and consider what he thought might have happened. This he did, and quite properly awarded a score. After that incident his refereeing was judged very harshly by the crowd, one wag calling out: 'No wonder you've only got this game!'

That was being overly critical. Harrison did rather well in the conditions, having the darkest of afternoons to work in and having to stop every few moments to flush the clinging Victoria Square mud from his and the players' eyes.

Morgan also kicked well, to make it quite a day for him. Along with the try, he scored from four conversions and three penalties, 21 points in all.

At Christchurch, when asked about Morgan's appalling performance against Canterbury and its consequences for the Lions, John Dawes had answered 'Duggie's a trier, lets leave it at that, shall we?' I drew the inference that he felt Morgan had become rather a liability to the team. Criticism was widespread. Morgan scotched it all in the Westport mud.

Apart from 'Duggie's' try the Lions scored six others. Peter Squires had two made for him and Jeff Squire one. They were all straightforward enough. Two of the others, however, were well-constructed and cleanly-executed. The first came when Morgan passed away to John Bevan, at fly-half. He went 'on the loop', doubling around Mike Gibson to take a second pass. A break appeared in the traffic ahead and through went Bevan, flicking up mud from his heels and scoring under the uprights.

Towards the end Bruce Hay went on a run along much the same path. He blasted in from fullback at great pace, collecting a snappy short pass from David Burcher on the way and belting away to score, again under the posts.

The seventh try, at least, created a debate that helped warm up the latter part of the match. It was scored when the Lions, almost cruelly, put on a huge scrum shove near the Combined line. Immediately the lightweight locals went into a backslide. The Lions pushed five metres forward and over the line, and the second rowers flopped down, all keen to get a score.

My initial reaction was that the try had been scored by Jeff Squire from number 8. Peter Bush, the *Truth* photographer and great friend of the whole wide world, reported from the sideline that Moss Keane had been the man. Afterwards it was settled. The Lions themselves awarded it to Bill Beaumont. So Beaumont it was.

When the Lions had relentlessly pushed their score up to 45, time ran out. The lighting had also run out, the camera lenses being 'open wide' since half-time. The sweat-soaked, mud-stained teams headed for the buses that would take them to their showers. Westport was doing its best, but it was not good enough.

The teams

Lions: Hay; Rees, Gibson, Burcher, Squires; Bevan, Morgan; Squire; Evans (captain), Beaumont, Keane, Neary; Cotton, Windsor, Clive Williams.

West Coast-Buller: Rex Mumm (Buller); Peter Teen (West Coast), Bruce Davidson (W.C.), Tony Mundy (B); Brian Morgan (B), Alan Ireland (B); John Gilbert (B); Brian McGuire (B); Neville Roberts (B), John Lee (captain) (B), Murray Sinclair (W.C.), Jon Sullivan (W.C.); Ritchie Banks (W.C.), Russell Mitchell (W.C.), Jim Steffan (W.C.).

Scoring

Lions (45). Tries by Squires (2), Hay, Bevan, Beaumont, Squire and Morgan; conversions (4) and penalties (3) by Morgan.

West Coast-Buller (0).

Referee: Graeme Harrison (Wellington)Wednesday, 29 June 1977.

14. Lions 13, Wellington 6. It was still raining three days later when the Lions kicked off, at Athletic Park, for the fourteenth match of their tour, against Wellington. The half-way stage had been reached and passed, thirteen games had been played, twelve were left. The tension was hard on; from here on in it was tough, brother, tough. In the immediate alert what was required against Wellington was a performance of firm authority in fulfilment of the players' obligations to the team and to British rugby. From the Wellington game what was needed was a new gear to shoot the side forward with confidence to the second test which now loomed near.

The All Black team had been announced after the Westport game. Doug Bruce in for Duncan Robertson. Bill Bush in for the ailing Kent Lambert. Sid Going still there.

There were no All Blacks in the Wellington team, the nearest being Andy Leslie and John Dougan who had worn the colours in the past. The Lions however, with their minds set on the struggles ahead, took them not lightly. For one of the few times on tour they named a near test line-up. Phil Bennett, Brynmor Williams and Graham Price all returned to active duty, not having played since their previous visit to Athletic Park. Bennett, it was said by some of the British press, supposedly well-informed, would not last the game out, his shoulder trouble not being completely healed. But Bennett did last, running and passing with most of his usual confidence.In the forwards big changes seemed imminent for the test. For the Wellington game Derek Quinnell was promoted to number 8 for what was clearly a personal trial. Tony Neary, a consistent player, won his first Saturday appearance since Napier. Then there was Gordon Brown, still needing matches to get fit after his suspension at home and his heavy chest cold in New Zealand. He was at lock, while in the front row came the two Englishmen, Fran Cotton and Peter Wheeler, both pushing hard to oust Welshmen from the test fifteen. None of these five had been in the so-badly-cleaned-out first test pack.

Wellington, in their typically dedicated manner, prepared most thoroughly for this match. For four of their team, Leslie, Dougan, Keown and Cleland, this was a crunch game, for they had all been in the Wellington team which had been beaten 47-9 by John Dawes' team in 1971.

Once again TV1 offered its videotape replay unit to help the home team prepare to do battle with the Lions. They came to Avalon and watched the tight, dour first half of the Lions match with Canterbury, plus their scattered confused second half against New Zealand Universities. The coach, Ian Upston, confided to me that he had been delighted with what had been shown to his team. 'The highlights programmes shown on TV', said Upston, 'tend to show only the good parts, while leaving out the dull or poor play. I wanted to show my guys the Lions in a full game, doing bad things as well, in fact being ordinary people.'

The bad weather that had diligently followed the Lions turned up in Wellington as well. Athletic Park was a clinging, cloying muddy mess by the time kick-off arrived. The decision by New Zealand rugby officialdom to play curtain-raisers at Wellington and almost every other venue, irrespective of the overhead or underfoot condition, was clearly stupid. The British were amazed that touring players should have to troop on to cut-up pitches to play vital games.

At Wellington the game that did the damage was just a social runaround featuring old-timers from bygone days climaxing a weekend on the tiles. It was a fixture that meant absolutely nothing, except perhaps as an exercise in nostalgia, and it could easily have been cancelled. There was a strong hint that the reason it was not cancelled was because of a tie-up between the New Zealand Rugby Football Union and a national brewery chain.

As it was the lines that mark the field were largely obliterated and the surface heavy and scarred when the big match started.

Once again Wellington's rugby public let themselves down by staying away from the match in droves. Little more than 20,000 were in the park for the action. As is their custom, officials blamed television for the poor attendance. The fact that the weather had been raining solidly for forty-eight hours before Saturday did not enter into one administrator's criticism. He blamed us for the poor crowd. Such, he told me, was the power of television.

But the game itself. As Fred Dagg would say, 'What a cracker!' Wellington, outweighed heavily, played courageously and cleverly and moved the muddy ball about all day. Dougan and Cleland, the two Petone five-eighths, were like workers on an assembly line, accepting their product and moving it on without question. This was a most admirable attitude from Dougan, who was still a cheeky and unpredictable player. His approach to the game was most commendable too. I made my customary pre-matchday visit to the park to see if all my gear was in place correctly. The park was empty apart from the odd ground staffer and television crew member. On the field, twenty-four hours before kick-off, was John Dougan. All alone, like an actor onstage without an audience, Dougan ran. He dummied, jinked, sprinted, rested, jinked some more. He played, by himself, a great game and there was not a rugby ball in sight. 'I was just getting a sighter', he said over his Saturday night beer.

But it takes two sides to make a match come alive, and the Lions contributed much, in a running way. The one aspect where Wellington was vastly inferior was at scrumtime. The Lions weight was awesome and the scrum's packing, power and tightness far too much for the Wellington eight. Peter Wheeler underlined his test chances by hooking three tightheads off Frank Walker. Such was the Lions heave that almost all scrum ball won by Wellington came to its halfback, Dave Henderson, all scrambled and shrapnelled.

At line-outs Wellington held their own through Keown, Brendan Gard'ner and John Fleming, which allowed Henderson to clear some running ball to Dougan and Cleland. Once it reached Ian May, the centre, that was it. May kicked often but never well and the Lions were able to build up from his errors.

Clive Currie and Warrick Proctor were Wellington's two stars. Both gave everything in defence, tackling hard and keenly, Currie's line-kicking was low and controlled into the wind, while Proctor's strong running through the centre tested the tourists many times. He brought gasps of admiration from the crowd on one occasion by chasing Andy Irvine from behind and catching him, no mean feat.

The Lions no doubt derived much comfort from the performances of Quinnell and Brown. Both were back into the fray in splendid fashion. Quinnell spoilt his otherwise excellent showing by some insufferably mad-headed play which severely tested the referee's tolerance. One was left with the feeling that it would be no surprise to see him sent off in a game on this tour, should he continue his foot-stomping, fist-waving and over-aggressive antics.

The referee, Colin Gregan, was a controversial figure. He never required scrums to be stationary at the put-in. Wellington were usually going backwards at this point so Henderson conceded a number of penalties for not putting the ball in straight. He usually had little alternative, as his scrum was always on the back-pedal.

Gregan also missed Wellington's best try-scoring chance. Flanker Paul Quinn, called 'Tungsten tough' by his team-mates in satire of one sportswriter's description of his play, tore away from a maul and headed for the line. Gregan was looking at something in the maul; he blew his whistle and was then surprised to see Quinn sailing away, and with the ball. The impetus of that Wellington attack was lost.

There was but one try in the match. The Lions led 9 to 3 at half-time, three penalties to Bennett to a good kick by Cleland, into the strong, cold, northerly wind.

After half-time, Dougan made one of his rare clearance kicks. Terry Cobner was quick off the mark and charged it down. Cobner then stayed close to the bouncing ball and soccer-kicked it over the line. He was clearly delighted to dive on it and score, hugging Gareth Evans for the line-up of photographers nearby. It was a just laurel for him to receive for Terry Cobner, again in this match, and increasingly on the tour, was a vital man for the Lions.

That made it 13 to 3, a sufficient gap to preclude a Wellington win. But they battled on, led inexhaustibly by Andy Leslie, who looked no different at number 8 than as All Black skipper in South Africa just twelve months before.

Richard Cleland got one other chance to kick at goal in the match.

He made it, two successes from two kicks from 35 metres, late in the match.

The Lions backs gained more in confidence with their performance. They were clearly much happier with Bennett back and not one person mentioned to me about Brynmor Williams being a weak link at halfback. This was because he was anything but that and like Bennett, relished the return to match play.

Both teams must have been heavy with leg-weariness near the end, the mud coating them all and weighing the ball down. The action continued right to the whistle however, when the scoreline read a Lions win by 13 to 6.

Everybody agreed afterwards that this was a game that would have been more splendid had the pitch been dry, but having a 'heavier pack on a heavy field', as Dawes put it, was the victory factor. Andy Leslie was of the same mind. 'If only the track had been better. Our guys wanted to play hit-and-run rugby, but being lightweights in the forwards on such a ground made it hard, too hard.'

As Leslie spoke to the press under a bare light in a cold Athletic Park dressing-room, the sound of singing wafted down the steamy corridor. But the noise came not from the Lions, rejoicing now that their tour was gaining in momentum again, but instead from Wellington who had given their all in the game for no winning return. Their cheerfulness was unending, their spirit a credit to their leaders and themselves.

And who cared if their exuberance spilled over into a masculine version of 'The Road to Gundagai' at the aftermatch celebration. There were only men there (no ladies invited, at Wellington) and some, it was said, were most upset at the bawdy ballad.

But I ask you. Is there a rugby man alive, of any age, who has not heard, nay sung heartily, a naughty song after the heat of the battle had cooled? To criticise was petulant. It was an act by officials who wanted the stuffy show to go their way and not express the spirit of the fifteen men who had run, tackled, shoved and jumped to such purpose. Wellington men, outweighted by the lively Lions.

The teams
Lions: Irvine; Gareth Evans, McGeechan, Fenwick, J. J. Williams; Bennett (captain), Brynmor Williams; Quinnell; Neary, Brown, Martin, Cobner; Price, Wheeler, Cotton.
Wellington: Clive Currie; Warrick Proctor, Ian May, Bernie Fraser; Richard Cleland, John Dougan; Dave Henderson; Andy Leslie (captain), Paul Quinn, John Fleming, Brendan Gard'ner, Mark Stevens; Al Keown, Frank Walker, Kevin Phelan.

Scoring
Lions (13). Try by Cobner; penalties (3) by Bennett.
Wellington (6). Penalties (2) by Cleland.
Referee: Colin Gregan (Waikato).   Saturday, 2 July 1977.

15. Lions 40, Marlborough-Nelson Bays 23. One of the nicest things that Marlborough offered as the venue for the Lions fifteenth match was sunshine. After the miseries of Westport and Wellington, Marlborough's weather was all brightness and brilliance. In fact the players in action at Blenheim's Lansdowne Park might have made the legitimate complaint that the sun was *too* bright. Catches were difficult to make looking into it.

The Lions had been unable to get out of Wellington by air on Sunday after their previous game because the weather was so foul. Monday was worse. About the only consolation was that the touring team could sit about the St George Hotel and read their newspaper notices from the Wellington game. Most critics agreed the tourists' front-five scrum power was now to be regarded with the highest esteem. As was the loose play, with Quinnell and Cobner becoming more dominant with each match.

'Confidence is the one quality our backs lack', said John Dawes after their latest Athletic Park showing. He was correct, although it was a staggering and telling admission to have to make. For all his personal interest and attention over the fourteen games and the innumerable practices, the backs had still not gained a firm positive approach, or a full understanding of each other. As I recall, it had not taken the 1959 Lions that long to reach a state of harmony and unison. Nor the 1971 team. Still, as Dawes did add, 'There is still time'.

Eventually by devious route of bus to Palmerston North and plane to Blenheim the Lions made it to the safety of the Criterion Hotel. The announced Lions team contained twelve changes from that which had played at Wellington. The backline was to be entirely different, with only Quinnell, Brown and Price retained from the pack.

There was a nice touch when the Lions arrived at Lansdowne Park in Blenheim to play Marlborough-Nelson Bays. When the playing members of that day's fifteen, plus reserves, went to change into their playing kit, the other players not required that afternoon set out on a stroll around the ground. They moved through the crowd, not in a showy manner, but simply to enjoy as much as they could of the sunshine. Young children pressed forward with autograph books, older fans stopped for a chat. Men like Andy Irvine, Moss Keane and Steve Fenwick obliged. The whole gesture was nice, just nice, and as warming as the sun.

The pre-game prospects gave the Blenheim team little chance of doing well. I inquired of the *Dominion's* touring correspondent, Phil Campbell, a long-time Marlborough stalwart, as to the strength of the team. 'If there are six in it from Nelson, then its got to be weak', replied a true Marlborough man. But the local team roared into their work and while they never, in all honesty, looked like winning, their pressure-cooker approach produced one of the most visually exciting matches of the tour.

The Lions won by 40 points to 23. Several of the locals played most noteworthy roles in the match's structure. At first five-eighth Jim Speedy was so efficient that it was hard to believe he had been shuttled between the Petone and Athletic clubs in Wellington without receiving due reward. He was a stylish player, with adhesive handling qualities and an excellent start-off point for a vigorous local back division.

Graham Rogers, the second five-eighth, scored both the home team tries and did so with great style and relish. His play about the field was so impressive that Jack Gleeson and the New Zealand selectors enquired, several days later, as to his age, obviously keen to involve him in the New Zealand Juniors team.

His first try came after a burst, 40 metres in length, from his centre Steve Marfell. Rogers stayed in support and as they say, after a time of wonder, a try was scored. The 'time of wonder' was that space of several passing seconds when the Lions could have made at least one, but probably a couple of tackles to end the rush.

The second Rogers' effort was a clear slicing run, late in the day. He picked a split between his opposites and charged through with an ease that must again have had John Dawes wistfully looking into the middle distance, hoping that what he had seen wasn't really true.

In addition to the tries, Steve Marfell helped the home team reach the highest score so far against the Lions, with five well-kicked penalties, none of which was really easy.

Of course while all this was happening and the crowd was exhorting the Marlborough-Nelson men to lift their game, the Lions were competing rather better in other areas of the play. They won the line-outs with ease and heaved the Combined pack back unmercifully in the scrums. At halfback, Douglas Morgan kicked four goals in the first half, two penalties and two from conversions, but was less attentive to his halfback duties. After the encouragement he had shown at Westport, Morgan lost ground again, possibly because of pain from a groin injury. At least it took him off the field before he compounded his reputation any further.

Brynmor Williams came on and immediately scored a try, as the result of a ruck following a thirty metre run by Jeff Squire.

The pleasure the Lions felt as they marched back to half-way was tempered by an arm injury Williams suffered in diving for the line. As he received attention it crossed my mind what might have eventuated had it been a serious ailment. Remember, Morgan had just limped off some moments before. As we all watched a strange mental picture of Ian McGeechan or John Bevan playing at halfback in the test match crossed my mind.

It must have been a frightening moment for the team, especially as young Brynmor did look in much pain. But he played out time, rubbing his elbow at every break. The crisis passed, as both recovered quickly after the game.

Of the five tries the Lions scored, none was better than Gordon Brown's, his first of the tour. Combined kicked through behind the Lions backline. Burcher went back, at half-way, and seeing the Marlborough-Nelson hordes approaching at great speed he, in an instinctive Welsh way, took the attack right back from whence it came.

He burst through the first line of defence and found the way clear for a run. Peter Squires was handy to the right. The movement continued on into the Combined scoring zone. Gordon Brown, going 'like crazy' to be up with the two speedsters, stomped up and took an in-pass for a splendid counter-attacking try.

The other scores went to Elgan Rees, who had a skittery match on the wing, Bruce Hay got another from fullback, and David Burcher followed up a high kick which Speedy missed, to make it five for the tourists for the day.

Mike Gibson, who dropped yet again the first two passes that came his way, derived some measure of satisfaction from his kicking performance, with four goals, all in the second half. These were Gibson's first goal attempts of the tour and put him on the imposing list of talented strikers in this department, Irvine, Burcher, Bennett, Morgan and Martin being the others.

In the end this was not anything like a complete win for the Lions. In fact it was far from it, the team being far too easily put off by the bustle of their lively opposition. Both teams were constantly and completely confused by the whistlings of Nelson Whittaker, the referee. He dished out 34 penalties in the match, which did not help the flow of play.

But though this win may have been unsure and unsteady it was, nevertheless, received with great delight by the tourists. 'We desperately wanted to go into the second test without suffering any further losses', Bennett told me. 'This really cheered the lads on.'

Yes it did. For the five matches that preceded the Christchurch test match had offered much in the way of testing rugby. There had been the springy, sprightly play on the hard turf of Timaru, there had been strong forward confrontations well won by the Lions against Wellington and Canterbury, there had been some outstanding running and passing in wet conditions at Westport and, to cap it all, there was victory in confusion at Blenheim. That was the key to it all right. In the five to get ready for the test at Christchurch, the Lions had dug deeply into their resources to win, but win they did. Could it continue?

We packed our bags and headed for Christchurch to see.

The teams

Lions: Hay; Rees, Gibson, Burcher, Squires; Bevan, Morgan (replaced by Brynmor Williams), Squire; Evans (captain), Beaumont, Brown, Quinnell; Clive Williams, Windsor, Price (replaced by Orr).

Marlborough-Nelson Bays: Ray Gordon (Marlborough); Brian Ford (M), Steve Marfell (M), Brian Hunter (M); Graham Rogers (Nelson Bays), Jim Speedy (N.B.); Peter Baker (M); Bruce Kenney (M); David Neal (M); Murray West (N.B.), Terry Julian (N.B.) (captain), Mark Best (M); George Paki Paki (N.B.), Kevin Sutherland (M), Joe Baryluk (N.B.).

Scoring

Lions (40). Tries by Hay, Rees, Burcher, Brynmor Williams and Brown. 2 penalties and 2 conversions by Morgan. 2 penalties and 2 conversions by Gibson.

Marlborough-Nelson Bays (23). 2 tries by Graham Rogers. 5 penalties by Steve Marfell.

Referee: Nelson Whittaker (Manawatu).   Tuesday, 6 July 1977.

8
The Second Test:
Christchurch

16. British Isles 13, New Zealand 9. There are many of the rugby public who substantially form their rugby opinions by reading newspaper reports of matches. If you had taken as gospel some of the press comment on the second test match between the Lions and the All Blacks played at Lancaster Park in Christchurch on 9 July 1977, then you would have been, a day later, firmly of the belief that it was the most violent and dirty game ever witnessed.

For this was the impression written into their reports by many of the fifty or sixty sports writers who were present that afternoon. They wrote of boots, knuckles, punches, knees, stiff-arms and other assorted human weapons used to inflict violence upon another man.

What hogwash! The second test match between the Lions and the All Blacks was certainly no place for men of faint heart or cowardly disposition, but it was essentially a poor display of rugby union by two teams, trying on a mucky park to play rugby up to their best qualities, but failing miserably.

The second test was played in the most critical atmosphere yet. For either side to consider defeat was reprehensible. The All Blacks victory meant they would draw the series and probably win it. The Lions, despondent at Wellington after the first test, needed a win to keep the success of the tour alive.

There is nothing surer than that this was a game of granite, with, undeniably, some violent streaks. But to call it 'the worst' was to overlook the many honourable aspects of an eighty-minute endeavour in which the two teams, with conditions against them, tried their darndest to play rugby of test match calibre — but failed.

It was a poor game. Some of the fighting was abhorrent. Putting in the boot, the rugby term that epitomises dangerous and wounding aggression, was evidenced more than once. But 'the worst' this was not, unless you are talking in terms of rugby expertise.

The All Black team for the match contained two changes. Doug Bruce came in for Duncan Robertson, and Bill Bush for the ailing Kent Lambert. Robertson lost his place on form, though there was considerable sympathy for him, as he had had to field in Wellington some of Sid Going's worst passes.

There was further saddening news for the team upon their assembly in Christchurch Grant Batty, that human expression of aggressiveness and most brilliant winger, was forced out of the match, and, most sadly, out of the game forever. He had given his injured knee a solid work-out at the All Blacks training session at Lincoln College. It was obviously not right. Radio New Zealand's John Howson, Paul Cavanagh of the New Zealand Press Association, and myself were the only men there from the touring press. We enquired in an official way of Ron Don whether Batty would be fit to play in the test and were told he was out, to be replaced by Bay of Plenty's Mark Taylor.

It was then that Batty dropped his bombshell. 'I'm retiring — this is it', he said, and Howson, a most diligent touring correspondent, dropped his jaw in dismay. He had a 'scoop' for radio on his hands. 'Retiring Bats? Are you serious?' Indeed the little bloke was.

It was typical of Batty that, as we stood there getting our interviews and generally offering sympathy for what was a sad moment, he cheerfully talked of other things. The weather, his family, my family, mutual friends. In the modest Batty way, there was no big issue. The long-standing threat had become reality. He had retired, no more no less — now let's get on with other matters.

Batty's departure, and the blow the All Blacks' chances took as a result, were added to further when Bruce Robertson also withdrew. He had suffered concussion playing for Counties against Auckland and was at training, though he looked pale and sickly. His place went to Otago's Lyn Jaffray, who was called back to test rugby to play his fifth test.

All this was upsetting to the All Blacks' pre-match preparations but still they soldiered on, holding a good winning chance, or so we thought.

The Lions on the other hand, had no pre-match sensations. Thirty players were available for selection for the first time on tour. Their test team was certainly predictable. Six changes were made, five in the forwards, ridding the side of those who had been so badly cleaned out by the ruthless All Blacks at Wellington. Gone were Keane and Martin, the locks, as well as Windsor, Orr and Trevor Evans. In came Quinnell, temporarily free of his knee problems, Beaumont, Brown, Cotton and Wheeler. The pack took on a new and stronger look. In the backs Gareth Evans gained his first full international cap, replacing Peter Squires. This one was not so easy to follow, for Squires had certainly never played badly on tour.

As was often their custom, the team trained badly. Dawes ran the backs, Cobner the forwards, in listless, lifeless sessions which seemed to mean very little. Elsewhere it seems the Lions did their homework well. The resolve hardened, the spirit knit and they were a far different proposition for the New Zealanders to face than had been the case at Wellington in the first test. To repeat, as they themselves must have done many times, this was a match they simply could not lose.

Once again New Zealand's extreme winter weather played a considerable part in deciding the pattern of the game. Heavy rain on the weekend prior to the test turned into floods, the waters and a Canterbury-Manawatu representative match turning the surface of Lancaster Park into a deep-rooted clog of churned mud. Though the weather improved overhead, the recovery rate of the pitch was slow.

Saturday dawned cold and clear in Christchurch; there had been a few solid showers in the early morning, and the field was desperately heavy. 'I've seen it worse', said Fergie McCormick, but even he had to concede that there would be little running rugby that afternoon.

Once again the match was telecast 'live' throughout New Zealand. Although the agreement between TV authorities and the New Zealand Rugby Football Union precluded any prior announcement of a live telecast, most newspapers predicted that those who stayed home would see the game as it happened. The Auckland Rugby Union made a change of policy from the day of the first test and scheduled its club matches to kick off at an early time so that the players could watch the test. They had not done this for the first test, leaving the ludicrous situation of senior matches being played out in front of empty grounds. The only people not at home watching the test on television were the players involved in those games. Fortunately common sense prevailed for the second test.

Before the match the New Zealand Army Band had delighted the assembled crowd of 50,000 with a precision display of marching and playing in rugby patterns. As the match played its eighty minutes out, I realised I had not seen better formations than the band had produced. They were very much one of the highlights of the day.

The Lions win and the tying-up of the series were due in a large way to the high-gear manner in which they began. The first twenty minutes, when they scored from two Phil Bennett penalties and a try by J. J. Williams, was in complete contrast to the many other dithering beginnings they had made on tour. But by improving that situation on this, clearly the most character-testing day for them, the Lions laid the way for their later victory.

There were other surprises. New Zealand used Mark Taylor to throw in at line-outs. He had been principally, in his rugby career, a second five-eighth, and had very little experience of the vital art of pitching the ball exactly to the nominated jumpers. He took time to find his length, as it were, and the Lions won several balls off his throws. The New Zealand rhythm was upset.

Also of surprise was the manner in which the Lions' pack moved so sweetly across the muddy turf. They made it first, via Terry Cobner, to most of the breakdowns in play and were thus able to turn these into mauls, where they were much superior.

The inclusion of Quinnell and Brown lifted the drive of the Lions' pack, while Willie Duggan, at the back, had his finest New Zealand game yet.

The All Black forwards, like a poorly-favoured racehorse, were slow away and never ran on until it was too late. Haden, bothered by a neck injury, was not the dominant force that he had been in Wellington, and Eveleigh and Kirkpatrick, by their slowness, indicated that they could be replaced for future games in the series.

One who did have a good game was Frank Oliver. Early in the proceedings, Farrell was absent from his fullback post and Gareth Evans kicked through. There was no All Black between Evans, the bouncing ball and the goal-line. Back went Oliver, galloping at surely his fastest rate ever, and forced Evans to make a hurried flykick, the ball running across the touchline. ('I had to use the after-burners in that one', said Oliver later, rolling his 'rrr's' in that delightful Southland way.)

In the rucks and general play Oliver was good too, and when any Lions considered taking more physical methods to stop or divert an All Black rush, the looming presence of Oliver often changed their minds.

At half-back Sid Going was in vastly-improved combination with Doug Bruce. But Going, you could say, cost New Zealand the match. He conceded three penalties, all in the first half, which Bennett gladly turned into points on the board. You cannot do things like that, no matter how doubtful you might consider the decisions, when the opposition has star quality kickers in abundance.

The best New Zealand back was clearly Bill Osborne, playing as well and as strongly as he had in the first test. Farrell at fullback was again a disappointment though, to be fair, he was rather better than at Wellington. Bryan Williams missed two simple penalties which could have turned the match New Zealand's way, and found the responsibilities of the goal-kicking role making significant inroads into his playing abilities. Mark Taylor made a useful replacement for Batty, being certainly as aggressive, while not looking a complete winger.

In the Lions backs, Bennett played much more physically than we had seen in earlier games, and guided his team's affairs well. It was a surprise to me that Steve Fenwick was voted 'Man of the Match', but those who voted him that award obviously were considering his defensive merits above anything else. Andy Irvine was, strangely, left out of the attack. He was even seen at one point when the All Blacks were on high attack, leaning casually against the goalposts. His talents were rarely employed.

The only try of the day came when Bennett lobbed up a short kick into the mud in the centre of the field. The ball skidded away from Kirkpatrick, and Cobner toed on. Gordon Brown made a run, to feed Quinnell then McGeechan. He unloaded to J. J. Williams whose dummied delay pass fooled Taylor, Going, and Bruce. Williams crossed for a superb try, the All Blacks clearly having expected him to kick ahead, as he usually did.

After a half-time score of 13-6 to the British Isles, Bryan Williams kicked one penalty near the end to close the gap up to four points. This prompted New Zealand to launch wave upon wave of attacks at the Lions. But the tourists held, and at the final whistle, blown by Brian Duffy of Taranaki, they sagged to the ground, arms draped around each other — the series was square. 'The show was on the road again.'

It might very well not have been that way. In the last moment Bill Osborne, with New Zealand on attack, nearly made a breakaway. Being caught partially he slipped a high ball to Jaffray on the burst outside him. Jaffray juggled it once, twice, and while reaching for it in the third motion had it plucked away under the goalposts by Gareth Evans. The try would have levelled things at 13-all and the All Blacks would probably have won, though at least one bitter type argued that Williams would have missed the kick anyway.

I asked Phil Bennett what he had been thinking about when

Jaffray was heading for the posts. 'Nothing really', said Bennett wist-fully. 'I was too busy praying to God.'

The violence that several pressmen wrote of was embodied in one real incident. Eveleigh made a late tackle on Bennett, a quite blatant one I might add, to which the Lions objected. They rushed from all quarters and the most fearful brawl erupted. Bill Beaumont was seen on TV to kick Sid Going on the ground. The All Blacks objected to that. The fight raged on, though eventually it was settled.

The only other incident of any substance involved a personal disagreement between Graham Price and Brad Johnstone. Price demonstrated his ability to head-butt and Johnstone went down.

These incidents were not pretty, and as an advertisement for the game did much harm. But it was hardly a dirty game. After reading the newspaper reports of violence and filth I made a small poll of the broadcasting commentators both Kiwi and Pom. All, to a man, agreed that their first reaction was not to consider it a dirty game at all; they saw it more as a typical test match, hard, *at times violent,* but not to be filed away under 'D' for dirty, dangerous and disgraceful.

The teams

British Isles: Irvine; J. J. Williams, Fenwick, McGeechan, Gareth Evans; Bennett (captain), Brynmor Williams; Duggan; Quinnell, Brown, Beaumont, Cobner; Price, Wheeler, and Cotton.

New Zealand: Colin Farrell (Auckland); Bryan Williams (Auckland), Bill Osborne (Wanganui), Mark Taylor (Bay of Plenty); Lyn Jaffray (Otago), Doug Bruce (Canterbury); Sid Going (North Auckland); Lawrie Knight (Poverty Bay); Ian Kirkpatrick (Poverty Bay), Frank Oliver (Southland), Andy Haden (Auckland), Kevin Eveleigh (Manawatu); Bill Bush (Canterbury), Tane Norton (captain — Canterbury), and Brad Johnstone (Auckland).

Scoring

British Isles (13). Try by J. J. Williams. Penalties (3) by Bennett.
New Zealand (9). Penalties (3) by Bryan Williams.
Referee: Brian Duffy (Taranaki).   Saturday, 9 July 1977.

9
Four in the North:
Matches 17-20

17. **Lions 22, New Zealand Maoris 19.** 'The show is back on the road again', said George Burrell after the second test victory. Indeed, that win had made the tour. By squaring the series at one-all the outcome would still be a question mark until the final whistle of the final match.

The happy band of Lions, intoxicated also, I may say, by other influences than their winning ways, now took their travelling road show to Auckland to play the New Zealand Maoris.

The. Maori side, coached by Waka Nathan, was confident of doing well. They had the test players — Tane Norton, Bill Bush, Bill Osborne and Sid Going — in their ranks as well as Eddie Stokes of Bay of Plenty and Vance Stewart of Canterbury, who had been 1976 New Zealand representatives. Waka Nathan played things way down low-key. He even made a radio interview outlining the weak points of his team, then after the tape was switched off, told the interviewer, 'Put your money on us!'

The Lions made a calculated gamble and rested ten of the test team, retaining only Fran Cotton, Terry Cobner, Willie Duggan, Steve Fenwick and J. J. Williams. It was widely felt that Dawes, Burrell and Bennett, the selectors, had undervalued the strengths of the Maori team and could suffer a loss.

The Maoris trained with their usual enthusiasm and built their match plan mostly around Sid Going. He and I had exchanged words at the aftermatch function in Christchurch. He took mild exception to my telecast remark during the first test that he was 'in for a dressing-down' for the way he had rushed in and tussled with

Trevor Evans and Terry Cobner. 'A lot of people disagreed with you, you know,' said Sid, who then related other deeds, of a darker nature, that he had seen in the ruck and which had prompted him to take his strong action.

My disapproval of Going's mayhem was based, of course, on what I had seen through the television camera lens. Perhaps Going did the right thing, to rush to the assistance of a team-mate; but what I had seen was a fight going on after the whistle, a fight that appeared to continue because of the action of several All Blacks.

Going and I parted friends, I hope, agreeing perhaps to disagree. I respected his opinion and believed him. My words, after all, were an instant reaction during a live telecast, an opinion that was on the soundtrack forever and could not be changed. But I stick with what I said. I have to, don't I?

Anyway, 'Super Sid' was back to his brilliant best in the first forty minutes of the Lions match with the Maoris. He spun out long, swift passes to his first five-eighth Eddie Dunn, then ran elusively, as well as controlling the Maori cunning and turning it into an attacking force which in the first half dominated the Lions.

Going scored two tries, both by slipping the Lions' cordon of defence close to the scrum. The crowd of 52,000, unlike the South Islanders, were all dedicated Going fans, and let the whole world know their pride, cheering wildly.

The Lions were totally bewildered in the first half, looking for all the world as if they were running out the after-effects of some huge celebration, which in fact some of them were. The Maoris led by 13 to 3 at the break, and minutes into the second spell were further ahead. Going spun the ball along the line to Dunn who, crunched by John Bevan, slipped it to Bill Osborne who made a dash in under the posts. The fullback, Joe Whiu (pronounced 'Few'), converted and the Maoris looked home and hosed, ahead 19 to 6.

The Lions, however, had other ideas. From this point on they built their game towards a dramatic and deserving victory.

Sid Going had been all-dominant in the first half. Doubtless further encouraged by copious supplies of line-out ball from Vance Stewart and Ron Lockwood with which to attempt further breaches of the Lions' defensive line, Going made a fatal mistake. His runs became commonplace, and the element of surprise was lost. Instead of varying his passing, kicking and running, and keeping his opposites guessing, as he has done on so many memorable occasions, Going's second-half performance was predictable and stoppable.

The Lions' fightback — a triumph, as George Burrell put it, for 'spirit, character and skill' — began with a tap-penalty seven minutes into the second half. Windsor stood in the dummy-half position and fed Tony Neary. The Englishman burst upfield through some shoddy Maori defence and linked with a rejuvenated Mike Gibson. The pass to Peter Squires gave him a run but Gibson, as is his way, stayed close and received a return which enabled him to score at the end of a seventy metre move.

Next came Phil Orr's big moment. Morgan kicked high behind the Maori winger, David Haynes. The ball bounced awkwardly on the drying Eden Park surface, one of the best on the tour, and Orr was soon plunging forward with the loose ball to score his first try for the Lions.

Gibson, at his near-best form, was also involved in the next two tries. He set up Bruce Hay in a sweeping back move, the result of excellent line-out possession won in the second half by Moss Keane and Allan Martin. Hay was scuttled by Joe Whiu, his opposite, but still managed to send Squires away for a try.

The Gibson, Hay and Squires tries were scored wide out and the conversions missed; with twelve minutes to play the Maoris still held the lead, 19 to 18. Then John Bevan made a clever little kick. behind the Maori backline and the ball bounced loose. David Burcher, through quickly, swung it away to the ever-present Gibson. He made a run of such speed that Squires was pressed to keep up. Gibson drew Whiu, who otherwise played excellently, and passed to the unbalanced Squires. In his easy run for the corner he suddenly pulled up, held by a hamstring, but there was no defence there and Squires scored the winnng try on one and a half legs. Again the conversion missed, but after seventy minutes of play the Lions had, at last, hit the lead.

The last Maori assaults were desperate, and the crowd roared its encouragement, but the red line held. 'It was our second best win of the tour,' said Burrell with a smile, in an obvious reference to the Christchurch test. Tane Norton, again the beaten captain, praised his team for playing an excellent first half and scrummaging well, but admitted that his team had 'lost concentration' in the second spell.

One of the most pleasing features of the game was the determined and controlled refereeing of John Pring. Three times he took individuals aside, and issued clear warnings. There was a potential flare-up between Murray West and Willie Duggan but after Pring's admonishment there was no further trouble. Pring's overall performance was excellent, quite the best of the tour I felt.

In the evening the Auckland Rugby Union hosted an excellent

15. 'Smile for the birdies, Gareth'. Terry Cobner has just scored the only try of the Wellington match and introduces Gareth Evans into the pose he strikes for the photographers.

16. Andy Irvine in full flight in the sunshine at Eden Park. Judging by the closeness of the crowd behind him it looks as if his own try line was close by. Another fast-clip counter attack on its way?

17. The final act of the match against Canterbury. The home team are ahead by 13-11 but Andy Irvine can win it for the Lions with this kick. He didn't often take the close ones, but this one he did, successfully, to win the game — even though he had other things on his mind that day . . .

18. . . . Mrs Audrey Irvine, Andy's wife, and baby daughter, who arrived safely in this world several days later. Doesn't Dad look proud? A front page picture for the *New Zealand Herald*.

19. Ruler, King, Lord of all things. John Dawes supervises training somewhere in New Zealand. The actual day could be pinpointed closer, as sunny practice sessions on this tour were almost as scarce as British Isles dropped goals!

20. Not even a white tornedo would get that gear clean. Tony Neary in the mud of Athletic Park in Wellington against the Junior All Blacks. The shame was that this match should never have been played. If not this day then when does a match deserve to be cancelled?

21. They say a well hit stiff-arm tackle is like being clubbed over the head by a hunk of four by two! Ask West Coaster Jon Sullivan — he knows. His debut in big-time rugby, for the Junior All Blacks, ended after just 16 minutes with this incident. The 'stiff-arm' belongs to Fran Cotton. Other Lions are Elgan Rees, Trevor Evans (7), and Jeff Squire (8). On the evidence of this photo Cotton should have been sent off.

22. Cotton in the action again in the Auckland match. 'Now hold it right there' Peter Wheeler could be saying to Greg Denholm (left). Cotton (right) had just stomped on the head of Denholm, who retaliated. All hell broke loose just after this picture was taken. Rugby was not the winner. Glen Rich is No. 8.

function at the plush clubrooms of the Otahuhu Rugby Club. The Lions turned up, which, in view of their absence after the test in Christchurch, was a surprise. There was much hilarity, with Billy Bush, the Dunn brothers, and Paul Quinn each doing a solo turn with the band.

Quinn, the Wellington flanker replacement during the match, gave an hilarious imitation of a Reg Clapp race call, describing a mythical horse race with 'Young Quinn' hopelessly trailing the field. As his race-call improved in momentum, so did 'Young Quinn's' running position, finally thundering home a winner, while all in the cabaret stomped, cheered and whistled. It was a grand end to a grand rugby day.

The Teams
Lions: Hay; J. J. Williams, Burcher, Gibson, Squires; Bevan, Morgan; Duggan (replaced by Squire); Evans (captain), Keane, Martin, Neary; Cotton (replaced by Clive Williams), Windsor, Orr.
New Zealand Maoris : Joe Whiu (Auckland); David Haynes (North Auckland), Eddie Stokes (Bay of Plenty), Geoff Skipper (Wellington); Bill Osborne (Wanganui), Eddie Dunn (North Auckland); Sid Going (North Auckland); Murray West (Nelson Bays) replaced by Paul Quinn (Wellington); Tuck Waaka (North Auckland), Ron Lockwood (Waikato), Vance Stewart (Canterbury), Tim Carter (Hawke's Bay); Bill Bush (Canterbury), Tane Norton (Canterbury — captain), and Leon Toki (Auckland).
Scoring
Lions (22). Tries by Squires (2), Gibson and Orr. Penalties (2) by Gibson.
New Zealand Maoris (19). Tries by Sid Going (2) and Bill Osborne. Conversions (2) and a penalty by Joe Whiu.
Referee: John Pring (Auckland).   Wednesday, 13 July 1977.

18. Lions 18, Waikato 13. Young Keith Quinn was at home in Lower Hutt one night, a rare domestic occasion on a three-month rugby trek. In several days' time the Lions were to play the red, black and yellow-jerseyed Waikato team.

Telephone rings. Young Quinn answers. A voice on the other end, slightly muffled, identifies itself and asks if he would like to assist the New Zealand Police Force. 'Why, sure', says Quinn, always ready to aid those who fight crime and violence in our streets. The request is simple. The caller speaks on behalf of a Police armed offenders squad and sharp-shooters who are holding an anti-terrorist exercise week at Shelly Bay, near Wellington.

'Can you', says the voice, 'tell us if Saturday's match is telecast live? We need to know. An armed offenders operation is scheduled for Saturday afternoon, but if you give us the nod that the game is on TV, we'll try and switch it to the morning.'

Of course I, and you, dear reader, both know of the tight-lipped agreement that exists between Television One and the New Zealand Rugby Football Union, with regard to the pre-announcement of live television. You can 'neither confirm nor deny' we are repeatedly told. But, of course there are exceptions. I admit, here and now, that I told my police caller with the muffled voice that the Waikato-Lions match, as far as I knew, would not be 'live' on TV. I broke the cone of silence. But, may I say in defence, I did it with police approval.

The match between the Lions and Waikato began on a hard pitch that seemed ideal for the running talents of Bennett and Irvine. Bennett had not played on a firm ground since the Southland game, over one month before, and Irvine had not seen one since Timaru, which he had insisted was perfect for his game.

So we expected big things from the Lions at Rugby Park, Hamilton. Waikato were a second division team and had won only one match out of five before the British Isles came to town. They had been bothered by injury, losing Murray Taylor, a gifted five-eighth, Andy Baker, a fullback tipped as a potential All Black, and their 1976 captain, Kevin Magill, a most promising number eight.

When the Lions won the first line-out and Bennett zigged once and zagged twice before passing to a running Irvine, the day had the potential of a repeat of Taumarunui and the second half at Timaru.

That did not happen however. Lifting their play in the first twenty minutes, as every local team does against a touring side, Waikato were able, with superior dedication, to earn much of the honour of this splendid rugby occasion.

The Lions won 18-13 but were 4-7 behind at half time, and only narrowly ahead (14-13) with as few as eight minutes to play.

Waikato were a gutsy lot. They had Trevor Irwin, a fullback out of the club, Kereone, that boasted D. B. Clarke as one of its former stars. Irwin scored a try by coming up, like Andy Irvine, outside his winger and then pushing, quite simply, past Bennett's poor tackle to go over in the corner. Irwin added a conversion and a penalty and played with great confidence.

In the centre was Kit Fawcett, the forgotten man of New Zealand rugby. Forgotten, in the sense that in all the talk of fullbacks for the tests, he was, quite callously I felt, left out of all consideration. He remained a player with many more innate skills than most of the more favoured test candidates at that time.

Fawcett showed me chewing-gum packing in his mouth, covering wiring on his teeth and jaw. This remained in position during the match, testimony to his determination to play even though he had not fully recovered from the effects of a broken jaw. He was a solid and sure player who kicked safely and tackled well. He was every bit as good as he had been, most of the time, in South Africa with the All Blacks in 1976. He deserved more, much more, than to be discarded by the 1977 New Zealand selectors as a rugby nobody.

At halfback was Kevin Greene, the Waikato captain, who led the team splendidly, passing the ball safely and with speed to his out-sides.

In the forwards the local star was undoubtedly Paul Anderson, who had been out of New Zealand since his previous game for Waikato in 1973. One of his bursts from a forward play was done with great speed. He gained forty metres, with blond hair flying, and fed Lehi Hohaia, another Maori second five-eighth prospect, who skipped along, only to have a scoring pass deflected away from Fawcett.

The Lions again looked vulnerable; their forward effort was deficient, including the lack of certainty to make the first sure tackle of an opposition surge.

The scrum was again the most potent force, pushing Waikato back time and time again. There were some goings-on, 'how's your father' it used to be called, in the front rows; this was resolved after a Waikato knee was raised, with force, into a Lion's face, and the two packs slugged it out, toe to toe.

My friends from the press, whom I trust implicitly at times like this, told me that, on the side away from the TV cameras, Jeff Squire, usually a most friendly chap, kicked a Waikato man on the deck. Their statements were confirmed several days later with a photograph in *Rugby News*. So the Waikato knee, and the Squire boot both deserve a place in that Museum of Mockery where foul rugby deeds lie.

The Lions scored three tries. Elgan Rees got two of them, in his most satisfactory performance of the season. Too often his elusiveness was not allied to any great purpose, and his running, though fast, went not directly through the traffic ahead. His second try, with a burst through Hohaia, was made of better stuff and young Rees was clearly delighted.

Andy Irvine, again left sadly out of much running action, scored the other try. It came after a Brynmor Williams blindside break, followed by a blinding burst by Phil Orr to clear the move to open territory. Williams again, then Burcher handled before Irvine, as extra man, sped in for a try that was seventy metres in length. Bennett's two penalties made the Lions score 18 and the match was theirs.

Ron Lockwood lived up to the literal meaning of his name, playing with teak-like hardness and forcing his way over for Waikato's second try late in the match, to give them 13.

The only cloud over the Lions' happiness was the number of injuries the team suffered. Clive Williams limped out of the tour with a knee ligament problem, similar to that which had sidelined Grant Batty. Ross Nicholson of Auckland, the same surgeon who had operated on Batty, made 'a good repair job' on Williams a week later, but the Lions management called for Charlie Faulkner to fly out as replacement.

Brynmor Williams also left the field under a cloud. He 'severely tore' a hamstring muscle but, strangely, failed to recognise the fact and played on. The severity of the doctor's initial report sent a wave of expectation through the press corps that Gareth Edwards, the great man himself, might be summoned as a further replacement. Alas, for the New Zealand rugby fan who would have enjoyed seeing Edwards in action again, Brynmor Williams recovered quickly.

Burcher heavily bumped his left knee and Squire badly ricked his neck, to add to the walking wounded.

After the longest speech of the tour, delivered by Waikato's President, Mr E. S. Beer, the aftermatch fun settled into a long celebration for the Lions. From Saturday to Saturday it had been quite a week for the team, first defeating New Zealand, then the Maoris and now Waikato. They were three important victories. But ahead were some tough games, amid the widely reported homesickness and disenchantment with touring life among 'the lads' who called themselves Lions.

The teams
Lions: Irvine; Rees, McGeechan, Burcher, Gareth Evans; Bennett (captain), Brynmor Williams (replaced by Morgan); Quinnell; Cobner, Beaumont, Brown, Squire; Clive Williams (replaced by Orr), Wheeler and Windsor.
Waikato: Trevor Irwin; Alan Clark, Kit Fawcett, John O'Rourke; Lehi Hohaia, Ross McGlashan; Kevin Greene (captain); Dick

Myers; Paul Anderson, Ron Lockwood, John Sisley, Ián Lockie; Dave Olsen, Pat Bennett and Graham Irwin.
Scoring
Lions (18). Tries by Rees (2) and Irvine. Penalties (2) by Bennett. *Waikato* (13). Tries by Trevor Irwin and Ron Lockwood. Penalty and conversion by Trevor Irwin.
Referee: Barry Dawson (Southland).   Saturday, 16 July 1977.

19. Lions 19, New Zealand Juniors 9. One of my most vivid memories of the 1966 British Isles tour of New Zealand was their game on Athletic Park in Wellington against New Zealand's Under 23 representatives, known then, as they are now, as the Junior All Blacks. The match was played on the bleakest of days and was won by Campbell-Lamberton's Lions by 9 to 3. The park was wet and heavy, and movement about the pitch was difficult and laboured. Two individual performances shone out like wide lights. One came from the New Zealand Junior fullback, Dave Laurie. He fielded kicks and ran across the mud in fine style. He looked an All Black in the making that day; the honour eluded him, though he was still playing first-class rugby ten years later.

The other star performer in the 1966 game was Cameron Michael Henderson Gibson. He darted this way and that, matched and bettered Laurie as an individual, and stamped the game as his own by making a right wing try for Dewi Bebb.

In 1977, eleven long winters on, Gibson came back to Athletic Park to play the New Zealand Juniors again. The weather was similar to the mud and rain of 1966 but in 1977 it was more depressing than ever. Heavy rain had fallen every day of the three visits the tourists had spent in Wellington. Athletic Park, famous we are told for its ability to drain excess water and provide a firm footing, became sloppily worse. It was bad, as you have read, for the test match. It was worse when the Wellington team had its own tilt at the Lions. But those conditions were sun and summer-like compared with the bog that was offered the Lions to play the New Zealand Juniors. Willie Duggan and David Burcher simply could not believe what they saw before kick-off and set off to climb the mountainous Millard Stand to record it on film. What they would have seen through the viewfinder was as heavy a field as is possible. In fact this ground went beyond that point, to being impossible, and there was a considerable case to have the game postponed or even cancelled.

When the two teams came out and played the opening minutes, tripping cautiously across the mud so as not to dirty their neat, crisp uniforms, the players were made to look almost foolish. What man of sound mind would otherwise discard his pride to suffer the humiliation of being slopped and thrown about on a field so mired and foul-smelling that nothing truly constructive could be performed on it?

The Lions were thoroughly brassed off at having to play the game, you could sense that. The Juniors were buoyed up by the fact that Mark Donaldson for one and Bevan Wilson for another, had only to play solidly to confirm their claims as senior All Black prospects. The team's youthful enthusiasm for the battle was a great start-off point for rugby action that was far better than I ever would have imagined.

The first manifestation of the Lions' gloom at having to play the match at all came after twelve minutes. David Haynes, the left winger who had played for the Maoris a week before, fielded a skidding kick at halfway. In a repeat of their match pattern he began to run, for that's what the Juniors did all afternoon. Finding Jon Sullivan, the West Coaster, nearby Haynes slung him a pass. Sullivan, handling in the big time for the first occasion, made several paces down the touchline and was then crunched in an upright tackle by Fran Cotton. It was not obvious to me straight away, but Cotton had included a strong right stiff-arm tackle in his assault on the new boy. Television replays showed that Cotton's action was close to that area of misdeed for which players are banished from the field. Cotton received a stern warning from Mike Farnworth, the young Auckland referee, but adopted a 'who me?' attitude throughout it all. It was a black mark against the Englishman.

The scoring opened when Bevan Wilson banged over a penalty from 25 metres, a strong kick, for the wind was brisk from the south. As he was setting the ball up there was great sadness as Mike Gibson limped off. One tends to fear the worst when injury strikes at 34 years of age, but Gibson was not hurt seriously; his experience told him that a hamstring twinge was warning of impending damage. Brynmor Williams take note.

The first Lions try came while the players were still recognisable. John Bevan, running wide in a blindside move, almost bumped into Bruce Hay, who was trying to join from fullback. The move stayed upright long enough to see Elgan Rees scoot in for a try in the corner. That's what it was at half-time, 4-3 to the Lions.

No sooner had the second half begun than the Juniors scored what may become the definitive wet-weather rugby try. Donaldson cleared a swift pass to Mark Sisam, his captain, then Stephen Pokere handed on to centre Dan Fouhy, who, with a canny sense of timing, sent Bevan Wilson away on an endless carve. His break was well clear of the Lions defence, prompting the question again: Was there a serious lack of planned defence in the Lions centre field?

Wilson was eventually blocked after running fifty metres, but Pokere came at great speed to toe on and dive ahead of Rees to touch down. 12,000 spectators whistled their approval, and Wilson's conversion made things look even better for the Juniors, ahead 9-4.

The speed with which Wilson and Co. had run and the fluidity of the move demonstrated that rugby of quality could be played in execrable conditions.

The Juniors, sent away admirably by Donaldson and Sisam, continued to run the ball all day. The Lions, with a change of tactics, took their game in close where the forwards were now lookalikes with their opponents, all caked in cocoons of mud. The switch produced results. The two tries which clinched the game for them came from close-quarter forward build-ups.

From one scrum on the Lions 10-metre mark, the Juniors were frog-marched (a particularly expressive term for this day). The scrum advanced fifteen metres before Doug Morgan, playing excellently, had the ball released to him for a high kick ahead. Alan Dawson (Sullivan's replacement) dropped the slippery projectile and Morgan worked the ensuing maul ball left to where Hay, J. J. Williams (Gibson's replacement) and Neary all handled before Windsor plunged over.

Morgan added a splendid conversion, later a penalty and in the last minute featured in the final score. The two packs of forwards, leg-weary and anonymous, so conjoining was the colour of the mud, wrestled in a maul close to the line. Morgan moved right when the ball came clear and slipped Jeff Squire into a scoring position. The big number eight went over, sliding on and on through the mire. Morgan's conversion and the referee's final whistle folowed. 19-9 in the nineteenth tour match.

In the showers afterwards some players stood fully kitted washing the mud off as best they could. Doc Murdoch, the cheery masseur and baggageman of the touring party, announced that whereas he could normally carry the team's gear bag hitched over his shoulder, this day he needed three of the Lions' hefty forwards to help him shift the watery, muddy uniforms.

In the press conference held under the stand in a steamy dressing-room George Burrell said 'it was a shame that the game had to be played at all under conditions like that.' John Dawes nodded in agreement, adding he 'wondered how all thirty players stuck it out to the final whistle.'

Someone asked why Douglas Morgan was limping late in the game. 'He's all right,' came the reply. 'He just had more mud on the right leg than the left!' That summed up the day.

The Juniors got more out of this pointless sporting exercise than the Lions. Donaldson played superbly, as indeed he had done for Manawatu-Horowhenua against the Lions. The unhappy memories of the kicking incident for that team were now, it was hoped, well behind him. He looked an All Black this day. So did Wilson — well, perhaps. A fine player, this young man had certainly impressed the Athletic Park crowds more than Farrell had done in better conditions in the test match.

The Lions quite simply and, on reflection, rather stupidly allowed the Wellington mud and rain to get them down. Their injury list, light in recent weeks, was mounting again and key players like Brynmor Williams, Clive Williams, Gibson, Squires and Cobner were all sick or suffering.

The side, already introverted, withdrew further into themselves. They still wanted to do well, they still wanted to win, but the increasing pressure of off-the-field stories of vandalism and loutish behaviour, the injury list, the thought of repeated hard training on slushy, smelly fields, the tough matches ahead and four weeks of the tour still to go, all made inroads into the team's strength of character.

The next few days, however, would see a change . . .

The teams

Lions: Hay; Rees, Gibson (replaced by J. J. Williams), McGeechan, Gareth Evans, Bevan, Morgan; Squire; Trevor Evans (captain), Keane, Martin, Neary; Orr, Windsor, and Cotton.

New Zealand Juniors: Bevan Wilson (Otago); David Haynes (North Auckland), Dan Fouhy (Wellington), Murray Watts (Manawatu); Stephen Pokere (Southland), Mark Sisam (captain — Auckland), Mark Donaldson (M); Graeme Elvin (Otago); Jon Sullivan (West Coast) — replaced by Alan Dawson (Counties), Alan Craig (Auckland), Wayne Graham (Otago), Glen Rich (Auckland); Rod Ketels (Counties), Gary Collins (Canterbury) and Mike Pervan (Auckland).

Scoring
Lions (19). Tries by Rees, Squire and Windsor. Penalty and conversions (2) by Morgan.
New Zealand Juniors (9). Try by Stephen Pokere. Penalty and conversion by Bevan Wilson.
Referee : Mike Farnworth (Auckland).Wednesday, 20 July 1977.

20. Lions 34, Auckland 15. Right from the moment the NAC Boeing 737s started delivering from Wellington to Auckland the British Isles touring party, the gentlemen of the media corps and assorted officials and supporters, the 'message' was quietly passed around — 'Auckland is ready, Auckland will win'.

Because the press camp followers are so often asked their opinions and forecasts, I eventually found the same fateful words passing my lips, spoken as though I had intimate knowledge of this Auckland side. This expression of Auckland confidence was based on three main considerations. Firstly, there was the complement of men who were the chosen Auckland team. They had a strong look about them. There were six current or former All Blacks: Colin Farrell, Bryan Williams, Terry Morrison, Bruce Gemmell, Andy Haden and Brad Johnstone. There was the speedster Tim Twigden, a centre, who had worn the All Black jersey as a reserve for the second test at Christchurch. Among the forwards were Glen Rich, the Junior All Black, Bruce Munro, a giant former New Zealand colt, and Dennis Thorn, the New Zealand University flanker. There were Mike Richards, Barry Ashworth and Ben Hathaway, each of them recent All Black trialists and contenders, and Steve Watt and Perry Parlane, long-time Auckland representatives.

With these names and reputations went other attributes, especially in the forwards, who were judged to have the physical properties necessary to beat the Lions. Munro, with experience of playing in Italy, stood six feet six inches above the earth's crust and Haden, as I have mentioned, has combined dimensions of height and weight that no All Black has ever bettered. This laid the foundation for a rugby structure that had, at its apex, such backline talent as Williams, Twigden and Morrison, who were all blistered by speed and powered by supercharged hi-octane running gas. The consolidation of individual talent and team experience was the second consideration in forecasts of victory for Auckland. The third consideration was the Lions.

The tourists faced Auckland's reputation and some heavy propaganda as they approached the match. It would be the first time they had to contend with a forward pack of equal proportion to themselves. They also had to face Steve Watt, by reputation the most accurate and methodical goal-kicker in the country. And the team also had to accept that in terms of morale, they were at the low-water mark of the tour.

For the previous two or three weeks that intangible ailment, homesickness, had entered the core of this Lions side. Outwardly they looked the same men, but inwardly they wanted a break from the unrelenting grind of training, training, and more training. There were other forces turning their minds towards home. Some New Zealand newspapers had vilified the team. During the week of the Auckland match one labelled them as 'louts and animals'. The team regarded these stories with contempt and scorn but their attitude towards New Zealanders was affected. In that particular week they would have favoured being anywhere else in the world but Auckland, New Zealand, with still a month of their touring torment to go.

So when the two teams trotted on to Eden Park under sunny skies more than a fair proportion of the 57,000 spectators at the ground had heard these stories and knew the backdrop against which the match would be played. They were there, waiting like spectators at the Coliseum in Roman days, except that in Auckland in 1977 it was Lions blood they were after.

No blood did they see. The rugby cut this British Isles team opened in Auckland's rugby pride drew no blood, so clean and cold was its incision. The 34-15 win to the Lions spoke wonders for their team spirit and inner unity. Simply, coldbloodedly, and with precision they carved the Auckland challenge to pieces.

True, Auckland played a brave part in the proceedings, running the ball to their threequarters with consistency and employing Bryan Williams, a winger without peer as an attacker, but the Lions performance was total for the first time on tour.

Ground conditions were good, after a hired helicopter had played its downdraft on the field for several hours. The British began quietly, if that's the word, while Auckland thundered in from the kick-off, fired as all local teams are with the fierceness of the build-up and the significance of the moment.

Scoring in the first half came mainly from penalties. Douglas Morgan got three, Steve Watt one, and Watt's was the best, being kicked, with his careful attention to method, into a strongish breeze.

The only try in the first half went to the British and was, if I may for once quote my commentary, 'a classic support play score'.

Phil Bennett, who had first demonstrated the Lions determination to do well in this match by tackling head-on the flying winger Terry Morrison, ran across field from a ruck. He was allowed, by the sluggishness of the Auckland loose men, to make considerable progress but only in a line parallel to the try-line. Then a high basketball pass bounced to J. J. Williams, who moved off at speed towards the corner. Andy Irvine, returning at last to his prime attacking role, ran up from fullback, like no New Zealander ever did, simply to support his winger should he have nowhere to pass when the defence came across. So the defence came across. Irvine got his pass. Try. Simple. Why had New Zealand no players possessed of this intelligence, speed and enterprise at fullback?

The conversion came from Morgan and it was 15-3 at half-time.

After the break Morgan scored with his fourth penalty and Watt with his second. Next thing we knew Bryan Williams had banged over a beauty from fifty metres. This was the Williams of old, taking the attempts only when it was known he could kick with aggression, taking a chance on being successful, and not being burdened with the knowledge that he *had* to kick them.

That made it 18-9 and I suppose Auckland might have swung the match had they scored next. But, as they say, if wishes were horses then beggars would ride.

Auckland at this juncture found themselves faced by a pack of such strength and guile that it became rare for them to win quality passing ball. The Lions forwards, with Tony Neary leading by admirable example, were superb at the mauls, overpowering at the lineouts and, may I say, great at scrum-time.

It was in this latter phase that Steve Watt, for all his praiseworthy goal-kicking, was scrummed out of consideration for All Black honours. Eventually he retired hurt, suffering a rib injury. His replacement, Greg Denholm, had scarcely taken his place in the lineout before Fran Cotton, earning another black mark, punched him in the face in a completely unwarranted welcome. Perhaps they had had a score to settle from their previous match in opposition, when Denholm had played so splendidly for the New Zealand Universities. But Fran Cotton . . . one wonders.

The play raged on and when Willie Duggan scored at a pushover scrum Denholm repaid the compliment on Cotton. Television showed it was a mighty whack Denholm delivered, albeit justifiably. The brawl which followed again brought the tour into disgrace. Dave

Millar, having controlled the game as well as he had the Canterbury match, saw early that Denholm was, in this case, the instigator; at the restart, he quite correctly awarded a penalty to the Lions at halfway. Millar was referring to Law 26, which forbids any molestation of an opponent after the ball is out of play; the penalty which must result is taken from where play restarts.

The whistling and cat-calling at this point made a mockery of the announcement directed to the crowd that 'booing does not occur' in Auckland. Admittedly, we who had followed the tour had heard much worse. But Auckland had joined the club.

Andy Irvine got in the act again by scoring another try, his eleventh on the tour. Then with a stylish swing-pass Irvine set up a try for J. J. Williams, the two men complementing each other perfectly as ever.

Phil Bennett himself got the fifth and last try. Doug Morgan, who had lifted his performance markedly in the last two games, ran wide and as the 1959 Lions had so often done, flipped up a backhand flick pass to Bennett cutting back. The captain was across in a blink and the Lions' joy was total. Big forwards rushed forward and cradled their captain's head under their enveloping arms. Scornful New Zealanders might have regarded their happiness as an intrusion of soccer clowning but the sight of a Welshman being hugged happily by Scotsmen, Englishmen and Irishmen was a telling on-the-field expression of integration and oneness.

As the clock on the scoreboard signalled no side Auckland, down by 34 to 9, made one final attempt to gain honour from the match. Perry Parlane, at second five-eighth, held the ball in suspended animation, waiting for the storming intervention of Bryan Williams, who took it at top flight. He simply zoomed past a flailing Irvine, something which Williams would no doubt remember in subsequent meetings, and with great power he was over. Parlane's conversion brought the final whistle.

The Williams lift in form was the only heartening asset for Aucklanders to consider as they drifted away. Colin Farrell, the other local hero, who had needed to play a 'blinder' to retain his test spot, had started well but fizzled out as his team did.

The Lions management, no doubt cock-a-hoop, held their press conference in a room among the musical instruments and bandsmen who had played before kick-off, which was somehow appropriate. The rugby music the Lions had played this day was of top-ten quality, a symphony conducted and executed with calm control of pianissimo and forte, and devoid of the disjointed attempts at harmony they had struggled with in earlier matches. We were all hum-ming the theme.

Burrell called the win 'a marvellous victory to go on holiday with', for the team was now headed for four days R and R in Waitangi. John Dawes said the reports of homesickness and depression within the side were 'nothing a good win won't put right'. How true. The party that night was another boomer. Bennett expressed the mood of them all when he repeated the happy phrase coined in Christchurch — 'the show is back on the road again.'

The gloom that closed in over Auckland with the arrival of darkness and the assimilation of such a massive defeat for the local team, became a cloud over the nation when the New Zealand team was announced for the Third Test in Dunedin.

There were six changes. Gone were some familiar and much-loved names, Sid Going and Kevin Eveleigh, and two of the Aucklanders — Brad Johnstone and Colin Farrell. At the aftermatch function everyone looked across the room at John Dawes. He was smiling.

If there was one day on the 1977 British Isles tour when the rugby balance reversed from tilting slightly New Zealand's way to bending back towards the Lions, let it be recorded that the day was 23 July 1977. And the place where it all changed was Eden Park in Auckland.

The teams

Lions: Irvine; J. J. Williams, Burcher, Fenwick, Gareth Evans; Bennett (captain), Morgan; Duggan; Neary, Brown, Beaumont, Quinnell; Cotton, Wheeler and Price.

Auckland: Colin Farrell; Terry Morrison, Tim Twigden, Bryan Williams; Perry Parlane, Mike Richards; Bruce Gemmell; Glen Rich; Barry Ashworth, Andy Haden, Bruce Munro, Dennis Thorn; Brad Johnstone (captain), Ben Hathaway and Steve Watt (replaced by Greg Denholm).

Scoring

Lions (34). Tries by Irvine (2), Bennett, Duggan and J. J. Williams. Conversions and penalties (4) by Morgan.

Auckland (15). Try by Bryan Williams. Conversion by Perry Parlane. Penalties (2) by Steve Watt and Bryan Williams.

Referee: Dave Millar (Otago).   Saturday, 23 July 1977.

10
The Third Test: Dunedin

21. British Isles 7, New Zealand 19. At 2.31 p.m., or thereabouts, on the afternoon of 30 July 1977, Dunedin's Dave Millar blew his referee's whistle and began the third test between the Lions and the All Blacks. Here is what happened over the next minute.

Bryan Williams kicked deep to Phil Bennett who, in turn, kicked back to find touch. Time gone: 11 seconds.

Brian Ford, a brand-new All Black left-winger, fielded another ball from the ball-boy and prepared to throw in. Time gone: 25 seconds.

Ford's throw-in was deflected directly down in front of the line-out, the new winger rushing straight in to gather and feed his encircling forwards. Time gone: 31 seconds.

The ball is freed to Lyn Davis, back in test rugby for his second cap. He sends out a perfect pass to Doug Bruce, Bill Osborne hands on, Bruce Robertson running at top clip holds the pass then chip-kicks ahead. Ian Kirkpatrick, to be a towering figure in this match, sprints hard to the loose ball short of the line, stoops to pick it up and steps over the line, to score what must surely be the fastest try in rugby history. Time gone: 45 seconds.

What a start for the All Blacks! The jubilation from over 30,000 spectators at the Carisbrook ground in Dunedin sent shockwaves reverberating through the air, to be heard several miles distant. The shock-response to the attack and move most notably affected (a) the British Lions, who never in this match truly recovered, and (b) the All Blacks, who were fired to full speed and power, leading to domination.

As the dominance became apparent the critics of this All Black team were jolted into the realisation that what was called by many a 'panic selection' was a classic case of superb judgment by the selectors, and Jack Gleeson in particular.

The All Blacks' 19-7 victory gave them a 2-1 lead in the series and was one of the most shrewdly-conceived and co-ordinated in recent All Black history.

For the Lions, the expectation of victory in the third test and a triumphant finale in the fourth came tumbling down into the Carisbrook mud, they were held in a reversal of form so powerful that men of great rugby stature within the British team were reduced to stunned silence.

New Zealand's skilful strategy was born in a small room away from the hustle and bustle of an aftermatch party at Eden Park in Auckland. Only moments before, the British Isles had ended the exercise that had humbled Auckland 34-15, to inject once again into their tour, the promise of a test series victory and the continuation of British dominance of world rugby.

When Messrs Gleeson, Stewart and Watson announced their team for the third test at Dunedin they made six changes. Gone were Farrell, Jaffray, Taylor, Going, Eveleigh and Johnstone. Brought in to fill their places were Bevan Wilson, Brian Ford, Bruce Robertson (back after injury), Lyn Davis, Graham Mourie and John McEldowney.

The initial response to the new team was one of total shock. At Eden Park, faces turned to where the Lions were tucking into food and drink after their satisfying victory. They beamed a vote of appreciation to the All Black selectors.

Later that evening Grant Batty flew with me to Wellington. We joined John Lindsay, coach of Otago's hard-rucking team, Tony Small, mentor of Hawke's Bay's superb effort against the Lions, and Gary Hermansson, frontman to the *Lions '77* TV show and former top-line representative Number 8 forward. These four men, all with high credentials and keen rugby intellect, obviously did not agree on all points, but they were universally agreed that too many men had been axed.

The most heated point of issue concerned Sid Going. His brilliance as a break-and-drive player had, after the second test, to be weighed against his inability to spark and supply a backline that was committed to running play. He had to go, for his passing inadequacies. Yet Grant Batty told New Zealand viewers, 'If I had to grade the All Black team of the first two tests in order of preference, I would have Sid Going at Number One. He is so strong and tough and his value to the team's cause is not always best seen by the watching public.

We just loved having him there.' True words indeed, and sad for Going that his career at this level seemed finished.

Kevin Eveleigh was another emotive point at issue. He was a popular terrier, who chased and cut down opposition backs in superb style. But the selectors needed more than that. The popular play on words at the time was that he was destructive, not constructive. What was wanted, the selectors reasoned, was a flanker who was both destructive *and* constructive. Such a man was Taranaki's Graham Mourie. Colin Meads, who rates as a rugby judge of the highest standing, called Eveleigh his 'man of the match' in the second test, and if Meads says that then it is praise indeed. But Eveleigh also had to go.

So too did Colin Farrell. He was a fullback gamble who had not paid out in dividends. He could not be classed as an abject failure — you got your money back; but he did not have resources beyond the soundness that is required in a top-line test match fullback.

Farrell's deficiencies were epitomised in one play in Auckland's match against the Lions. On the stroke of half-time Douglas Morgan had kicked through to him at the Auckland 22-metre line. All that was required of Farrell was to retrieve, kick out and take the half-time break. He retrieved all right, but then turned his back in a sluggish motion on the oncoming Lions, and moved off to run the ball. His misjudgment of the situation was made total when he was collared after several paces, the ball wrenched from his arms, and kicked behind the Auckland line. Only the closest of shaves prevented the Lions from scoring a try under the bar. Farrell, unfortunately for one so young and keen, had to pay for errors and omissions like this.

There were other changes. Brad Johnstone, from the front row, made way for John McEldowney, a Gleeson favourite. 'I guess I had two bad games, the second test and the Auckland game,' said Johnstone disappointedly, 'but I'll be back.'

Winger Mark Taylor was gone too, not so much for ineptness, but because the selectors felt the need for a specialist speedster, and one who would provide expert throwing in at line-out time. Brian Ford, at 26 years of age no winger's fledgeling, was summoned from Kaikoura to play the test. He was clearly delighted and grasped his chance firmly. Lyn Jaffray, ball juggler extraordinaire of the second test, was dropped with the return of Bruce Robertson to the centre position. An interesting and welcome addition to the reserves was Mark Donaldson, whose indiscretion at Palmerston North had been forgotten; his playing talents were accorded proper judgment.

What a team! What alarm it caused! The Lions enjoyed the whole affair. On Sunday night, tucked away from the rain and wind in their Waitangi Hotel on their three-day holiday, they shushed the dance-band floor-show into silence and raised their glasses to toast the New Zealand selectors. 'For allowing us to win the series', they said.

Dunedin again brought rain to the touring team. In its all-enveloping way it had closed in around the heights of the city, leaking down in gentle mists for ten days prior to kick-off. The ground at Carisbrook, free from action for most of the previous five weeks, took a lot of water, but played out the eighty minutes well. In complete contrast to those non-thinking unions who had staged successive saturated Saturday matches and then added pointless curtain-raisers to many of the Lions' games, the Dunedin reasoning was gladdening to the extreme. Full marks.

Test day dawned fine and clear with the streets of Dunedin lightly awash with overnight rain. The All Blacks breakfasted early in the Beach Hotel, a homely establishment away from the city bustle. Staying at the same hostelry, I had been impressed by the quiet, iron-willed build-up of the New Zealand team. There was no trumpeting, chest thumping, or 'we're gonna do 'em' approach. Just commonsense resolve. One could feel it.

The British scrum machine, unchanged from that which strongly moved the All Blacks around the Lancaster Park mud in the second test, repeated its dominance of the New Zealanders at Dunedin. And in the line-outs, Bill Beaumont, now a craggy and critical member of the Lions line-up, and Gordon Brown, the Scotsman whose form had improved in every match, leapt higher more often than the All Blacks and won rule here too. With this wealth of set-piece possession, and Phil Bennett and Andy Irvine among those in the back division to throw it to, this was a game the Lions should never, never have lost. But for the first time on tour the backs did not just play ordinarily. At Carisbrook, Dunedin on third test day, they were woeful!

They were bad as a set; so predictable, stumpy and stodgy of movement that they looked for all the world like one of the many boring, staid provincial backlines they had run rings around so often on this tour. It was as if some magic wand had touched them, relieving them of all talent and gift, turning them into a tardy band of stragglers, devoid of invention.

This same magic, waved so wickedly against the tourists, brought confidence and co-ordination to the re-arranged New Zealand set. Only Bryan Williams, Bill Osborne and Doug Bruce remained where they had been at Christchurch; different men lined up in the other positions. Denied, by the Lions pack, a sure supply of ball to attack with they made full use of the scraps offering, like hungry hounds at a butcher's shop door.

With handling as sure and as brilliant as I could remember from an All Black team, Bruce, Osborne, Ford and Williams directed strong incursive attacks at the Lions' frail backline. These four were brothers-in-arms to the three stars of the day.

Lyn Davis was one. It was he who accepted the shredded possession from scrum and line-out and delivered fast, clean passes to Bruce.

Bruce Robertson was another. He punched holes in the confidence of his opposites with darting runs of immense power and character.

And the third hero was Bevan Wilson. This young man, blessed with boyish features so smooth one has to look closely to see if he shaves or not, came in to the fullback role as if it had been waiting for his arrival for years. He was immediately at home, turning back high balls from Fenwick and Bennett with all the surety one associates with a well-capped veteran. He ran in strongly to some attacks — not too many, but not too few — and he found touch after touch with superbly struck line-kicks. His presence, in such good form, lifted the All Blacks' level of play up several notches, the others could tear into their *own* work, without worrying about the last line of defence, which had been their problem at Wellington and Christchurch.

Wilson it was who was called up after Kirkpatrick had scored his first-minute try (his fiftieth for New Zealand), to attempt the conversion. The boy grew into a man in this moment. From wide out he kicked, with his usual rural efficiency, a goal that must have been agony to make. All the talk of fullbacks, failure, fallibility and Farrell must have been in the back of his mind. Yet Wilson's kick was safely through the posts without a centimetre of deviation.

The clock said one minute gone. The Lions were down 6-0. And Tane Norton, who was in his fourteenth year before Wilson was born, shouted congratulations through the tumult to the new discovery as he ran on back to position.

The match was New Zealand's. There were many more forays and diversions in the absorbing struggle before their victory was won, but the match was only New Zealand's.

The Lions bounced back, Willie Duggan slipping over for a try after only four minutes to close the gap to 6-4. But the tourists played without clarity or, as John Dawes and George Burrell put it, without the 'character' which had seen them through so many tight squeezes before.

At the root of their problems was Phil Bennett. For the first time on tour he was captured by an opposition match plan. On this occasion it was Taranaki's Graham Mourie, the new flank-forward, who trapped and held the Welshman. Instead of committing himself to tackle Bennett at all costs, as Eveleigh would have done, Mourie ran up to 'Benny', threatened him by his quickening presence then moved outwards to make tackles. Bennett was forced for the first time to feel the heat of pressure from a fast-following loose forward. He did not react well. He kicked, usually directly to Wilson, nearly always to hand. He passed poorly, setting up the only new test cap in his team, David Burcher, for a miserable day; and when Bennett ran he met a blackening wall of determined defenders who scarcely allowed him to essay his sizzling sidesteps.

Other problems arose for the tourists. J. J. Williams and Brynmor Williams both left the field injured, J. J. in the first half and Brynmor after the half-time break. Their replacements were Ian McGeechan, who went to the left wing, and Douglas Morgan, the improving half-back.

The All Blacks took their lead to 10-4 when Andy Haden followed up to a set-up ruck which had resulted from strong running by Bruce, Robertson and Ford. When Haden applied his strength to the ruck, the ball slid loose for him to clutch gleefully and dive over.

So the score remained till Andy Irvine closed it up to 10-7 shortly after the break, with a penalty goal. This was the only goal-kicking success of the day for the Lions, who had cause to wonder what had happened to their usual unerring accuracy.

The three-point gap inspired the Lions to begin their strongest bid for the match. Their forwards, plunging the scrums forward, broke up the New Zealand pack time and time again, driving them back in confusion and disarray, a truly staggering sight. 'A bad patch here, chaps,' said Jack Gleeson later, as we sat in the TV lounge of the Beach Hotel and watched the replay. 'Tighten up, tighten up', he repeated to himself, though everybody heard it. But the Lions' efficiency and determination up front, often epitomised in bursting runs by Quinnell and Cobner, could achieve no break-through. Mourie, Knight and Oliver tackled like demons. Kirkpatrick, playing, as Tane Norton put it, 'the most important test of his life', was superb. McEldowney, the new man at prop, weighed in with strong-man action, as did Bush and Haden. Tane Norton, a losing captain in his previous test, had his head 'on the block' in this game and contributed a lot more to the general play than he does normally.

The turning point came when an All Black break-out, after Doug Bruce charged down a sluggish Bennett kick, swept downfield with Williams forcing Steve Fenwick to soccer-kick the ball away. From the resulting line-out play Fran Cotton was penalised. Bevan Wilson kicked the goal and the lead again went out to six points. Irvine then missed a sitter, as Bennett had done too, and Wilson came next to attempt another penalty. Again the flags were raised. 16-7 and relief in the All Black camp. Frank Oliver, the fullback, told me that as the ball soared on, straight and true, he said to himself, 'Wilson, my friend, you're in this team for a while, I think.' How true.

The Lions' fire, from here on, was sputtering and sparking, with no bright flame. Andy Irvine had again joined the unemployment bureau, so seldom was he used.

The All Blacks, now driven like a raging fire in the fern, were all-dominant. Haden made a strong 50 metre burst, his legs turning over slowly, yet eating up the ground in seven-league strides. Brian Ford in aggressive form, crossed the Lions' line enveloped in defenders, but the try was not awarded. 'A good call by Dave Millar', said Tane Norton. 'He couldn't see it in the mass of players; neither could I.'

The match ended without the customary explosive counter-attacks by the Lions. They were not there this day, blunted by an All Black team that was outgunned in the head to head contests for ball yet were brilliant at the back-play build-ups and broken forward surges.

In the last moment Ian Kirkpatrick toed a loose ball upfield, Ford helped too, and soon the All Blacks were winning an attacking maul with the Lions all confusion. Davis had a moment to consider which side to move. He chose the correct option and sent the ball out to Bruce Robertson. The big Counties man disregarded the overlap positioning itself outside him, and calmly drop-kicked a goal. The whistle blast signalled, as well, the end of the test and New Zealand had won 19-7.

The Lions lined up to clap and congratulate their New Zealand op-ponents off the field, a generous gesture, in view of the massive publicity the bad side of this tour had engendered. There had not been a fight or a fist in the match, a credit to all thirty men.

Jack Gleeson, coach, selector, assistant manager and mentor of this team, stood much later in the crowded bar of the Beach Hotel. Beside him were his jubilant co-selectors. Around him raged a wingding party. The 'boys' were in celebration. The noise was deafening, the mood high.

'What's next, Jack?' I asked. 'The fourth test', he replied, winking his famous wink. 'Smug Jack?' said I, again. 'Not smug, Keith, satisfied — that's all.'

The teams

British Isles: Irvine; J. J. Williams (replaced by McGeechan), Burcher, Fenwick, Gareth Evans; Bennett (captain), Brynmor Williams (replaced by Morgan); Duggan, Cobner, Brown, Beaumont, Quinnell; Cotton, Wheeler, Price.

New Zealand: Bevan Wilson (Otago); Brian Ford (Marlborough), Bruce Robertson (Counties), Bryan Williams (Auckland); Bill Osborne (Wanganui), Doug Bruce (Canterbury), Lyn Davis (Canterbury); Lawrie Knight (Poverty Bay); Ian Kirkpatrick (Poverty Bay), Frank Oliver (Southland), Andy Haden (Auckland); Graham Mourie (Taranaki); Bill Bush (Canterbury), Tane Norton (Canterbury — captain) and John McEldowney (Taranaki).

Scoring

New Zealand (19). Tries by Kirkpatrick and Haden. Conversion and penalties (2) by Wilson. Dropped goal by Robertson.

British Isles (7). Try by Duggan. Penalty by Irvine.

Referee: Dave Millar (Otago). Carisbrook, Dunedin. Saturday, 30 July 1977.

11
Three to Get Ready:
Matches 22-24

22. Lions 35, Counties 10. The Lions were a subdued lot Sunday morning after their test loss at Dunedin. At the airport on their way north faces were blank and staring and their mood was quiet.

The Sunday papers brought no relief. The *Sunday Times* ran 'Scent of Series Triumph in Wind! in two-inch-high front page head-lines. The *Evening Star — 7 O'Clock* screamed 'All Blacks Ahead!' over a full-page picture of Dunedin's (and New Zealand's) latest hero, Bevan Wilson. The Christchurch Star Sports said 'All Blacks All the Way'.

The only paper, of the Saturday night and Sunday morning variety, which did not run the New Zealand test victory as headline was the *Sunday News,* which instead dallied with a tasty little gem headlined 'They're Lousy Lovers! — A Kiwi girl tells of sex in the Lions' den'. Ugh! The story served only to harden the team's dislike of New Zealand and New Zealanders.

So it was on next to Pukekohe. The Counties-Thames Valley team, trained by Hiwi Tauroa and Joe Wright, the coaches of the two unions, looked a sprightly bunch. Bruce Robertson was there, a re-doubtable rugby figure in this area. Around him were backs of talent; Buff Milner, the 1970 All Black utility back, was to play on one wing, with Bob Lendrum, a 1973 New Zealand test player, at fullback. The halfback, Mark Codlin, was rated highly by the locals.

In the forwards was John Spiers, one of the much-loved characters of the second All Black tour of Argentina in 1976. With him were John Hughes, an All Black trialist of several seasons ago, and be-tween those two was Andy Dalton, one of the liveliest hookers met on tour. Elsewhere in the Combined team the players were of solid value only. The locks were short by international standards and the loose men only average in speed.

So the Lions decided to use men who had not played since the New Zealand Juniors game, a fortnight before. Therefore, nine of the team had their first match in fourteen days and another, Charlie Faulkner, the replacement, made his first New Zealand appearance. The Lions selectors, in generous mood, gave the front row over to the three Pontypool men. Faulkner, Windsor and Price relished the chance to bring further honour to their club.

Tony Neary, in recognition of his excellent form in recent games as a creative flanker, was elevated to captaincy for the first time, but once the Lions took the field it was soon obvious he was not going to receive a major effort from his team. Six of them — Hay, Gibson, Bevan, Trevor Evans, Keane and Martin — were now foundation members of the midweek fifteen, and they played like it.

A match like this one I call 'just another day at the office'. Sure, there were moments when the crowd of 30,000 yelled their heads off and other times when expertise and skill sparkled, but overall this was no day for golden memories.

What was nice was a typical Pukekohe day. Bright sunshine, so rare in this murky New Zealand winter. Lush green grass, so inspiring after so much training and playing-field slush.

The Lions led by 12-0 at half-time. Douglas Morgan, the solitary halfback after Brynmor Williams had to depart the tour through his hamstring injury, kicked two penalty goals and converted a try scored by Bruce Hay.

The set-up for the opening score was one of three that came directly from a scrum pushover attempt. In the first, Squire eventually relinquished the ball in the push ahead, Morgan slipped it away to the advancing Hay, and he went across untouched.

The rest of the spell the Lions backs blundered about, like some scratch combination getting together an hour before kick-off. Burcher continued to let his early tour form slip well into the middle-distance and Gareth Evans disappointed, not for the first time in recent games.

Six of the forwards had not played for a fortnight, so were slow to the early rucks and mauls. Keane and Martin trundled about field like two great cart-horses.

The second half brought a transformation and it took an incident of ill-temper to trigger it. David Burcher took a kick in the back of the head from one of the locals — 'just a bit of slipper', someone said, but still a black mark. Next, Douglas Morgan tripped one of his opposites. For his trouble he received as healthy a boot in the backside as you would ever wish to see. A general fracas broke out, but watching it became difficult when one saw what was happening to the ball.

It seemed a kick came down on the Combined team's right wing side. Don McMillan, the winger, one of only two Thames Valley players in the team, leapt ahead of Gareth Evans for the catch. Securing the ball, he did precisely the wrong thing, running back inside the upcoming Lions backs. This is the area of the field familiarly known as 'suicide alley', for cutting back inside at speed a player is often vulnerable to, at best, a strong forward tackle or, at worst, a 'stiff-arm' defensive reaction. 'Wrong way McMillan' received neither as he broke clear on a diagonal run, some seventy metres out. There was no British cover defence; most of them had forsaken rugby for punching.

McMillan raced away, an incongruous sight. There he scuttled, much like Grant Batty had done in the Wellington test, with red hair flying. Behind him, running second, was Mike Gibson, flagging somewhat, while in third place came the referee, Peter McDavitt. In racing terms 'daylight' was fourth, for the rest of the teams, if not actively involved in the fighting, were disengaging in some humiliation. McDavitt signalled the try to McMillan, Gibson heaved and puffed, for he had chased long and hard for one his age, and the crowd knew not where to look. Over here, the longest fight of the tour with no referee to stop it; over there, a runaway try of mammoth proportions.

Later, when both teams had settled down, Counties-Thames Valley gained some more glory. Alan Dawson, the New Zealand Junior reserve, made a cut and run dash. The Combined loose men made a quick ruck and spun the ball. Graeme Taylor and Brian Duggan handled in the five-eighths and then Duggan turned the ball in to Lendrum, up from fullback. His try, under the posts, was converted by Lendrum himself.

These moments of grandeur for the home lads were not, however, indicative of the true run of things. The Lions, with Martin, Keane and Price concentrating more at the line-outs, secured enough possession to press on. The tries had to come.

They all came from scrums. One was a pushover. Neary pleaded with his front row to win the strike and then when the ball was safe in the second row the whole eight heaved. The Combined scrum went back five metres and Doug Morgan dived forward to score. The sight was awesome indeed.

In another pushover attempt Jeff Squire released the ball for Morgan to pull exactly the same move as in the first half. Hay came up. Try.

Hay's generosity bubbled over in the next move. Morgan, in superb touch in these later matches, robbed Codlin of the heeled ball. Neary leapt delightedly for it and fed Hay, in again at speed. The little Scotsman could have scored but slipped it on, in a charitable gesture, to Evans.

Evans scored again near the end, after receiving a kind bounce from a kick through by Burcher. Morgan landed goals galore, six in all, for a personal tally of 19 points, and the Lions won by 35 to 10.

One area where Combined did well was in the scrums. Though outpushed at every set-down, hooker Andy Dalton secured three strikes against Bobby Windsor which, when placed alongside the scrum efforts of other provincial teams, placed Dalton in the highest class. Jack Gleeson was sitting in the stand.

Bruce Robertson, no doubt still elated after his superstar stuff of Dunedin, did not occupy centrestage much in this match. He received some over-close attention from David Burcher early in the match but let it not worry him. He also took a bump on the head and several on the knees, which might have persuaded him to think of honour and duty at a higher level and keep out of mischief.

The teams
Lions: Hay; Gareth Evans, Burcher, Gibson, Rees; Bevan, Morgan; Squire; Neary (captain), Keane, Martin, Trevor Evans; Faulkner, Windsor and Price.
Counties-Thames Valley: Bob Lendrum (Counties); Buff Milner (C), Bruce Robertson (C), Don McMillan (Thames Valley); Brian Duggan (TV), Graeme Taylor (C), Mark Codlin (C) (replaced by Phil Sheehan (TV)); Alan Dawson (C); Hank Harbraken (C), Joe Rawiri (C), Roy Craig (C), Peter Clotworthy (C); John Spiers (C), Andy Dalton (C — captain), John Hughes (C).
Scoring
Lions (35). Tries (2) by Gareth Evans, Hay (2) and Morgan; penalties (3) and conversions (3) by Morgan.
Counties-Thames Valley (10). Tries by Don McMillan and Bob Lendrum; conversion by Lendrum.
Referee: Mr Peter McDavitt. Pukekohe Stadium. Wednesday, 3 August 1977.

23. Lions 18, North Auckland 7. His name was on the tip of the tongue of everyone, yes everyone, that I met in Whangarei. Sid Going was a 'great bloke' according to the man who handed us the rental car keys at the airport; Sid Going 'will *get them*' according to the receptionist at our hotel; 'I know Sid personally', said the unknown man standing in the bar. Indeed, all of Northland knows Sid personally. Even if they had never ever spoken to him, such was the affection for the man and the concern they felt for recent trends in his rugby career, that they all did seem to know him intimately.

The locals carried their love for the man out to Okara Park, venue for Northland's big rugby day, and by their vocal appreciation, directed at his every move, conveyed their abiding love and loyalty for the bald little man wearing Number 9.

Lyn Davis had done a quite splendid job for New Zealand in the Dunedin test. He cleared the ball well from its usually scrambled delivery, and the backs functioned with more flair and fluency than in the first two tests, when Sid Going had been the halfback. But to hold such an opinion, or worse, to express such an opinion in Whangarei was the surest way known to get oneself in the dickens of an argument.

Anyway, for the record, I too was hoping that Sid Going would play well for his province against the Lions and I felt, beforehand, that his team would have a fair chance of toppling the tourists. We had heard that big Hamish Macdonald was 'steamed up' for this game; Joe Morgan was another who, it was said, was going to 'lie down and die' before any Lion passed him. Like Sid Going, they had points to prove, for in 1976 they had been All Black test players. Macdonald was a veteran of 12 tests and 48 matches in the New Zealand colours. An average leaper at line-out time, he came into his own in the tight, pushing departments of the scrum and was still a highly-rated forward. Morgan will always be one of my favourite players. A smooth, steady second five-eighth, he has the hardness and toughness of a Graham Williams or Kevin Eveleigh. His tackling was as solid as a kauri tree and his general play and reflexes were top-class. Though neither had made the All Blacks in 1977 it was entirely possible that they might be required again.

The Lions rolled into Whangarei a tired group, having travelled eight hours by road from Pukekohe when short bus rides and a plane trip could have covered the same route in a quarter of the time. There were rumblings about the team's hotel. 'The rooms are not big enough to swing a cat', said one team member. But the sun was shining. That is, it did up until one hour before kick-off, when a steady shower for a quarter of an hour reminded the Lions again they were still in New Zealand.

Andy Irvine kicked off to the roar of 32,000 fans, many of them settled on the high embankment that makes Okara Park the most spectacular rugby ground in New Zealand.

The Lions halfback was Alun Lewis, who had been called out from London to replace Brynmor Williams.

After two days in the country, and with no rugby for four months, Lewis was thrown into the line-up to mark Sid Going. Some prospect!

In every tour there are matches which promise much yet never come off a spectacle. This was one. The Lions' winning margin of 18-7 looks nice enough on the summary scoreboard, but it was one of their most disappointing presentations of form all tour.

Again all the trouble stemmed from their backline. Phil Bennett, whose slide in performance had many of the British critics calling for his replacement as a test player, seemed to lack application again in this match. He passed extremely poorly, ran across field far too often, and not once was seen urging his team on. However he did goal-kick well, landing five goals from seven attempts and scoring 14 points in all.

Bennett's dithering at fly-half caused all sorts of trouble in the backline. Fenwick and McGeechan were always crowded and Evans and Rees, on the wings, were never run into any position of advantage. And for the first time on tour Andy Irvine was below par. His attacking forays were few and not always for advancement and he, like Bennett, passed poorly. Irvine's concentration, as tight as wire normally, lapsed badly on one occasion. Mike Gunson, the hometown fullback, joined a back move and kicked ahead. The ball, projected too far, went behind Irvine and over the goal-line. Irvine's return to touch the ball down was casual and, on turning, he slipped on the wet grass and the ball tumbled forward. David Haynes, playing his third game against the Lions, had followed up, probably just to cover Irvine should he decide to make one of his cuts against the tide of play. When the ball fell from Irvine's arms, Haynes was close enough to react quickly, dart forward and score.

At halfback Lewis looked good, within the bounds of lack of match practice, but with Douglas Morgan's play improving all the time, Lewis would scarcely threaten as a test candidate.

The Lions' forwards again won the line-outs and scrums comfortably but then seemed to consider their work done. 'They were pushing when they should have been out chasing', was the way Jeff Butterfield, of the 1955 and 1959 Lions, put it.

Terry Cobner limped off with a damaged knee ligament, looking as though the tour might be over for him, and Tony Neary came on.

While there was so much indifferent play from the Lions, North Auckland were opponents playing with great audacity and pluck. 'We knew we had no really tall forwards', said Sid Going, the skipper, afterwards, 'so we wouldn't get much ball, but we figured our young team could match or better them in other phases of play'.

And, by golly, they did too. Facing a team with so much ball they halted attacks and set up their own opportunities by tackling like tigers. The crowd roared appreciation, especially every time Super Sid pulled a red shirt down. Sid made more tackles in this match than I had ever seen him do. His example fired up his fellow men, and their pattern of defence was exemplary.

It was not until four minutes from the end that a break came. The Lions won a ruck, Lewis lobbed a ball to Bennett, who sent it on to McGeechan. On the North Auckland 22-metre line and in centre field McGeechan began to move. He cut back inside, sidestepping all the way, beating man after man. Not since Gisborne in match number three had we seen him play like this. The try came under the bar and McGeechan, a quiet tourist, almost blushed with pride. Clumsy though the Lions backs were, it did seem McGeechan, on his performance in Whangarei, would get back into the test side.

So the game meandered on. Denied possession, North Auckland never really got a sniff of the opposition tryline, while the Lions fluffed about trying to organise a workable back division. Such was the game.

The only talking-point about the forward display was the number of line-out penalties. Jeff Walker of Otago whistled away all afternoon, awarding 34 penalties in all, a high percentage of them coming from line-outs.

Peter Sloane and Tuck Waaka were bruising forwards of high standard. Macdonald and the 1970-73 All Black, Bevan Holmes, lost out in the line-outs through lack of height. Peter Wheeler would regard this game as one of his best on tour.

At the end Sid Going and his nephew Charles, a most talented-looking centre, tried to place pressure on the Lions line. There was no way through and the game ended at one try each but 18-7 to the tourists.

After the match I spoke with Barry John, the most brilliant of the 1971 Lions backs. 'I think our forwards are superb', he said, 'so today I was looking to the backs for an improvement on their third test form. Sadly, though, nothing to report . . .' and the great man gazed off into the distance, searching for words. 'Ye gods, if we didn't have this pack we'd be in trouble', he concluded.

Sid Going came out to appear on TV and said he thought his team had gone 'extremely well', allowing for their limitations in height, weight and experience. I asked him if he enjoyed the third test and the All Blacks' play. He nodded and expressed genuine pleasure that they had won. 'Do you think this is the end of the road for you, as far as international rugby is concerned?' I asked. 'It looks like it', said Sid, beaming a bright smile. That smile, I am sure, went into thousands of homes that night and won more sympathy for Sidney Milton Going. If this was to be his last big rugby appearance, he had bowed out with a high quality performance of his usual toughness and brilliance.

He walked off. In the deserted ground the only noise was the chatter of typewriter keys from the press box. No doubt many of the words being written, by New Zealanders and overseas pressmen, would be about him. The rugby field was his stage, his audience a throng of admiring Northlanders, in whose hearts he would never be replaced.

Writing in the *Sunday Times* Alex Veysey said, 'I have seldom, if ever, heard a crowd give itself so devotedly and wholeheartedly to one player. For all the tributes which have been heaped on Going through the years this one, on his home stamping ground, might well have been the ultimate.'

I agree entirely. The noise level whenever Going touched the ball in this match was Northland saying 'Thanks' to one of the greatest players ever seen in the game, anywhere.

The teams
Lions: Irvine; Gareth Evans, McGeechan, Fenwick, Rees; Bennett (captain), Lewis; Duggan; Quinnell, Brown, Beaumont, Cobner (replaced by Neary); Orr, Wheeler, and Cotton.
North Auckland: Mike Gunson; Lloyd Roberts, Charles Going, David Haynes; Joe Morgan, Eddie Dunn, Sid Going (captain); Harley Sowman; Tuck Waaka; Hamish Macdonald, Bevan Holmes, Ian Phillips; Wayne Neville, Peter Sloane, Chris D'Arcy.
Scoring
Lions (18). Try by McGeechan; penalties (4) and conversion by Bennett.
North Auckland (7). Try by David Haynes; penalty by Mike Gunson.

Referee: Jeff Walker (Otago). Okara Park, Whangarei. Saturday, 6 August 1977

24. Lions 23, Bay of Plenty 16. Rotorua, that place of fusty odours and sulphurous steam, conformed depressingly to the meteorological pattern of the tour by attracting heavy rain almost as soon as the Lions arrived in town.

The team was quartered in the Travelodge, away from the Whaka thermal region but some players, followed faithfully by television cameras, did their tourist bit and caught the Prince of Wales and Pohutu Geysers in full display.

Unfortunately, as often this winter, the damp out-of-doors kept many of the team indoors. The gloom was not helped by the news conveyed only six days before the fourth and final test, that Terry Cobner and Derek Quinnell would not play any more on tour; they would be missing from the fourth test line-up.

Cobner's ligaments, torn in the Whangarei match, were so bad by the time he reached Rotorua he could hardly walk. Quinnell had completed eighty minutes of rugby against North Auckland and afterwards considered a slightly sore hand just another rugby trifle, but in the ensuing twenty-four hours his hand swelled and a broken metacarpal bone was diagnosed. So it was goodbye, in the playing sense, to these two, who had contributed so vitally to the strength and driving-power of the Lions forward pack. Cobner should, I believe, have been captain of the Lions. His adherence to hard Pontypool-New Zealand-type forward drive was discovered by the Lions at precisely the correct time — after their first test trauma. Much of the excellence of the British Isles mid-tour success was due to him, and his principal disciple, Derek Quinnell. There were some, close to the team, who considered the fourth test would now be 'game, set and match' to the All Blacks, for the Lions were not the same forward unit without these two tough Welshmen.

Still, George Burrell and John Dawes seemed full of good cheer when they broke the sad news to the touring media people at a special 'shout' for the press at the Travelodge. On the floor below the news spread quickly through a rival function in honour of a contingent of Welsh supporters. Their later singing was no doubt designed to rise up and motivate the Lions, especially the test Welshmen, to a final victory at Auckland.

But there was one other bridge to cross before Eden Park.

Bay of Plenty was yet another New Zealand provincial team that looked capable of extending the Lions. With the 1976 All Blacks Greg Rowlands, Eddie Stokes, Mark Taylor and John Brake in the backline, the Lions weakness there was sure to be probed. The British mid-week pack regulars — Moss Keane, Trevor Evans, Jeff Squire and Bobby Windsor — were reinforced by Charlie Faulkner, Gordon Brown, Willie Duggan and Graham Price, and looked too massive for their Bay of Plenty counterparts.

With Peter Squires still suffering from his Eden Park hamstring, Gareth Evans desirous of a rest after six matches on end, and J. J. Williams suffering continuing pain from his third test thigh injury, Phil Bennett volunteered to play on the wing. This was a bold decision by Bennett, who had lost form so seriously in recent matches.

On match day officials at the International Stadium were talking about a crowd of near 50,000. In the end they were short of that mark by some 20,000 but it was still a big day for Rotorua rugby.

The pitch was in excellent order despite heavy rain the night before. The pumice base of the stadium ground is extremely porous and the rainfall served only to cushion the upper soil surface, with no loss of foothold.

Greg Rowlands, an excellent running fullback in this match, kicked off. The Bay forwards, with a couple of relative unknowns in Barry Spry and Dave Matuschka roaring about like keen kids at a lolly scramble, looked a set capable of infiltrating the Lions plan of attack. The home backs, fed in excellent fashion by Teddy Davis, moved the ball crisply. Taylor missed a big drop-kick but soon Brake landed a bigger one, to the delight of the home crowd. Their encouragement was loud and strong, even after Mike Gibson had moved the ball crisply to David Burcher for a try, and Bennett followed with two of his five penalty successes.

The Bennett goals took his tour total to 112, second behind Barry John, who was watching from the stands. The only other Lion to hoist a century in New Zealand was Bob Hiller in 1971.

As a winger Bennett seemed to enjoy himself thoroughly. While not skilled at the winger's trade, his open running style raised great excitement each time the ball neared him.

At ten points to three against, Bay of Plenty were rewarded for their backline initiatives. The ball spun out from a line-out to Rowlands, and again on to Mark Taylor, who had spun out also. Nicely set up, Taylor steamed 35 metres at top clip to score. Thrilling stuff.

The next incident was complete sadness. Mike Gibson was seen to pull up, holding again the hamstring muscle that had slightly pulled in the Junior All Blacks game. He grimaced in pain and raised his head skywards, no doubt in complaint to the Goddess of Good Fortune, for she had sadly neglected him on this tour. Against Bay of Plenty he had looked purposeful and sharp, *perhaps* the key to restoring the penetration of the test backline. His runs were quick, his passes always safely to the man, and his penetrative movements mostly in parallel to the touchline, in other words, dead straight.

Mike Gibson, at 34, might yet play again for Ireland, for he is the only top-rated back they possess. But this would be his last match appearance in New Zealand. As he limped off, the crowd was slow to realise that one of the great men of modern rugby was departing the New Zealand scene.

Two Rowlands penalties and Bay of Plenty had the match all tied up at half-time.

The second spell was excitement all the way, with the Lions gradually, but only gradually, asserting their power at line-out and maul. Scrums were clear-cut their way, enabling Alun Lewis to send away running passes to John Bevan.

Bevan passed less often and kicked more often than necessary, but his punts were usually well-positioned to bustle the fielder.

The Bay kept the ball moving from hand to hand, even though it was coming less frequently from their forward; Graeme Moore, the right winger, benefiting often from an opportunity to skip along.

The try of the match followed another penalty each to Bennett and Rowlands. From a maul, Alun Lewis moved right, just five metres in Bay of Plenty territory. His pass sent Elgan Rees away and the little man cut and sliced his way down the touchline to the 22. There he jerked infield, and at tip-top speed he whizzed through for his try of the tour. Bennett could not convert although his fifth penalty followed later, to complete the scoring at 23-16.

There was much satisfaction in the end for the Lions players for they had been engaged in battle with a torrid and victory-hunting Bay of Plenty side.

George Burrell, rather coldly, said his team could have won by 40 points had they sustained their effort. This gave no credit to Matuschka, Spry, Alan McNaughton, Mike Connor and the others in the Bay pack, plus the excellent backs I have mentioned, all of whom contributed to a sparkling match.

The Lions forward summaries again made excellent reading and Jeff Squire was one who 'delivered' for his team when they needed it most. But after Gibson had gone, the backs resumed the bumbles

23. Two into seven doesn't go. Only Terry Cobner and Willie Duggan of the British Isles are in sight in this shot taken from the third test in Dunedin. The All Blacks, in abundance, are Doug Bruce (10) Ian Kirkpatrick, Andy Haden, John McEldowney, Frank Oliver and Lyn Davis.

24. 'It's history now', skipper Tane Norton could be saying in the dressing room after the third test at Carisbrook. The series cannot be lost. Bryan Williams looks happy but the realisation of the moment has not yet hit Ian Kirkpatrick.

25. Two tests played and two victories under his belt. New All Black fullback Bevan Wilson of Otago comes off the field at Eden Park in Auckland having played in front of 57,000 at the stadium and an estimated world wide television audience of eleven million. A far cry from his home town of Omakau, Otago which has just one shop and one pub.

26. I challenge you to find a sad face in the crowd! They have just seen Lawrie Knight score the winning try at Auckland in the fourth test, the try that was to be the clincher in the series for the All Blacks. The only sad faces belong to Douglas Morgan (9) Ian McGeechan (13) and Phil Bennett, who made the last desperate but unavailing chase of Knight.

27. Willie, Willie, why did you do it? The final test match at Eden Park in Auckland is saved by the All Blacks and lost for the Lions with Willie Duggan being held up short of the line in the last minute. Many felt if he had held it at the back of the 5 metre scrum the match could have been won for the Lions by a pushover try.

28. The aftermatch. Facing the press at the end of the fourth test John Dawes (left) and George Burrell are tight lipped and drawn. 'We were beaten only once in the series but lost three times,' said coach Dawes. But hang on John, aren't you looking at things through rose coloured glasses?

29. Before and after. The two tour faces of Phil Bennett. The smile of pride and expectancy at the tour's beginning . . .

30. . . . and the agony of defeat and personal disappointment at tour's end. Bennett caught alone with his thoughts as the crowd sings 'Auld Lang Syne' after the fourth test at Eden Park.

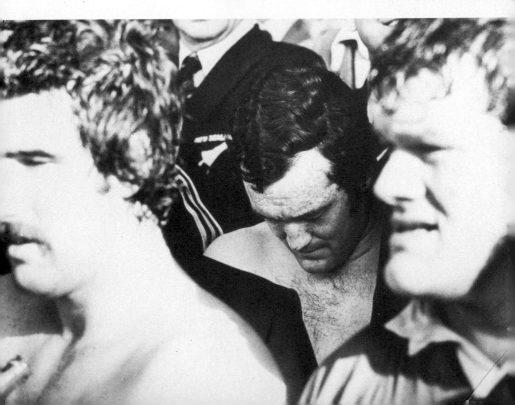

and fumbles of Whangarei. Their flounderings were too bad to be true.

The Lions' New Zealand record now showed 21 wins and 3 losses. This match marked the continuation of Lions' world dominance of state and provincial representative teams. They had, in 1977, gone completely through New Zealand without losing a provincial game, as they had done here in 1971, and in South Africa in 1974. The previous non-test losses were, of course, to Queensland in 1971 and New Zealand Universities in 1977.

But — one match and one question remained. The last encounter of 1977 was four days away. For the fourth test could the bumbles and fumbles, homesickness, weather-weariness, media-wariness, boredom, embattled isolation and disenchantment with twenty-five match touring, be put aside for eighty minutes of rugby excellence? And the honour of a series shared? Could it, would it, be all worthwhile?

At Invercargill the stream of rugby travellers had its birth. Up the South Island it flowed and across Cook Strait. From east and north the tributaries entered the human river, leading to Auckland's Eden Park. The Bay of Plenty match had been won by the Lions. Only the fourth test remained.

The Lions packed their bags. They summoned up their total mental reserves. They had but one objective in their lives. To beat the All Blacks.

The teams

Lions: Hay (replaced by Irvine); Rees, Gibson (replaced by McGeechan), Burcher, Bennett (captain); Bevan, Lewis; Duggan, Squire, Brown, Keane, Trevor Evans, Price, Windsor and Faulkner.

Bay of Plenty: Grey Rowlands (captain); Joe Kamizona (replaced by Tony Compton), Eddie Stokes, Graeme Moore; Mark Taylor (replaced by Robin Moon), John Brake; Teddy Davis, Mike Connor, Alan McNaughton, Bill Jones, Barry Spry, David Matuschka, Bo Keepa, Russell Doughty, Jim Helmbright.

Scoring

Lions (23). Tries by Burcher and Rees; penalties (5) by Bennett.

Bay of Plenty (16). Try by Mark Taylor; dropped goal by John Brake; penalties (3) by Greg Rowlands.

Referee: Norm Thomas (Manawatu). International Stadium, Rotorua. Tuesday, 9 August 1977.

12
The Fourth Test: Auckland

25. British Isles 9, New Zealand 10. Willie Duggan really is a nice bloke. He is typically Irish. His hair on tour was always slightly dishevelled, his shirt-tail was often found outside his trousers, and his skin was as white as the snow which doubtless falls in winter on his hometown of Kilkenny.

Duggan was a most necessary cog in the wheel that, accelerating about mid-tour, turned the Lions forward pack into a powering unit of accord and strength, the best ever seen in New Zealand. Duggan played his rugby with devillish commitment, throwing himself upon ball and man regardless of physical risk or harm. Sometimes it was thought, he hurled himself upon ball and man regardless of the best tactical needs of the moment. Towards the end of the tour family business demands might well have called him home earlier than planned, but he stayed to do battle at Eden Park.

Perhaps it was over-keenness and not lack of rugby intellect which drove Willie Duggan, just seconds from the full-time whistle and the end of the tour, to pick up the scrum-ball he had under control at his feet at the back of a Lions pushover try attempt. As it had been throughout the match, New Zealand's scrum machine was in a sad state of disarray. New Zealand were leading by 10 points to 9 but were going backwards from a defensive five-metre scrum. The Lions, with their power, could not be prevented from heaving on until the line was crossed and the try scored. But impatiently, even crazily, Duggan chose to pre-empt the near-certainty of the pushover momentum. He elected to withdraw his head from its slot, stoop and pick the ball up and plunge forward for a solo try. In this moment, honour and parity on their three month tour of New Zealand were lost forever for the Lions.

Duggan was held up as he made his plunge. The All Black defence forced another scrum. The impetus of the British attack was lifted. The New Zealanders were able to clear. The referee, Dave Millar, blew for full-time soon after and the All Blacks had won, the scoreboard said so anyway, by 10 points to 9. Had Willie Duggan not chosen to pick up by hand the tourists must surely have scored their pushover try and the series would have been shared at two tests each. Duggan's incorrect choice assisted the All Blacks to take the series three matches to one.

Right from the kick-off in this last and most critical match an uncanny tension lay over Eden Park, the players and the 57,000 spectators; it was doubtless felt by the millions who watched the live telecast.

The first twenty minutes were viewed in whispered silence. In that time things looked ominous for the All Blacks, as the Lions scrummed with tremendous strength and were untroubled to win the line-outs, even without Cobner and Quinnell. The two newcomers, Jeff Squire and Tony Neary, confirmed the depth of Lions forward play by turning in loose men's games of such magnitude of purpose that the New Zealanders were further assaulted when they might have expected some respite.

There were other changes in the Lions team, one brought about by injury and one by necessity. At the team's Thursday training at the Tamaki Club in Auckland, J. J. Williams gripped his leg and crashed to the ground in agony, being soon assisted by George Burrell to leave the pitch, the scene and the tour. This rushed Elgan Rees into test rugby, years before his time I might add, to partner Gareth Evans. These two surely constituted the worst pair of wingers ever to play in a Lions test threequarter line. The other change saw David Burcher return to the also-ran's bench, as his showings in Dunedin, Pukekohe and Rotorua had in no way matched the heights Ian Mcgeechan reached at Whangarei and Rotorua.

There was much discussion as to who would play halfback. Alun Lewis had done well enough in his two games since coming to New Zealand, with the promise of better things to come. Douglas Morgan, on the other hand, had flourished under his new title of 'number one' halfback, now that Brynmor Williams had gone. The rumour was that John Dawes preferred to play Lewis in the final test. There was no doubt his pass was long and direct but like a shuttlecock hit with power it did tend to fade. In the end, in deference, we were told, to those who had soldiered on for three months, Morgan was picked as test halfback.

On New Zealand's side, the only changes made from the team which had surprised and won the admiration of New Zealanders in the third test came in the props. Kent Lambert had quickly recovered from an appendectomy and was given, along with Brad Johnstone, the task of bolstering the All Black scrum front row. Johnstone should never have been dropped after the second test; at the team's scrum practice at Mosgiel before the third test he had embarrassed the selectors by the strong manner in which he dominated his replacement, Bill Bush. Johnstone was also vital to the front position in the line-out, where New Zealand had lost so badly at Dunedin. Misfortune struck again however, when Johnstone pulled a hamstring at training and had to withdraw. John McEldowney moved into Johnstone's place and Bill Bush came in as reserve.

Eden Park was at its postcard best for the match. The sunshine streamed down on a solid playing surface. Stands and terraces were tightly covered, brightly coloured. Cameramen waited, ready to burst into their own sideline dashes.

Television viewers saw a nice touch underneath the Number One grandstand in the moments before kick-off. Tane Norton and Phil Bennett shook hands after the toss and exchanged pleasantries for a few seconds before taking their teams out into the sunny arena. Every seat in the house was sold. The interest in the match had built up to such a point that tickets were as rare as sunny days and many changed hands at vastly improved prices. This was a game which, for the tourists, was a repeat of their Carisbrook dichotomy. Their backs were again best forgotten, so poor were they on attack; their forward superiority at line-out and scrum became an embarrassment once the ball moved beyond Douglas Morgan.

In the first twenty minutes, played, as I have said, in a tense silence that would have delighted a city librarian, the only score came from a Bevan Wilson penalty. The Lions backs, Bennett in particular, were up offside. That raised a cheer from the earnest attendance but silence greeted Douglas Morgan's equaliser after twenty-five minutes. It was gripping stuff.

The All Black forwards, as at Carisbrook, were finding difficulty winning the ball quickly or delivering it accurately; the result was that Lyn Davis was having a most difficult job sending his backs off on attack.

But it made no difference. The Lions attack, with Brown, Beaumont and Duggan winning a high percentage of set-play ball, was stultified once the ball reached Phil Bennett. Their prematch policy had been, so Dawes said, 'to eliminate errors behind the scrum' but they had failed to do that. Bennett on many occasions kicked ahead seeking a new line-out position, with the result that his team's most generative attacking weapon, Andy Irvine, was unused most of the day.

To be fair though, Bennett was not permitted much space to move in. Once again, Graham Mourie ran like the wind, with 'get number ten' firmly imprinted on his thinking, Morgan was unable to pass the ball the greater distance Bennett needed to shake off Mourie's attentions.

Further out Steve Fenwick played a type of 'crash-ball' game, as the British call it, seeking to power through tackles whenever he took a pass. One had to admire the Welshman's hardness, for one so slightly built.

So it was that the pattern of the game was set. New Zealanders watching were horrified at the ease with which the All Black pack was bettered, but consoled and delighted that the wheel had turned the full circle so that the New Zealand backs, again spear-headed by Bruce Robertson's brilliance, were a vastly superior set than their opposites.

After thirty-three minutes the Lions forwards peeled from the back of a line-out. Fran Cotton made one of his stylish set-up passes to Bill Beaumont, who ran down to just ten metres from the All Black line, and with Graham Price and Steve Fenwick running off him a try looked on. A quick ruck, well won, and Douglas Morgan moved wide, spinning through Bevan Wilson's tackle to score. It was a cleanly executed 'Willie Away' move, much in the manner of the All Black packs who had created it in the nineteen sixties. Morgan landed the conversion himself, to take his personal tour tally to 98. Sadly though, from the Lions point of view, this was their last score of the tour in New Zealand.

Winning no ball, tane Norton harangued the troops in black at half-time about that issue and Ian Kirkpatrick was seen chiming in with vehemence as well. Men like these, who had worn the New Zealand colours for years and who had known the frustrations of 1971, 1972-73 and 1976, would never concede dominance to an opponent, especially one lacking a swinging attack to capitalise on the forwards' crunch.

In the first twenty minutes of the second spell the situation did not change. The Lions remained on top in the forward struggles, scrumming well, although Norton did gain one surprise tight-head heel and, with Haden and Oliver not succeeding with many of their leaps at line-out time, marching on to a winning line-out count. One paper said it was 35 to 13, but it was scored for me at 28 to 14.

They were helped in the loose by Tony Neary playing a rattling good game. He put far more squeeze on Doug Bruce and Bill Osborne than Cobner had ever done and in this regard was one of the players of the day. Doug Morgan was another. From mid-tour his form rose at every appearance. Never a long-passer, he was instead a tough ruthless competitor who played up to the limit of his skills. So the Lions were on top in the play and they were ahead on the scoreboard, still by 9 to 3, but with no more points in sight. Bevan Wilson, coming back to earth a little in this game, where he had to face the realities of test rugby away from familiar surroundings, missed several kicks at goal from penalties. The thought passed through my mind that if New Zealand was to lose this match here was another of New Zealand's good young fullbacks, in the Fawcett and Farrell mould, putting his neck on the block ready for the verbal axing that the fickle public would not doubt administer.

In his general play Wilson was sound. Bill Osborne and Bruce Robertson were, in the centre, masters of a defensive screen that was never beaten in the series. On the wing Bryan Williams played right up to the expectations of the huge crowd.

The All Blacks were not helped by injury forcing two on-the-field changes in their line-up. Brian Ford gashed his knee badly and hobbled off, Mark Taylor coming on. John McEldowney left later, walking unassisted from the field with a shoulder injury. Bill Bush appeared in jersey number 20, and won the loudest cheer of the series from the crowd.

While McEldowney was off the field came the surprise play from the All Blacks which, while not turning the sway of the game there and then, certainly became the take-off point for New Zealand's winning effort. A scrum was called. New Zealand's put-in. With McEldowney absent some reorganisation of the front row was required; Lawrie Knight formed up with Lambert and Norton. Imagine the surprise when no other New Zealand forwards packed down. A three-man scrum! A brand-new rugby ploy had been invented.

In the manner, I imagine, of Cliff Porter and the old wing-forward days, side-ranker Graham Mourie put the ball in. The Lions pack made their usual massive push but Norton's hook had only five instead of fifteen feet behind. British heads popped up from the scrum in disbelief to find the ball well gone. Davis worked the play left, Mark Taylor and Andy Haden handled well and broke through. As a successful yard-winning ploy thus was the three-man scrum born!

The Lions managed to hold that particular rush but began to wilt under the relentless heat of a New Zealand team determined not to lose the game. One might even surmise that the three-man scrum and the sheer cheek with which it was used dislodged the tourists from their own resolve. After all a team that cheeky must be brimful of confidence in its own ability.

Bevan Wilson closed the gap to 9-6 with a penalty for hands in the ruck. Fifteen minutes remained with the series still in the balance. It is in times like these that individual errors can change the course of a new match and rewrite the record book of international rugby. The Lions made two in the last five minutes and by these crimes they would be judged as tour failures and sentenced to be remembered only as a mediocre touring side.

The first of their two false moves came as Phil Bennett sought too much distance from a defensive kick and missed touch. Bill Osborne caught the ball delicately on his fingertips and ran up to half-way. His kick back to the Lions was of such perfect height and length that Osborne himself was able to pressurise Steve Fenwick who waited underneath. Fenwick hurriedly flung the ball to Peter Wheeler who somehow was nearby. Graham Mourie arrived at top speed to crush Wheeler, and the ball was forced upwards by the explosion of Mourie's charge. Lawrie Knight, who to that point had not contributed significantly to the cause, reached up and secured the ball in his big hands. He had ten metres or so to travel, which he did amid a tumult of commotion as New Zealanders realised that this was the try that would clinch the test series for the All Blacks. Wilson missed the conversion but who among the Kiwis present or watching on television cared? The scoreboard showed a one point lead to the All Blacks with just four minutes to play. Four minutes later Dave Millar blew for no side as the Lions ran the ball through their back line. Again it was 'too little, too late'.

In that short time Duggan had committed his blunder, which, with the Bennett kick to Osborne, determined the outcome of the match and the series. There was no way the All Blacks could have stopped the pushover try being scored. 'Their front row was up, we were on our way,' Gordon Brown told me.

At the end, when the final whistle blew, I looked for Phil Bennett. He had been backing up the last back move which Andy Irvine had come into, desperately seeking a way through an All Black defensive screen which, right then, could have stopped a tank. Irvine knocked the ball on. The whistle blew and with the victory roar from the crowd Phil Bennett stopped dead still. His head dropped and he was frozen to the spot. Bryan Williams was standing quite near and in a consoling gesture touched the little Lion on the arm. There was no reaction. Bennett's head was down. The battle had been lost. Three months of gruelling travel, training and personal trial was over and as captain, Bennett would have to bear the brunt of being, for this tour anyway, a loser.

In that clamouring moment of exultation for the All Blacks, as they flooded the field, Bennett was quite alone.

For the All Blacks life was good. Tane Norton appeared in the grandstand for the farewell ceremony, to receive an ovation that would have delighted a politician. The pressures on him and his team, heaped so high by a doubting New Zealand rugby public after the second test, were all forgotten. Victory was the medicine that cured all ills.

'It was a lucky win,' said Frank Oliver over his aftermatch beer, 'but, by God, we'll take it.'

'Who'll care how lucky we were thirty years on,' added Gary Seear, who had watched as a reserve all the tests from the grandstand.

'It was great to be part of it,' said Brian Ford, walking stiff-legged from the gash on his knee.

Jack Gleeson, a most modest victor, put the success of his team down to 'Just two things, pressure and tackle. That's what I told them, pressure and tackle.' Adding then, with his famous wink, 'I also told them to remember it's an eighty minute game, no more, no less.'

To Phil Bennett's eternal credit he appeared on nationwide TV a short time later, standing barechested and pale under the glare of the arc lights which warmed the area under the grandstand, out of the gaze of the delighted throng milling outside. Fans at home by their firesides were given a bonus. Bennett spoke quietly, expressing in his usual polite manner the team's disappointment at losing, etc. The words were lost on me. They did not matter. The expression on Bennett's face told all. His eyes were hooded in heavy distress and unresisted weariness; his shoulders fell away sharply, not held up any more by the proximity of a won match and a tied series.

The expression and posture were not born of anger and frustration, just complete and total disappointment.

Bennett knew his side had thrown away, by two late errors, the chance of honour and satisfaction from the game and the tour. Instead, after being the better side for much of the fourth test, they had committed sins of misjudgement, and by these deeds would be remembered.

The teams

British Isles: Irvine; Rees, McGeechan, Fenwick, Gareth Evans; Bennett (captain), Morgan; Duggan; Neary, Beaumont, Brown, Squire; Price, Wheeler and Cotton.

New Zealand: Bevan Wilson (Otago); Brian Ford (Marlborough — replaced by Mark Taylor, Bay of Plenty), Bruce Robertson (Counties), Bryan Williams (Auckland); Bill Osborne (Wanganui), Doug Bruce (Canterbury), Lyn Davis (Canterbury); Lawrie Knight (Poverty Bay); Ian Kirkpatrick (Poverty Bay), Frank Oliver (Southland), Andy Haden (Auckland), Graham Mourie (Taranaki); John McEldowney (Taranaki — replaced by Bill Bush, Canterbury), Tane Norton (Canterbury — captain), Kent Lambert (Manawatu).

Scoring

New Zealand (10). Try by Lawrie Knight; penalties (2) by Bevan Wilson.

British Isles (9). Try by Morgan; conversion and penalty by Morgan.

Referee: Dave Millar (Otago).   Saturday, 13 August 1977.

13
Postscript and
Post Mortem

One place the Lions really enjoyed was Fiji. The relief of getting out
of New Zealand and the warmth and welcome of the Fijian people
(plus, of course, the sunshine) convinced the team that this was the
most enjoyable stop on tour. 'This is the life', said Charlie Faulkner,
relaxing beside the hotel pool. 'Next time the Lions come they
should play twenty-five games in Fiji and one in New Zealand!' That
was said in Faulkner's nicest manner, for he was one who was
reluctant to go home, his three weeks on tour having given him a
taste for more.

There was a good deal of light-hearted banter as to who would
play against Fiji. 'The first fifteen names out of the hat,' Dawes joked
at one point, but in the end he bowed to injury worries and the
strength of the Fiji team and released a side that included eight of
the fourth test combination.

The hospitality was something else in Fiji and in the Lions' state
of relieved euphoria, having rid themselves of New Zealanders (I
was the only Kiwi reporter there), they settled down to relaxing and
some drinking sessions. 'We lost a day here somewhere,' said
George Burrell to the aftermatch crowd. He was not referring to
crossing the dateline or losing his calendar.

Sixteen members of the party, including some British pressmen,
ran up a restaurant bill of $700! 'The food was nice,' Moss Keane
recalled the next day, 'ah, but the wine was terrific,' and he rolled
his eyes back into his head in satisfied reverie. When the party returned to the hotel, Keane was ceremonially thrown into the swim-
ming pool, clothes and all. 'As I can't swim,' he said, 'I got into im-

mediate difficulties.' He was hauled out and the festivities went on. This happened on the Monday night, only sixteen hours before the team was to play the might of Fijian rugby, in rampant and hungry mood, at Suva's Buckhurst Park.

The Lions' attitude and devotion to winning in Fiji were not all they might have been. Not that it mattered. The next afternoon, when Fiji beat the 'Famous Lions' by 25 to 21, was one of the most exciting and enthralling sporting occasions I have witnessed. For a start there was the crowd: all 20,000 of them were drummed into a ferment of excitement, because Fiji, who had beaten Tonga soundly in a recent three-test series, had a great chance of winning.

It was a truly colourful sight. The ground is backdropped by the waving coconut palms and the Pacific Ocean; and the pitch, all year round, is as hard as rock.

Fiji ran the ball at every opportunity and deserved to win. They scored five tries, some of them thrilling and all containing excellent authority in their execution.

To their credit the Lions contributed fully to the spectacle, not for any great running moves — they were more content to kick for position than spin the ball, but for the style they contributed to the spirit of the occasion.

In the scoring, the Lions drew up to 21-all, but then Vuato Narisia, the flanker, took a pass from his captain, Pio Bosce Tikoisuva, and dived, like an Olympic swimmer off the blocks, for the winning try. The noise was deafening and the clamour loud and rapturous; the score enabled Fiji to notch its first-ever win over a major touring team.

As the players left the field, Fiji's famed Police Band played 'Isa Lei', the Fijian farewell song, then 'Now is the Hour'. The team boarded the windowless vehicle still in their playing gear, and as they drove away the emotion of the day reached its climax. The happy crowd pressed towards the slow-moving bus, the Lions waved and shook hands by the hundreds, and the band played 'Will Ye No Come Back Again?'

Nobody in the touring party minded losing, as the Fijians' delight was infectious. The fact that the referee had failed to whistle some dreadfully obvious forward passes and had blown a penalty count of 22-4 against the Lions was quickly forgotten.

For the record the teams were:
British Isles: Irvine; Gareth Evans, Burcher, McGeechan, Bennett; Bevan, Lewis; Squire; Neary, Beaumont, Martin, Trevor Evans (replaced by Brown); Faulkner, Windsor and Price.

Fiji: Kemu Musunamasi; Joape Tuinikoro, Qele Ratu, Senitiki Nasave; Wame Gavidi, Pio Tikoisuva; Samisoni Viriviri; Vili Ratudradra; Vuata Narisia, Ilisoni Taoba, Ilaitia Tuisese, Rupeni Qaraniqio; Nimilote Ratudina, Atonia Racika, Jo Rauto.
Scoring:
Fiji (25). Tries by Narisia (2), Joape, Racika and Rauto. Dropped goal by Pio Tikoisuva; conversion by Rauto.
British Isles (21). Tries by Bennett, Beaumont and Burcher. Conversions (3) and penalties (1) by Bennett.
Referee: Mr Sefanaia Koroi.

It was the ultimate irony that the match was played in bright sunshine, on an almost windless day, and on a firm field. Fiji offered, in weather terms, what, in 1977, New Zealand never could. There is no doubt that the Lions' backline progress would have been more marked had the New Zealand pitches been more firm.

The rain that followed the tourists around New Zealand was almost too much of a coincidence. It was as though the Meteorological Service had decreed that rain should be laid on for every stage of the Lions' itinerary. After the Auckland match, where the park was softish after overnight showers, John Dawes told the press, 'If God belongs to us as well, he'll stop it raining.' Alas, for the Lions, it never did. By my calculations, eleven of the twenty-five tour games were played on sloppy fields on rainy days. A good slice of the remaining games were on grounds soft from recent showers.

Where the weather really hurt was in the days between the games and constant training in damp conditions. Wet gear, muddy boots, cold hands, and cheerless dressing-sheds do not help the daily grind. The Lions made light of the weather in the early days but it soon disheartened them, far more than their morale should have allowed.

'It's a shame we have to play rugby in weather like this,' said Burrell before the New Zealand Juniors game, a sentiment I agreed with. That match should not have been played. Forget the money through the turnstiles; no human beings should have been subject to the degradation of behaving like pigs slopping about on the mud-hole that was Athletic Park that day. Add to that the New Zealand-France match in 1961, on the same ground, which was played in a super-chilled Wellington gale; or the New Zealand-Scotland match in 1975 at Eden Park in Auckland where snorkels and flippers should have been standard issue to the players; and one is forced to the conclusion that mud, wind and water are *never* judged bad enough by Rugby Officialdom to warrant a tourists' game being called off.

I have previously mentioned that the team came adrift from its New Zealand public because of unwillingness to meet, talk with and understand local people. Whether this was the team's doing or not will probably never be known.

In the latter days, the personnel of the team also grew away from their management. Although John Dawes had stated early in the tour that he was a 'player's man', his side eventually grew disenchanted with him, the feelings becoming quite open as the fourth test drew near.

There were several areas of dissension. Dawes appeared very keen to play Alun Lewis, the replacement scrum-half, in the final test team, disregarding the efforts of Douglas Morgan who had battled, without much praise, but with steady improvement, throughout the early days. When, after much discussion, the team was announced with Morgan, it was clearly a compromise to meet the players' wishes. One Lion told me there would have been 'bloody hell to pay' had Lewis won the No. 9 jersey for that match. Morgan, as you will recall, went on to play the game of his life at halfback, encouraged no doubt by the fact that he knew his team-mates were with him.

Dawes also got badly off-side with his team over the last dance of the tour held at the Royal International Hotel in Auckland. It seemed the touring members of the press party, both New Zealand and British, had been invited by members of the team to come in and enjoy the fun. This they did, but were soon weeded out by John Dawes. 'Out!' he said to every journalist and reporter he could see, including Mervyn Davies, the great Welsh and Lions number eight forward who, but for an injury misfortune, could very well have been captain of the 1977 team. Several members of the Lions fronted up to Dawes in a very direct manner, demanding to know why their guests had been ejected. The All Black fourth test team looked on bemused. The high-handed action diminished the public and press opinion of the Lions' team spirit.

The rift widened, and in Fiji it was obvious that few of the Lions would do more than pass the time of day with their coach. He was a lonely figure.

This British Isles team had a strong bond of brotherhood with each other. Their team spirit was staunch and intense. In the end, though, their bond was entirely to each other and to their captain, Phil Bennett, whom they really appeared to love, even more so during the late days when the pressures of the tour and its captaincy were taking their toll.

John Dawes was always ready and more than willing to appear on television. When he was required to wait for videotapes to record or microphones to be readied, Dawes was patient and uncomplaining. 'I know the difficulties of your job', he told me once, but his tolerance of television did not spread itself to other media.

At the after-game press conferences Dawes treated some of the writers' questions with indifference and high-handedness that verged on bad manners. He refused to answer hypothetical questions, when sometimes they offered significant openings for his views. He sidestepped difficult queries with sarcastic quips and offered little or nothing in the way of constructive comment about the opposing New Zealand teams. Several times I heard him give one and two-word answers to press writers' queries, then minutes later step in front of television cameras to elaborate at length on more or less the same question.

He had, during the tour, a continuing conflict with several of the British press that bordered on open warfare. Clem Thomas, a big, bluff and thoroughly likeable Welshman, was one who was forever on the receiving end of Dawes' wrath. Mind you, Thomas gave as good as he got during the tour and, in his final assessment of the team, joined other writers from both countries in condemning Dawes and Burrell for mismanagement of the party.

One of the British media contingent in Christchurch was so moved by a verbal attack he had had to endure from Dawes that he hoped the Lions would lose the second test. 'At least that'll put him onto the long slippery slope out of British rugby.' Strong stuff. Strong feelings.

When I asked Dawes after the fourth test whether he considered he had had a fair press hearing he replied, 'From some, yes. Some have been fair and accurate, others have not been fair and have been unkind, not remembering that the lads out here are people who are doing it for the love of the game as amateurs, not professionals. It's about time those writers who have been unkind put their own house in order.' Strong feelings again.

George Burrell should not be left out of a bad news chapter. As manager he was a total disappointment. Gone was the genial leader of 1975 who had cheerfully led the Scottish team through New Zealand. In his place in 1977 was a man antagonistic and suspicious of the press, indifferent to hospitality, intolerant of local officialdom, unreasonably restrictive of his team's freedom, roused to flashes of anger, and damned difficult for everybody to deal with.

Which was a shame, for he was one of the best rugby aftermatch speakers I have ever heard, able to come up with a different humorous story for each match, and as well, he was a thorough expert on rugby law.

There is no doubt that his peformance on tour will earn him as much criticism as has been received by any manager of a touring rugby team.

At Rotorua he and Dawes hosted a very pleasant function for the media men. The chat between the previously feuding parties of the British press and Lions management was light and friendly, in contrast with the bitter exchanges which the two groups had had earlier in the tour. Though the drinks were copious and free, and the hospitality from the two warm and peaceable, there were still some of the pressmen who could not forget. It was 'too little, too late', said one.

Although he probably did not realise it at the time, those words were probably the most concise and informative description of Dawes' and Burrell's public relations I have heard. Too little, too late.

The two never seemed to be embarrassed by the consequent bad publicity, though Burrell did show signs after nearly three months that it was getting a bit much for him. 'I wouldn't do this job again if you paid me a million quid,' he told me that night in Rotorua. 'This is an incredibly difficult and lonely job. If I was being paid the money Don Revie was I wouldn't mind the criticism, but I'm not.' One could have almost felt sorry for him at that time. It *is* a lonely job, being a manager under the glare of so many pressures (and pressmen).

Dawes' selection policy was to give as many players as possible chances to win test match places. He and his co-selectors, Burrell and Bennett, never chose a top test-quality combination until the week of the first test in Wellington. While it is an upright sentiment to give everyone a chance to prove his playing worth, all the successful rugby tours of modern times have, early on, sorted out their players into Saturday and Wednesday teams. It is a harsh fact of life for the Wednesday players.

'But we didn't know our top side in those early matches,' said Dawes. 'We came out to New Zealand with a party of thirty players and all we knew was that one or two test places were secure. We were determined that every player be given his chance, to get a fair crack of the whip.'

Worthy sentiment indeed. Had the tour been a success Dawes may have gone down in history as the ultimate 'player's man'. When it was not prosperous in victory terms, his actions must come under closer scrutiny and criticism. The fact was that Douglas Morgan never played a full match in halfback combination with Phil Bennett until the twentieth game of the tour; the second and last time they combined in a full match was the fourth test!

The first test forward pack had not played together before that match. There was much dithering about in the selection of pack leader before that test, no fewer than five being used in the first ten matches — Fran Cotton, Trevor Evans, Derek Quinnell, Nigel Horton and Terry Cobner. This particular procrastination slowed down forward development, the improvement only coming when Terry Cobner was chosen as permanent pack leader, after the Wellington test. (Tony Neary was much later nominated as his deputy.) Cobner proved the ideal man for the job, drilling the forwards from that point into the admirable unit they became. But, like other things, that, too, could have come too late.

These were some of the problems the team faced in playing their tour. They never played to their full potential, they were slow developers, they had a 'hot streak' in the middle of their tour which they were not able to continue, and there is sufficient evidence that their slide in performance at the end of the tour was partly due to the diminished regard they had for the principles and performance of their coach and manager. And that, dear friends, was bad news for the team and its chances.

14.
Lion Power

And now for the good news. Much of the rugby the Lions played was totally admirable. Parts of their game, goal-kicking for instance, were awesome. The power of their scrum and their expertise in the maul were educational to New Zealand, while the skill and daring of several of their backs were delightful to watch.

Someone wrote a letter to the editor of *Rugby News* during the winter to ask whether Keith Quinn was 'in love with Andy Irvine and Phil Bennett — or are they just good friends?' He had obviously gained this impression from the many praiseworthy comments I had made, as tour commentator, about their play.

Well, my friend, let me make a statement. In the rugby sense I admit to having an affair with the genius of Bennett's footwork, the mastery of his goal-kicking and the cheekiness of his approach. I also admit to total affection for the speed of Andy Irvine, great admiration for the length and power of his goal-kicking, and the highest regard for his ability to maintain the momentum of an attack and create extra scoring opportunities by staying in close support of the men he passed to. (Mike Gibson shared this talent.) With regard to their play, in a rugby-love sense, I admit I was smitten.

What afflicted me with a heavy heart, though, was the sight of Bennett's form and confidence on the wane and of Irvine's diminishing involvement in the team's attack. Their superiority was not sustained over the whole tour so their entry into the echelon of truly great players who have toured New Zealand was never quite achieved.

Irvine clearly ranked as the number one star player of the tour. He continued, with distinction, the British Isles' proud tradition in the fullback position, and in attacking terms I have no hesitation in saying he is a street better than J. P. R. Williams. On defence, so vital in test matches, Irvine was not quite as sound. But rugby is a game where tries get points and points win matches, so Irvine is now the greater player.

Irvine began his tour of New Zealand bouncing up and down on the spot in the chilling cold of Masterton, having come on as replacement for Bruce Hay. His hands remained in his pockets while he waited for play to come his way. Early though those days were, that was to become symptomatic of the use of Irvine on tour. Every try he scored or assisted appeared to be the result of his own initiative, and it will be a teeth-grinding, head-shaking memory for the Lions that he became an unemployed attacker, especially in the last test.

The standard tactical fare served to Irvine in the first part of the tour by New Zealand rep teams was the sky-high punt, designed to unsettle the Scotsman and exploit the shaky reputation he had for mishandling the high ones. Hawke's Bay tried it and on occasions the Lions looked dreadful going backwards. Irvine was the target for the Garryowens but claimed that the errors at McLean Park were not his doing. 'If you look carefully at the TV replay you'll see that I never dropped one ball,' he says. 'J. J. Williams missed one, but the rest we got.'

Somehow or other though, the rumour of Irvine's susceptibility under high kicks was passed around. When he came on, again as replacement, at Gisborne, the Combined team changed tactics in mid-stream to start bombing Irvine with towering kicks. He took most of them.

In the next match Taranaki tried the same stunt. Paul Martin, the first five-eighth, can kick as high as anyone in New Zealand. When he did the crowd roared their loudest and Irvine waited for the ball and the Taranaki forwards to arrive at the same time, a fearsome prospect. He came through with flying colours. Irvine knew he had won that battle. 'I'm quite happy if they kick me the ball like that, because then we get it and gain the initiative,' he said at the time.

For the next sixteen matches Irvine set alight his 'hot streak'. His form was superb, based on fast running, classical sporting instincts for the unexpected, and bred-in-the-bone rugby nous.

His five tries at Taumarunui were clear-cut and exciting, and the fourth — where he joined an 80-metre move after Bennett had split the defence with two massive side-steps — was named 'Top Try' for that month in TV1's competition. Most of the 19,000 entries voted for Irvine. He rated it his best of the tour. 'I liked this one because four or five of the lads handled and it was a team effort.' Understatement again, but typical of Irvine, the man. He was a quiet person, possessed of a soft lilting Scots accent that won him friends everywhere. His modesty in the face of heaped praise was completely natural. When I approached him for a film interview as he packed his bags to fly home nothing was too much bother. 'Sure, sure,' he said, struggling with lengths of twine to contain his bulging suitcases. When I informed him we considered him the 'player of the tour' he looked up, somewhat surprised. 'Thanks Keith, you're very kind,' he said. That was Andy Irvine, busiest player on tour, top try scorer, and thorough gentleman.

To the All Blacks' everlasting credit they bottled Irvine up for all but a few runs in the test series. Only late in the fourth test did he run with any length. The rest of the series he was kept severely in check by strong All Black defence headed by Bruce Robertson, Bill Osborne and Bryan Williams. The impression of their tackles obviously stuck with Irvine. 'I've never seen a team mark so well and put us under so much pressure . . . I hadn't given New Zealand back play much thought, but I'll certainly go back with the myth shot that the All Blacks have no backs.' Most of Irvine's tries were scored from entry into the backline and then 'running-off' one of the outer players, notably J. J. Williams and Peter Squires.

The only real flaw in the gem that was Irvine was his defence. Possessed of only a light frame, his tackling was not of the 'rock-like' consistency his team would have liked. Fortunately this blemish was not over-exposed in the test matches.

Bennett I cannot accord the same total admiration. The introduction of Graham Mourie into the All Black team for the third test showed his decline from top form. Bennett at the start of the tour and Bennett at the end were two different men. In the early days he was lively and alert, at the end only efficient and completely predictable. His passing fell away dreadfully and his discipline let him down on several occasions, the most glaring being in the fourth test when he over-kicked a touch-finder, and Bill Osborne's return kick led to Knight's series-clinching try.

Mourie made Bennett's life miserable in the third and fourth tests. The Taranaki flanker's runs from scrums and line-outs were designed to cramp Bennett with 'pressure and tackle', Jack Gleeson's winning match-plan. This they did to the letter.

As a person Bennett was like a new boy in school. He was shy, polite and quiet, not often seen in the company of New Zealanders, and a figurehead captain in terms of social responsibilities. One wonders, for instance, how many Christmas cards he would be sending to friends made in New Zealand? Which is sad, for Bennett's quietness, almost a stand-offish attitude, belied the very human qualities he could exhibit.

Only once did I really see his face light up. That was in the television interview I did with him after the second test. 'We're delighted,' he said — with a smile almost, but not quite, coming into view.

In the early days at Masterton, Taumarunui and New Plymouth, Bennett, on the field, was as lively as a firefly. A ball that was delivered to him in a position only slightly conducive to running was sufficient and he would be away. His head would sink low, the ball held to his chest with one hand. With the dip of a shoulder, a last-second signal, his side-step would explode, several metres wide — with his backline breaking in support.

His form was on the rise till the first test, but in the instant Sid Going scored, Bennett, a desperate tackler, was buried under Willie Duggan's weight, suffering a nasty shoulder injury. From that moment the Welshman's game nose-dived. This decline, and the lack of a replacement or remedy, was compounded by bad passing and alignment by his outsides. The Lions' back play developed no further. Thus did a rugby tradition end, and the likelihood of a series victory.

Mention must be made of goal-kicking, for both Bennett and Irvine, as well as Douglas Morgan, were of a class well beyond most, if not all of the New Zealanders. Morgan was the best. His highly-difficult kicks out of the mud at Athletic Park against the New Zealand Juniors were made to look easy, and at Gisborne, Westport, Auckland and Pukekohe he landed limit bags with straight shooting.

Bennett was a kicker from instinct, who seemed to 'ease' the ball towards his target rather than 'bang' them as Irvine did. Their background in soccer gave them a style, rhythm and success rate that was far superior to the rigid techniques used by New Zealanders.

Which brings me to the strongest aspect of the team play of the 1977 Lions. In many respects their forward endeavour, rucks and line-outs excepted, was of the best quality ever seen in New Zealand. Their shoulders, trunks and thighs, in every scrum combination and throughout the span of every match, were an aggregation and application of muscle power that the New Zealanders could not match. Searching for the secret of the Lions' scrummaging success kept New

Zealanders in debate all winter long. After all, their scrums were only eight men pushing, as had been every other scrum in rugby since the 1930s. How then did these Lions get their power?

It was based on several significant points. The props held their usual solid positions, but with the put-in and the weight they received from the second-rowers they then pushed in an upward manner, coming up underneath their opponents rather than trying to push straight through them off the ball. Many was the Kiwi scrum that found its props jerked upwards at the British application of weight.

The Lions also said 'look after the inches and the yards will come.' Unlike the old days when, on the call 'weight!', packs would try to drive for yards of gain, the Lions' second row would shift their feet only inches forward at a time. The combined effect of the inches gained invariably became a momentum that sent most New Zealand packs into a backslide.

The application of weight came from the superb upper body development of most of the Lions' scrum men. Their grasp of each other at the formation was therefore tighter and more strongly knit; held in that position, the scrum moved forward as a complete unit locked together by steel-like grips. It was interesting to note the high body positions of the lock forwards. Whereas New Zealanders have always called 'sink!' just before a scrum to remind the locks to go as low as possible, the Lions never bothered with this. Beaumont and Brown, in the tests, locked the scrums with their posteriors held much higher than the norm in New Zealand. And the scrum went forward.

The New Zealand selectors admitted after the third test that they had 'no answer' to the Lions' power at scrum-time. There was so much dominance, in fact, that the All Blacks invented the three-man scrum as a desperate means to hook the ball quickly. It was a sound idea, accepting at the same time that its very conception was based on a total beating taken in eight-man shoves.

The New Zealand test eight held up well in the first test, but with the subsequent inclusion of Beaumont and Brown as the Lions locks and the loss of Kent Lambert, New Zealand's top prop, the balance of forward play tipped alarmingly towards the Lions.

That the tourists became obsessed with their scrum power, as Jack Gleeson suggested, was true. Who could blame them when their forwards looked up from scrum, maul or line-out to see bumble-footed backs casting the golden possession away? The disappointment of the tour was that the Lions did not develop tactics to exploit consistently their forward dominance. When they did, in some games, the end product was not as visually interesting as the 'fifteen man' game but was much more effective and successful.

Against Counties-Thames Valley each of the five Lions tries came from a scrum. One was a classic pushover score. From a decision which led to a five metre scrum, the Lions forwards talked intently together while an injured player was attended to. On the restart, Tony Neary, the day's captain, insisted the scrum go down tight and hard. He banged his hands across the shoulders of Moss Keane and Allan Martin as they set themselves in the second row, insisting that they be perfectly set. On the ball being put in, Bobby Windsor made the hook, the ball hung at the feet of the locks and then on Neary's screamed command from the flank the pack almost ran forward. The Combined pack was smashed, and in the scramble at the back Douglas Morgan dived forward and scored the try. The control exhibited at the back of the scrums was always better when Jeff Squire was there, as he was that day. It was a subdued Counties pack that picked itself off the floor after their alarming experience of Lion strength.

As Barry John said, 'If we didn't have this pack this year, we'd be history.' It was ironic that a week after the Lions left New Zealand TV1's 'Sports Extra' replayed scenes from the 1967 New Zealand/Wales match at Cardiff in which the All Black pack completely overran the Welsh scrum. The wheel had turned full circle in a decade.

In mauls it was the same story. Strength of shoulders and forearms enabled the Lions to rip many a ball from their opponents and 'smuggle' it back to the waiting halfback. And whereas New Zealanders made second-phase play by charging into a first-tackle ruck situation, the Lions did the same by bursting from the back of a scrum but maintaining an upright position once the tackle was made. Willie Duggan was particularly adept at this move which, in the second test in particular, committed the New Zealand loose forwards to making the tackle, thus losing their mobility as destroyers.

At the unhappy area of the game that is called line-out, the Lions did not exhibit the greatness they had at scrums and mauls. Yet their top jumpers, Beaumont and Brown, won decisive advantages over Oliver and Haden. Most of the ball won was much better presented to the halfback than the sprayed possession New Zealand received.

The Lions' most impressive forward performance was when Terry Cobner led them against Wellington, after the dismal showing in the first test. The team had called a special meeting without their managers and Cobner had taken over the speaking. His powerful rhetoric moved his teammates to rally to his call and lift the forward play to great standards. As Cobner took over the forward responsibility for the tour, he rose splendidly in his status within the team. The balding Pontypool man would have made a decisive, strong and bold test captain.

John Dawes stated at tour's end that the only satisfaction he could gain from a losing tour of New Zealand was the knowledge that his side clearly beat the All Blacks at what has traditionally been their own major strength. 'I've never seen an All Black team so comprehensively beaten in forward play,' he told me.

The sadness for the Lions was then that their forward strength was not matched by backline strength and skill. Given a richness of possession, the test backs could not put points on the board.

Undoubtedly this 1977 Lions team found playing in the shadow of the 1971 and 1974 Lions teams a huge handicap. 'Almost an impossible burden to bear,' said Dawes. Agreed. The final word should go to Chris Rea of the 1971 team, who toured New Zealand again in 1977 as a BBC commentator. 'If we had had the forward dominance over the All Blacks in 1971 that we had this year then we would have beaten New Zealand by 40 points.'

True words, even allowing for prideful parochialism. But the statement sums up the tour. The forwards were mighty, the backs flighty. Nowhere near as good as in the past.

'All our yesterdays are gone,' said Mervyn Davies at Whangarei. He and the other touring ex-Lions had to face the fact that Bennett's team of 1977 had good and bad points. The bad outscored the good, and so the series was lost.

15.
The Good, the Bad
and the Battlers

John Reason, the forceful and perceptive rugby writer for the London *Telegraph,* had a theory about why the 1977 Lions were such inept or unwilling socialisers when they left the team enclave to mingle with New Zealanders. (Reason's opinions tend to be diminished by New Zealanders, who still smart from the thorniness of the barbs he wrote about our national game in 1971 and 1972-3, but his perception of the game is on a higher plane than most of his critics and colleagues admit.)

Reason says that the public school influence has gone from British rugby. 'There are no more Tony O'Reillys and Andy Mulligans impressing New Zealanders with their wit, wisdom and background. This 1977 team is more like a Welsh working-class team, they're not used to socialising, it's not in their nature.'

His theory was borne out by the nature of Phil Bennett's Lions. They had little time for chatter with locals, they were awkward with New Zealanders generally, and avoided the 'heavies' — rugby parlance for bores who talk only rugby.

To me the team seemed to lack a 'character', a real hard-case, harum-scarum, guitar-strumming comic who could relieve tense occasions and enliven dull, wet days. Every team needs one, indeed they can almost be built into selection patterns so vital are they on a three-month tour.

The Lions tended to be unrelaxed, without a team jester. It was sad that Geoff Wheel had to cry off the tour, for apparently he is such a man, capable of fun and geniality whatever the hour. John Dougan, the Wellington ex-All Black five-eighth is such a one — his cheerfulness is overflowing and his repertoire of songs unending. Life is fun when he is around.

But let it not be said that this Lions team was without 'character'. They had genuine affection for each other, and the prospect of cliques forming among the separate national groups was soon forgotten. 'It's like being married to 29 fellows,' said Bobby Windsor, when asked about life on tour. 'We all get on well and there's been no friction. Becoming really close on tour — and winning — is what makes it all worthwhile.'

The Lions thought nothing of sitting in a grandstand, or in a bus, with an arm affectionately draped around a comrade's neck, or leaning comfortably on another's shoulder and thus sharing the pleasure of an occasion.

Travelling to Fiji at the tour's end, Bobby Windsor was going through his usual inexorable agony over air travel. He leaned forward, fingers in ears at take-off, to try to drown the howl and roar of the jets, obviously so upsetting to him. During the flight every man in the team must have come down the plane at one time or other to clasp Windsor's shoulder, massage his neck or make other comforting gestures to ease his misery. They were like that. They cared when one of their own was not up to his best. They were not afraid to show it.

The most touching gesture occurred at Buckhurst Park in Fiji after the last match. Phil Bennett stood, in his exhausted state, at the end of 80 minutes of vigorous tropical rugby, and personally thanked all of his exhausted teammates as they stumbled to the bus. It was not a verbal thank you, but a hugging, back-slapping, face-patting, hair ruffling, pat-on-the-backside farewell for each man which clearly said 'thanks chum for seeing this long struggle through to the end.' A devoted captain paying respects to his team. They enjoyed it, for they all loved each other.

In playing terms some of these Lions were successes, some were not. I have divided their performances into three categories — the good, the bad and the battlers.

Irvine and Bennett, the two near-greats of the tour, I have dealt with elsewhere in this chronicle. That they could not always employ their greatness was one reason why the series was lost.

Also in the top group I rate, in alphabetical order, Bill Beaumont, John Bevan, Gordon Brown, Terry Cobner, Fran Cotton, Tony Neary, Graham Price, Peter Squires, Peter Wheeler and J. J. Williams.

Terry Cobner played only ten minutes of football in the three weeks prior to the first test. Yet in the test he was able to give his everything, playing right up to the high reputation he had brought from Pontypool. His elevation to the permanent forward leadership lifted both his and the team's performance. Had he been available for the fourth test his influence might just have won the day.

On a personal basis Cobner had a mixed time in New Zealand. In the early stages he was keen and vital, with some time for on-the-field humour, as he showed at Timaru when he went around the beer cans that had been thrown at the players, searching for one that had some refreshment left. But depression lowered itself about him when, after the Waikato match, he suffered a poisoned leg. In Hutt Hospital he talked of retirement, of his dislike for long, weather-blighted tours, and was generally bowed down. He recovered for the third test but was not quite the player of old. His top-flight performances were spread over just six games and were a decisive influence on the upsurge of the team as they went into the second half of the tour.

I went looking for Cobner after he had captained the Lions to their important win over Canterbury. We wanted an interview to air his views on forward play to New Zealand television viewers. But Cobner could not make it. Long after the other players had showered, changed and prepared to move out of the dressing room, he still lay, in his muddy playing kit, drained of every ounce of strength, along a bench.

The improvement in Lions forward play not only dates from the time Cobner took over the pack leadership but also from the time Bill Beaumont came into the top side. Beaumont's non-selection in the original Lions' party was staggering, as he was quite clearly a better player than Martin and Keane. Beaumont's lucky break, to become sixth choice lock, was to replace his England teammate, Nigel Horton, who suffered a fractured thumb against Otago. As it turned out, the English influence in forward play became greater than that of the Welsh, and Beaumont led the way. He was a superb scrummager and as a number three line-out man bested Frank Oliver in the last three internationals. With Gordon Brown, Bill Beaumont gave a lot to the Lions' forward effort.

A graph drawn of the form of Tony Neary would show an upwards line all the way. His play at the beginning was well below that of an international flanker. He took weeks to discover that the speedy flanker role needs to be spiced with physical involvement. Where he stood off at the start, he was 'into it' in the end. Indeed it could be said he played better the more his beard grew. He stopped

shaving the day of the first game and by the end he had a set worthy
of an Elizabethan sea captain or courtier.

Jack Gleeson said of him: 'We admired Cobner, but Neary was a
much quicker flanker in pressurising our backs. We were disappointed Cobner couldn't play the fourth test as we knew it would be
harder to move the ball with Neary there.'

What a shame Fran Cotton marred his tour with malevolence. His
slugging of the young West Coaster, Jon Sullivan, was reprehensible,
as was his fistic welcome to Greg Denholm in the very next game at
Auckland. Denholm came on as a replacement and stood in the line-
out. The ball came in and — biff! — went Cotton right into
Denholm's face. Later he stomped on the Aucklander's head in a
collapsing scrum, for which Denholm delivered a punch and earned
a penalty.

Cotton was a better player than this, his strong propping keeping
him in all the top games after the first test. Perhaps the most in-
triguing feature of his game was his smile. In fights, furores and
fisticuffs Cotton would be there, in the thick of it, smiling. Early on,
he was named captain against Hawke's Bay and was not a success.
'He didn't say one word all match,' said a local forward. He was not
offered the leadership again.

Peter Wheeler was neglected at the outset. He later became a test
choice and, like the other Englishmen who played the fourth test,
won his cap ahead of a Welshman. Wheeler was a quickish hooker
of the ball and a lively forward who policed the front of the line-out
expertly. His try at Timaru, a splendid forward charge, sprung from
his alertness in this area. A big part of the Lions' line-out superiority
in the last three tests was due to the highly-accurate nature of the
Leicester Tiger's throwing-in.

Of the nine Welsh forwards in the team I would only rate Cobner
and Graham Price as truly successful. Only two forwards played all
four tests; Graham Price was one. This he did with no show or fuss.
In fact in the four internationals I can only recall him in individual
play twice. Once when he chased Batty at Athletic Park in the
runaway try, and the second when he went down after a tussle with
Brad Johnstone. His work-rate in line-outs, scrums and mauls was of
the highest calibre and in every way this quiet Welshman was a
credit to himself and the game.

Gordon Brown was another gifted tight forward. And a lovely
bloke, much more gentle than his fearsome appearance on the field
suggested. During the second test he played with one shoulder
packed with sponge rubber, giving him a Quasimodo appearance. In

the TV commentary I dragged out the hoary old chestnut, 'there he is, the hunchback of Troon,' for which Brown was delighted. 'I had five phone calls from families who had lived in Troon and wanted to meet me. It was great.'

Brown was great value as team choirmaster and lock forward; after lack of fitness had upset his early tour form, he became a first-ranking test man.

John James Williams, who had 'J. J.' tagged onto his name, so as not to confuse him with J. P. R., Brynmor, Clive, Bryan, Alun, Barry, and all the other players, referees and commentators who bear that name, was a class winger who exhibited flashes of rugby genius. His kick-on try through the mud at Masterton, where no hands were used in a 70-metre move, showed meticulous application to a slippery, planing ball. His perfection of the art of kicking ahead, to use his uncommon speed to chase and beat defenders, was a vital weapon for him and his team. It was in the second test that he scored his best try, choosing to dummy and run when the All Black defence expected him to kick ahead as per usual. Sadly that was J. J.'s last major act of the tour, as he was taken from the field in the third test with a leg injury. He broke into tears under the grandstand, so great was his disappointment. He did not play again on tour.

It will surprise some that I rate John Bevan and Peter Squires among the successes of the tour, for neither received adequate recognition from the Lions' selection panel. Bevan, behind his Elton John spectacles, looked a studious type and played that way. He was cleanly efficient at all times. He could, when he chose, scoot through a gap at great speed. His kicking was uncommonly accurate, and he rarely missed touch. He was the perfect foil to Bennett's flare.

Squires was, next to J. J. Williams, the best winger in the team, but was inexplicably left out of the second test XV. His replacement by Gareth Evans plainly embarrassed some of the Lions. Squires had much more talent and speed and was in great intuitive touch with Andy Irvine, who often 'ran off' him from fullback.

So those were the twelve men who could go home with pride. In the Battlers Club are Willie Duggan, Trevor Evans, Charlie Faulkner, Steve Fenwick, Mike Gibson, Bruce Hay, Nigel Horton, Alun Lewis, Ian McGeechan, Douglas Morgan, Phil Orr, Derek Quinnell, Brynmor Williams, Bobby Windsor. Some did not get the best and fairest treatment from the selectors.

Carwyn James claimed part of the failure of the Lions' backs was due to the lack of a player in the centre who could punch straight through and run hard. 'There's too much lateral movement,' said

James. Gibson might have fixed that up, but there were indications that there was no confidence in him doing the job. He was out of form early on, but when the flashes of the old Gibson returned he was not given the Saturday games to fit in to the test pattern. Was he too old? Perhaps, for he was slower than in past days, but he did not play in a losing Lions team all tour, something that only he could boast of.

Phil Orr also got a shabby deal from the selectors. I never saw him play a bad game, but after being in the losing first test front row he thereafter played only four full games out of sixteen. He was fit all the time, being reserve for eleven of the remaining twelve matches, including the three tests. Another champion bloke, too.

Centres Fenwick and McGeechan, the test pair, were big disappointments. Fenwick played crash-bash rugby all tour in repeated attempts to break the line; McGeechan's dancing feet could take him through, but only rarely. Fenwick was often over-aggressive in the tackle which over-compensated for other backs who often failed to make the crunch. McGeechan gained some kind of distinction, being the only player to appear in all five tour defeats.

Brynmor Williams could well have made the top drawer of talent had not injuries cut him down at the vital time. His favoured dive pass was big, swinging and exaggerated, but he and Bennett created a workable halfback combination. Williams was a lovely lad whose command of the Welsh national tongue made him a regular interview subject for the BBC's Alun Williams.

The other halfback, Douglas Morgan, could not have been a popular selection as, in the early days, so many of the British critics were wishing him homewards at the slightest cut or bruise. After the Canterbury game, where he played 'like a hairy goat', he was called an 'embarrassment' to the team by one of the British journalists. Morgan must have relished the games which followed, when he built up his form in goal-kicking and halfback play, to make him a popular player's choice for the fourth test. A good tour.

Derek Quinnell was one who was not allowed, through injury, to play up to his best pre-tour form. He always looked mean and aggressive but was far too slow for even the tight-loose flanker's role. When he had to change his jersey at Whangarei his unfitness was revealed — the 'spare tyre' on his waistline was there for all to see. Several times Quinnell went ultra-close to earning the referee's ultimate displeasure and being sent off.

Bobby Windsor, Jeff Squire and Trevor Evans were three men who had one test apiece and performed steadily. Evans won distinct-

ion as the unbeaten mid-week captain, while Squire, the best con-
troller of the ball at the back of set scrums, deserved selection for the
fourth test. Windsor suffered from a heel injury early on but was
back to push Wheeler for his test spot near the end.

Terry Cobner told me one night the funniest thing he heard all
tour was Moss Keane talking to a Fijian Indian, with Bruce Hay in-
terpreting. Hay, like Keane, had the broadest of broad accents, and
enjoyed his tour in a quiet way. His only attacking play seemed to be
a high kick-and-rush move, but his bravery in the face of charging
New Zealand teams was unflinching.

Willie Duggan played all four tests at No. 8 and played hard and
well. The only drawback was the lack of rugby logic that, in perhaps
an Irish sense, often came into his play. He conceded penalties here
and there, threw punches, bullocked into tackles and held on too
long on too many occasions. He was a lovely boyo though, and in a
tour where the drop-goal played no part for the team, he had the best
attempt — just missing from 40 metres against Auckland!

Nigel Horton was sorely missed, as his locking game was shaping up
strongly till he had to head home with a broken thumb. He was one
man who appeared keen to mix with the locals at social functions.

Which leaves just Alun Lewis and Charlie Faulkner to consider
among the 'battlers'. Both came out to New Zealand at short notice,
and had to adjust quickly to a well-knit social and footballing group.
Faulkner, the judo expert, was extremely proud to play three times
in a Lions front row with Price and Windsor, his Pontypool club-
mates, and relished his short time in New Zealand. Lewis, the
stocky London Welshman, played satisfactorily in his three games,
especially in Fiji.

Now to those six individuals who did not have such happy tours:
David Burcher, Gareth Evans, Moss Keane, Allan Martin, Elgan
Rees, and Clive Williams.

Elgan Rees and Gareth Evans were two wingers who did not
come off as selectional gambles. John Dawes named them in a TV
interview. 'Those two didn't show their true potential,' he said,
adding, 'back home they each had that special something called flair
but never displayed it in New Zealand.' That was for real. Evans,
when full speed was reached, bobbled about from head and shoulder
like a tired 400-metre runner, while all the dash that Rees had was
worthless because it carried him anywhere and everywhere on the
paddock but nowhere fast! Rees, a good-looking boy, tried his hardest and burst into smiles with each good thing he did, but just was
not good enough to be a Lions winger. Ditto Gareth Evans.

David Brucher started at Masterton as though he would be a first choice test centre. Thereafter his play drifted along, not driven by any apparent ambition. He played badly in the third test, admittedly not helped by some slack passing from inside, and was summarily dropped.

Clive Williams never really got into his tour. He propped in nine games, including three on Saturdays, and scored a valuable try against Manawatu-Horowhenua, but was never a candidate for a test place. Not so much a disappointment as a non-contender.

That leaves two locks, Martin and Keane. Allan Martin was big and beefy, and when he donned a monkey mask at Westport to interrupt some TV interviews, he was very funny. He was not so amusing, however, when Bill Osborne zipped past him in the Maoris match, when Martin's strength and weight, if applied, could easily have prevented a try being scored. Martin, who, like Irvine, became a father while in New Zealand, played the first test and was well beaten in the line-outs by Andy Haden. He then faded into mediocrity, and was sentenced to lock the Wednesday scrum with Moss Keane, the big Kerryman. Together the two of them thundered along, from mid-week to mid-week.

Keane played the first test with Martin, but was well beaten by Frank Oliver for No. 3 line-out ball. The huge Irishman then played only five times in nine weeks, being cast aside by the selectors. Keane played honestly and burned inside with desire for more games. They did not come.

He was, however, one of the nicely-chiselled comic cuts of the team. They called him 'Rentastorm', which he did not take kindly to at first, as it stemmed from the door and glassware smashings of New Plymouth. Keane thereafter behaved pretty well and won the hearts of many with his droll humour and Irish wit. Too bad he was so broad — a lot of it was not understood!

16.
A Team Only Plays
as Well...

When the All Blacks turned back the rugby challenge of the 1977 Lions they won with points on the board, they won against the tide of possession and, this was the great satisfaction, they beat the British Isles tactically. They were not outsmarted as many believed had happened in 1971.

The tactical plan that Jack Gleeson, his co-selectors and leading players formulated was aligned against the strengths of the Lions team. The old expression 'you can only play as well as the opposition lets you', rang true in 1977 for New Zealand. Mind you, it took two tests before the selectors found the combination to implement the tactical plan, and they had to take calculated and considerable risks to develop that combination.

The plan developed thus: Jack Gleeson perceived at about the half-way stage of the tour that the Lions realised their backs were not coming on as they had hoped. The Lions then changed their tactical plan, to place more emphasis on their scrum. Jack Gleeson takes up the story, '. . . they became obsessed with their scrum power and began messing about, holding the ball in the back and pushing around. This lack of quick heel gave our backs time to move up flatter in the defence role, as they could see the Lions were in possession. We were then able to catch their backs behind the advantage line when they were passing. They were going backwards while we were on our way forward to the breakdown. Next we picked teams who were strong in the backs, both attack and defence, so that we could stop them there and then probe their weak three-quarters.'

It was a winning formula for New Zealand in the third and fourth tests, capitalising on the Lions' employment of their strengths, and applying Gleeson's catch-cry, 'Pressure them and tackle'. The winning formula was the making of Jack Gleeson, as coach, convenor and mentor of the 1977 All Blacks.

By nature I guess you could call Gleeson a conservative man. He is quiet, as is his home town of Feilding. He is a successful businessman, having an interest in several hostelries in the lower part of the North Island. His home pub is 'Gleeson's Empire' in Feilding, a tavern just off the main street, where business is brisk and turnover solid.

I made a trip, with a television film crew, to the tavern at the beginning of the 1977 season, to try and find for our viewers the philosophy and attitudes of Jack Gleeson, the new All Black rugby coach.

He speaks with well-considered deliberation and dry humour, and a lot of words were exchanged between us on a most pleasant day.

I can never forget the conclusion of our filmed interview. At the end of all my researched questions about Jack Gleeson, Gleeson's All Blacks and the Lions of 1977, I asked him just one more, the kind you ask when you are winding up a programme. 'Do you think then, we can maybe win this coming series . . .?' Gleeson looked across the table at me, almost sharply, deliberated for just one second, then said, 'We will win the series.' There was no more. He stopped speaking. I asked no more questions. The firm statement of fact allowed no doubt and left no opening for further questions. We folded away our film gear and, in time, set off for home with 'We will win the series' ringing in our ears.

That statement was the first of many confident and positive things Gleeson said during the season. He never once wavered from the extraordinary confidence he first expressed that day in Feilding.

The interview played on television several days later and his assurance was thus conveyed to the rugby public. Many disagreed with his boldness because not all of them were behind Gleeson in those early days. There was still much sympathy about for John Stewart, who had been so mercilessly blamed and dumped as convenor of selectors by those who know best in the New Zealand Rugby Union, simply, it seemed, because the All Blacks lost the 1976 series with South Africa.

It must have been a test of character for Gleeson to come in as convenor with J. J. Stewart still on the panel, knowing the great affection 'J.J.' was held in by senior All Blacks. Indeed one player who appeared in tests against the Lions, and who I had better not name, said to me he 'didn't like Gleeson at all — he's just a mouthpiece for J.J.'

Gleeson won through. At the end of the series his confidence and success had won him the confidence of his charges. They would have died with their boots on for him in August where they might not have in May.

It was a long and difficult road to victory. The Lions were a hard team to beat because they were in possession of the ball so much of the time, and that is where Gleeson's tactical ploy of gaining parity and initiatives from British strengths represented the clear thinking of a first-class rugby intellect.

Mistakes there were along the way. It was crazy, plumb crazy, for instance, to go into a test series without a specialised goal-kicker. The confidence shown in Bryan Williams taking the attempts at goal in the first two tests was based on reasonable logic, for he *could* kick, but his record as a regular kicker was in no way as high as his percentage of success was for kicks just taken to 'have a go'. There is a difference. Williams, in the third and fourth tests and for Auckland against the Lions, was his usual relaxed aggressive self as opposed to the rigid nervous man who had played at Wellington and Christchurch with the burden of all the goal-kicks on his mind. Gleeson himself has admitted that his second test team was deflated by an early, easy penalty miss Williams had made. 'There's always an early penalty in a test match; we had hoped for it,' he said. That miss may have lost New Zealand the test. Thankfully Bevan Wilson, the Otago fullback, was brought in for the Dunedin test match. Williams was able to concentrate again on backline defence and attack, and played so much better, freed from worry.

And talking of fullbacks, here was another area of contention. Colin Farrell was a bad choice for the first two test matches though naturally, I have the advantage of making that statement in hindsight. However it still defeats my search for logic that Farrell was not among six fullbacks named to play the New Zealand Trials, yet was chosen to be All Black fullback a month later. Not plumb crazy, just plumb curious.

Farrell, after two confused tests and playing below his form, had to go after Christchurch, if only to give those men playing ahead of him confidence for the third test match. 'Farrell was clumsy and inarticulate as a fullback and lacking judgment,' said Clem Thomas. 'They must replace him.'

Bevan Wilson was hard to fathom. He played very well in his

Dunedin test debut but essentially in a ball-catching, touch-finding role. And yes, I hear you remind me, he did kick some goals. He conveyed vital confidence by doing only safe things and doing them well. There was great praise for his courage, and he deserved it, for facing high kicks in a first and crucial test match would chill the nerve of many a man. But, as Graeme Crossman, the former All Black, said on television, 'There was a euphoria of relief' — a nice phrase for it — 'about Wilson, and we shouldn't get carried away with him yet.' Quite correct. Wilson at Auckland in the fourth test found things quite different. He missed two handy penalty kicks, which could have been necessary in the final analysis, and did not go quite so surely. His big trials may come with continued selection, with more involvement expected from him as his confidence grows.

Maybe I am being too harsh. After all he completed two tough test matches doing nothing remiss where Colin Farrell had done plenty. Joe Karam, the man the All Blacks still missed this year, said during the tour that 'all the other fourteen players want from a fullback is reliability, catching the ball and finding touch.' And that was Bevan Wilson.

The talk about All Black fullbacks was fascinating, especially before the first and third tests. 'Rowlands?' said the Bay of Plenty people. 'Currie?' said Wellingtonians. 'Cederwall?' said T. P. McLean in the *New Zealand Herald*. 'Lendrum?' said the selectors, Gleeson and Stewart, trooping off to watch him play. 'Whiu?' everybody said, after New Zealand Maoris had played.

Mains, Heffernan, Barrell, Richard Wilson, the list goes on. All received scads of publicity, championed by their local sportswriters and fans. The talk was lively, but one name was not mentioned much. Christopher Louis Fawcett, of Waikato. Remember him? The New Zealand selectors obviously didn't.

Kit Fawcett would have been the ideal choice for New Zealand test fullback in 1977. Why he was overlooked, even from the trials, is beyond me. He remains the most skilful running back with experience of top-line fullback play in New Zealand. He can run, kick for touch and attack, kick goals, pass, tackle, do everything. I admit he made mistakes at fullback on the South African tour, but he missed only two or three kicks for touch all tour. He seemed sacrificed for a missed high pass which Johann Oosthuizen intercepted to run away, like Batty did this year, to score — and win a test. He is confident and outgoing, but those are qualities essential as part of the 'cheek' of an extrovert rugby player.

After he had played well for Waikato, as a centre, I spoke with Kit

Fawcett. 'I'd like to get back in,' he stated, 'but I'd do it differently next time. I enjoyed my time as an All Black and if they want me in a couple of years I'll be here.' It was good stuff, I wanted to record it on film. 'Sorry mate,' said Kit. 'I'm playing it quietly this season, still learning the game. I've learnt a few things.'

Grant Batty was one who agreed that Fawcett could have done the fullback job more than adequately in 1977.

Why, I wonder, was his confident and outgoing personality not understood and encouraged more by the New Zealand selectors? Was Fawcett judged guilty of permanent incompetence by the public and the selectors because of the reports of some critics and because television replayed his South African 'errors' time and again? Fawcett would have fitted admirably into the powerful backline combination that Gleeson called for.

'I've always been a great believer in New Zealand back play ability. We have the greatest backs in the world,' Gleeson said. 'We were convinced that was how we were to beat these Lions. So we selected a side for the third test that was capable of moving the ball to our three-quarters. We didn't panic as some people suggested.'

If it was not panic, the third test selection sure looked like it. Sid Going was dropped, Kevin Eveleigh went, plus four others. It was one of the most perceptive selections, as it proved, of the rugby decade though there were *many* doubters at the time.

Ex-All Black selector, Jack Finlay, summed it up for me nicely during the season. 'I'm absolutely delighted with what Gleeson is trying to do with the team. In the 1950s when a test match was on I could have gone home, gone to bed, put a blanket over my head and stayed there all weekend, and I'd *still* know what kind of dull football they'd be playing. They had fourteen blokes to kick it out and one to throw it in!' Finlay was impressed and so were the public, but only after the third and fourth tests had been won and Gleeson's and the team's firm commitment to move the ball had been put on display.

There were casualties along the way. Batty had been forced into retirement and the selectors had to decide that the indestructible Sid Going was not the halfback to beat the Lions.

In towns north of Auckland it was, of course, the wrong decision; for Going, in those parts, is the toughest, headiest, match-winningest halfback in the world. Gleeson and his selectors again were proved correct. Lyn Davis was obviously a better man at moving the ball, so he came in. It was 'thanks Sid, see you later.' Even the All Blacks' best player (as many thought Going had been in the first two tests) had to make way if he was not the ideal man for the new pattern.

At the dropping of Sid Going the Lions, at Waitangi, reportedly toasted the New Zealand selectors 'for handing us the test series on a plate'. They did not perceive his departure as the key change in a policy to run the ball. They saw it only as panic.

The decision not to play Kevin Eveleigh in the third test brought social divisions in the Feilding area where both he and Jack Gleeson reside. 'Business fell off for a while,' smiled Jack at Dunedin in the afterglow of victory. 'I'm sure they'll be back.'

As a rugby flanker Eveleigh was a demolition expert while his replacement, Graham Mourie, was a construction worker. Eveleigh could cut down runners to perfection, but the play tended to stop at that point. Mourie, on the other hand, not only tackled but tore in and ripped for the ball at breakdowns as well as running off, sometimes devastatingly, the other forwards or the backs.

Eveleigh is certainly not finished with New Zealand rugby. He is too fine a player for that. But again, the pattern called for 'pressure and tackle', not just 'tackle', so Mourie was the better choice.

The key test match for New Zealand was, obviously, the third at Dunedin. To take six risks changing the team and be accused of panic only made the All Black victory all the more startling. In the first test New Zealand had quickly won ascendancy over a British pack that was much weaker than those chosen for the later games. This was converted into 16 points before the Lions realised they were winning no ball, so stayed up flat in the backs to block off the New Zealand back moves. Tane Norton, as captain, read this perfectly and called for more kicking from his five-eighths in the second spell to avoid breakdowns in centre field. It worked. New Zealand won.

In the second test Batty's retirement and Bruce Robertson's withdrawal were critical, while a neck injury to Andy Haden upset the forward rhythm. The Lions played much better and deserved to win. So the series was one-all going into the third at Dunedin.

Here was where the All Blacks played their master card. With the Lions' evident confidence, six new All Blacks and talk of panic by the selectors, Ian Kirkpatrick came forward, making a strong plea for the new men to 'help me through my most important test ever'. He has such standing within the team, the pledge the players fashioned around his plea was of the type that is broken only by death.

Bolstered by the confidence of their coach, lifted by their captain's call for special effort, and charged with 'helping' their most senior player in his 'most important test match ever', this new-look All

Black team charged from the kick-off.

We all remember well what occurred in the next 45 seconds. A line-out, the first of the match. Won quickly for New Zealand by Brian Ford's fast winger's reaction, in forming a maul, the act of a man keen to get involved in his first test match. Freed to Lyn Davis, in only his second test in thirteen years of representative play, his first reaction was to the team's 'move the ball' commitment. Out through Doug Bruce, Bill Osborne it went, to Bruce Robertson who chip-kicked ahead. A melee formed around the bouncing ball and the All Blacks plunged forward for the try. And who came up with the ball! Ian Kirkpatrick himself. Although the end was seventy-nine playing minutes away, the team's co-ordination and spirit had been proved and the try was the seal on the promise they had made to each other, only moments before in the dressing-room, to assist one of their real champions through a personal crisis.

'That Kirky,' said Duncan Robertson late that night, 'he's, he's . . .' and he could not find a word expansive enough to express all that was felt for the big Poverty Bay farmer, who was in his tenth year of wearing the silver fern. The others felt the same. The test, obviously, had not been won with his try alone, and indeed there was a period when the Lions forwards threatened to win, such was *their* dominance — but Kirkpatrick's try, made by the commitment to use the backs, confirmed the New Gleeson Pattern as a winning one.

The series victory, finalised in the fourth test and in dramatic fashion by a late try to Lawrie Knight, proved a personal success story for the team's captain, Tane Norton. He called the shots on the field, changing the tactical pattern, and lifting the players, reminding them of who they were and who they were representing. Norton did all this while not being anywhere near the All Blacks' top player. He did not seem to have the upper arm strength and weight to be a great mauler, did not often feature in running hand-to-hand rushes, and was not noted for dragging men down in crunching tackles. What he did have, in abundance, was pride in becoming All Black captain and determination to lead a victorious team. When the fourth test was done and the narrow victory won, Norton's delight was total. He waved to the crowd at Eden Park and they waved back with equal joy. Moments later he was human enough to express on television the belief that he personally had not played well in the series. A humble winner, a champion.

What reads as a 3-1 margin to New Zealand could have been reversed, had the Lions exploited their forward power more swiftly

and employed more finesse (and Andy Irvine) in their backs.
I do not believe, as some writers have said, that New Zealand
were lucky to win. They deserved the success because they were the
better *team,* but this did not excuse or conceal the obvious short-
comings, some quite alarming, that crept into their game.

The scrum, for instance, absolutely broken by the power of the
Lions. The line-out, where in only one test, and that against second-
rated British jumpers, did the count favour the All Blacks. And goal-
kicking, even with Bevan Wilson in the team, still fell a long way
short of British standards. These areas would have to be worked on
to restore New Zealand's traditional strength. But whereas the forwards were beaten in front-line activities, other facets of play had a
depth of talent where standards are extremely high.

The New Zealand loose forwards were faster, better tacklers and
handlers, and more hard-nosed of intent than their opponents.

Back play reached heights of achievement and promise that had
not been seen for decades. Bruce, Osborne, Taylor and Ford were
strong links in the powerful probing unit, with a whiplash application
to defence. Bruce Robertson confirmed his 1976 form as one of our
great players, the same class as Batty, Williams and Going, the top
New Zealand backs of recent years.

'Robertson is the greatest,' said Batty on his retirement. I agree.

17.
The Series in Review

When one writes the account of a rugby tour, as I have done for the first time this year, some conclusions emerge to add to the observations based on the struggle of the day, the successive provincial opponents, the development of a team identity, or the shaping of its test series adversaries. All of which have been dealt with in preceding chapters.

It had been a spine-tingling winter for rugby-watchers.

The Lions flew away not really understanding how they lost the series, some not believing they had been beaten at all. They left with the same shackles as they had arrived in — short of several key players, deficient in management, sociability and a series-winning tactical plan. Their potential not realised.

The All Blacks thanked their lucky stars — and their selectors. John Stewart's development of attacking back-play had flowered in Jack Gleeson's and Tane Norton's 1977 All Blacks and the spectacle of purposeful, thrusting five-eighths and threequarters was a joy to behold. It won the series.

Television took the matches to New Zealand, Britain, France, South Africa and Australia. Never before had so much consecutive television time been given to the game and flashed simultaneously into so many homes. Every point scored in every match was seen on screen, twenty-six matches and three months of twice-a-week rugby, supplemented in New Zealand by interviews, panels, forecasts, post-mortems and 'top try' competitions. Saturation, some people said. Magnificent, said others.

I spent the winter of 1977 perched in and on exposed rugby grandstands, criss-crossing New Zealand by airway and highway, and alternately inspired, occupied, bored and bone-wearied by it all. I travelled in the amusing and amazing company of other television broadcasters and crews, radio commentators, gentlemen of the press (and 'press' is certainly a wide-ranging word), and the lively ones who sprout cameras from their foreheads.

We fellow-travellers were semi-attached to the team, neither on the outside nor on the real inside. We were more restricted in access to the players, for interviews and for friendship, than with previous touring sides of my experience. Their sociability, whether by edict or group instinct, was substantially reserved for the team and its private occasions.

They adopted a protective screen against uninvited well-wishers — opponents of the day and of yesterday, administrators great and small, past heroes of the rugby field, future and never-to-be All Blacks, touring team supporters — a peculiar affliction these, enthusiasts and addicts (Rugby Anonymous, where are you?), ladies of true and other virtue, bores and bludgers, Anglophiles and benefactors, Old Uncle Tom Jockstrap and all. Thirty-two fishbowls. One could not blame them for self-protection, if it had not become a serious affliction.

It saddened me greatly that during the course of a turbulent, tough and occasionally dirty tour not one player of the hundreds involved earned expulsion from the field of play, as the ultimate punishment for a rugby misdemeanour. If referees are reluctant to dismiss players in top matches, indeed appear to have been instructed not to do so, something must be done to restore their total authority with regard to vicious play, otherwise rugby's image as a noble sport will be tarnished beyond repair.

I work for television, the only medium that can isolate and repeat acts of rough play as they actually happened. I am often accused of a morbid interest in such incidents, of deliberately embarrassing the perpetrators and referees, and of harming the game itself by replaying the worst as well as the best aspects of a match.

My reply is that a match and its highlights especially are news and must be given coverage accordingly.

In addition to recording for posterity, if the year 2077 is interested, the acts of skill, courage and intelligence that are the whipcracks of a match, the television camera is a unique witness to illegal acts. It thus helps, often conclusively, to establish the guilt and innocence of individuals, as well as showing extenuating circumstances.

It is my opinion that acts of violence on New Zealand rugby fields in 1977 merited the expulsion from matches of a number of players. None were. I will look next year for a strengthening of attitude from rugby's top brass towards violence in the game.

With the remainder of the many and varied aspects of refereeing during the winter I, like most New Zealanders, am reasonably satisfied. I felt that John Pring's handling of the tourists' game with the New Zealand Maoris and Dave Millar's display when the Lions played Canterbury, were the two outstanding refereeing performances of the tour. The Canterbury match was hard, clean and exciting and Millar exercised firm control at all times. John Pring, at Auckland, blew a very fair whistle for the Maoris-Lions game and after three fistic confrontations, issued sufficiently stern alarums that thereafter the match was very cleanly fought.

I hold with the view that no side coming on tour in New Zealand should ask for neutral referees. It's not that I think they receive generous treatment from New Zealand referees, but rather that our whistlemen to a large extent go through touring teams' matches with the attitude of 'look at me, I'm bending over backwards to show you I'm being fair'. That in itself is not an indictment of them, rather it is a compliment, and the kind of thing you do not remark upon in referees when you watch the All Blacks in action overseas.

As it turned out line-outs were the one major area where New Zealand interpretation differed greatly from the British approach. At the conclusion of the tour both Burrell and Dawes had strong feelings that what they had seen in New Zealand would require re-appraisal by the International Rugby Board. Said Burrell, 'The line-out causes world-wide concern. It should be a fair contest between two chaps jumping for the ball, two-handed. This, as we've seen in New Zealand and in the rest of the world, is virtually impossible at the moment.'

The British tourists were disappointed with the unsporting crowds at those venues where boos, catcalls and scorn were directed at the Lions, solely because they were in opposition. Of course they invited some of this reaction by overt and illegal acts and by the unpopular image they had developed off the field.

Most of the adverse crowd reaction was undeserved. It stemmed from memories of the 1971 series and the first-ever defeat by Britain, exasperation with the Lions' goal-kicking competence and New Zealand incompetence, and the apparent development of flag-waving rugby nationalism that produced a win-at-all-costs attitude in some spectators.

It also produced some distinctly unpleasant episodes. The hundreds of young men who sang a personalised and insulting song to the tune of 'Campdown Races', at Lancaster Park and Carisbrook mainly, should hang their heads in shame. The only word for the worst expressions of crowd prejudice is 'hooliganism'. It is not supposed to exist in New Zealand rugby.

The fourth test in Auckland in 1977 was a classic example of the high-pitched desire for victory which now pervaded New Zealand rugby. The first twenty minutes of that game were watched in a nail-chewing, nerve-wracking silence by the crowd of nearly 60,000. Most of them were intent, vitally so, on seeing what the signs and portents of the match were going to be. 'Would "we" win and send these arrogant, ill-mannered Poms home with their tails between their legs?' The transformation to total, mind-blowing, whistling, stomping ecstasy, when Lawrie Knight scored his try with just four minutes to go, confirmed my belief in this matter.

There is no doubt that twenty-five matches in New Zealand were far too many for any touring team to have to play. A tour of that length and longer was fine in the 1950s and even the 1960s, in keeping with the 'simpler' life then. Rugby was, to young men in those days, a more important priority than it is in the fast-moving world of the 1970s. Men of the age of the 1977 Lions are the adult products of teenage years where girlfriends and the money to buy a cherished first car were readily available. Affluence and alternative activities make inroads into the lifestyle of the 1950s and 1960s, when rugby was 'King' over all things. The attitude in 1977 is that other pursuits score highly in competition with rugby: things like job, social status and family, weighed heavily on the professional men of the Lions team. Their time is valuable, and three-month tours are too long.

The answer is for the International Rugby Board to consider the players more in the future and the spectators and cash registers less. Shorter tours simply have to happen, or overseas teams will continue to tour with watered-down personnel, as the Lions did, to the detriment of their team strengths, their playing record and the playing honour of their nation. In New Zealand the ideal tour should now be no more than fifteen games, spread over seven weeks. Three test matches and twelve other games.

Combined teams should also be eliminated, as no provincial team with its own status likes to relinquish established team-mates and fit a proportion of 'token' players from an adjacent union, generally less-experienced players, into its established playing patterns.

I suggest the New Zealand Rugby Union should allow teams that finish high up in the divisions of the Radio New Zealand Championship to have, as 'reward', a game against the next season's touring team. The top six teams from Division One could each have their own game, along with the top two sides in both the North and South Island Second Divisions. These latter four would obviously comprise some of the mid-week games; the others could come from the familiar national splinter teams, Maoris, Universities and New Zealand Juniors.

This plan would increase competitiveness in the middle part of the Division One championship table, which is, under the present system, 'safe' from relegation and the downward slide to smaller crowds and lesser gates that go with it. Teams would battle for the championship, but also for the Top Six, to win a prestigious match on their own against a top-class touring team.

For teams that miss out, tough break. That's life. They would have to improve in the next season to earn the big attraction and the big gate that an international match would bring.

Another requirement of provinces which host touring teams should be the assurance that they make every provision to present their showpiece playing-surface with as little damage from previous matches as is possible. In this regard in 1977 the Wairarapa-Bush, Manawatu, Canterbury and Wellington unions are just four which deserve chastisement for playing meaningless curtain-raisers or previous Saturday games on the substandard playing-surface of their grounds.

The weather that so foully swept New Zealand in 1977, churning rugby fields into messy mud heaps, cannot be prevented. But commonsense in keeping grounds ready for the big occasion is not difficult and it should be obligatory. New Zealand rugby grounds came in for a stack of well-founded criticisms in 1977 from British folk, who see their own international venues maintained in the best condition by considerate ground committees. Keeping grounds free of matches for three and four weeks to ensure top shape for top days was a necessity which escaped some New Zealand unions in 1977.

'Our rugby will be just great, in two or three years' time.' So says Jack Finlay, the former All Black selector. He was referring, no doubt, to the style and attitude of the All Blacks as shown by their approach in 1977. The continuation of the development of running backs was steadily replacing the safety-first instincts of New Zealand five-eighths and threequarters. The commitment to safety-first principles had left the backs in a subsidiary role in All Black team patterns in most of the post-war years.

One lesson which was hammered home in the Lions matches this season was that at no time can New Zealand forward play be neglected during the development and exploitation of backline techniques. The loss of power in the New Zealand test scrum against the Lions was alarming, especially as there was 'no answer' except for introducing the three-man scrum as a counter, a move which was more of a gimmick than a solution. The line-out work in the second, third and fourth tests was not good either and clearly front-five standards in New Zealand are at the poorest ebb for years. Frank Oliver and Andy Haden, while showing admirable dedication to ripping into mauls and rucks, simply could not counter the increasing British line-out dominance. Props like Johnstone, McEldowney and Bush were good players but no match for the champion props the Lions produced at scrum time. This was one shock the 1977 Lions hammered into the heart of New Zealand forward play. Future international series will not be won by the All Blacks without improvement in these power areas.

Currently I rate France, as seen on television, number one rugby nation in the world. Then I rate New Zealand, Wales, England, South Africa, Scotland, Australia and Ireland in that order. South Africa does not rate highly for me, as their 3-1 win over New Zealand in 1976 was not convincing, being very much a 'home ground' affair, with powerful influences in their familiar playing conditions and referees. Outside South Africa the Springboks would be diminished.

In terms of rugby the 1977 Lions tour was not an overly enjoyable one to cover, but then neither was the All Black tour of South Africa in 1976. In South Africa the touring players were feted like kings, but had to weigh that enjoyment against being in such a troubled country.

The Lions, on the other hand, missed one of the greatest satisfactions of a rugby touring side, that of making friends.

So they flew away, first from Auckland and then from Suva — the good, the bad and the battlers. They had an enviable unity, they possessed remarkable strengths and skills, they filled the grim New Zealand winter with spectacle and excitement, their potential flowered vigorously, and then they faded and were out-thought in the final days.

Postscript
The 1977 British Lions played a match together on their return home to Great Britain. They beat the Barbarians Club by 23 points to 14 in a match played at Twickenham on 10 September 1977. For the Lions tries were scored by Peter Squires, Andy Irvine and Gareth Evans. Phil Bennett kicked 2 penalties and a conversion. Irvine kicked a penalty goal.

For the Barbarians Club tries were scored by J. P. R. Williams, Ray Gravell and David McKay. Gerald Davies kicked 1 conversion.

The Lions team was: Irvine; Squires (replaced by Rees), McGeechan, Fenwick, Gareth Evans; Bennett (captain), Morgan; Duggan; Neary, Brown, Beaumont, Quinnell; Price, Wheeler, Cotton.

A capacity crowd of 60,000 saw the Lions in adventurous mood, their backs playing well for once, but the forwards were held at scrum and line-out by an experienced Barbarians pack. The Barbarians team was made up entirely of players who had not made the touring team. They had additional support from the three French loose forwards Jean-Claude Skrela, Jean-Pierre Bastiat and Jean-Pierre Rives.

18.
Records and Statistics

Note: The 1977 tour of the British Isles team concluded with a match against Fiji. This has been included in two tables: Match Record and Appearances on Tour. All of the other tables exclude Fiji. The match against Fiji has not been listed as a test match.

MATCH RECORD

1.	v.	Wairarapa-Bush	at Memorial Park, Masterton	won 41-13
2.	v.	Hawkes Bay	at McLean Park, Napier	won 13-11
3.	v.	Poverty Bay-East Coast	at Rugby Park, Gisborne	won 25-6
4.	v.	Taranaki	at Rugby Park, New Plymouth	won 21-13
5.	v.	King Country-Wanganui	at The Domain, Taumarunui	won 60-9
6.	v.	Manawatu-Horowhenua	at Showgrounds Oval, Palmerston North	won 18-12
7.	v.	Otago	at Carisbrook, Dunedin	won 12-7
8.	v.	Southland	at Rugby Park, Invercargill	won 20-12
9.	v.	New Zealand Universities	at Lancaster Park Oval, Christchurch	lost 9-21
10.	v.	NEW ZEALAND (FIRST TEST)	at Athletic Park, Wellington	lost 12-16
11.	v.	South Canterbury-Mid Canterbury-North Otago	at Fraser Park, Timaru	won 45-6
12.	v.	Canterbury	at Lancaster Park Oval, Christchurch	won 14-13
13.	v.	West Coast-Buller	at Victoria Square, Westport	won 45-0
14.	v.	Wellington	at Athletic Park, Wellington	won 13-6
15.	v.	Marlborough-Nelson Bays	at Lansdowne Park, Blenheim	won 40-23
16.	v.	NEW ZEALAND (SECOND TEST)	at Lancaster Park Oval, Christchurch	won 13-9
17.	v.	New Zealand Maoris	at Eden Park, Auckland	won 22-19
18.	v.	Waikato	at Rugby Park, Hamilton	won 18-13
19.	v.	New Zealand Juniors	at Athletic Park, Wellington	won 19-9
20.	v.	Auckland	at Eden Park, Auckland	won 34-15
21.	v.	NEW ZEALAND (THIRD TEST)	at Carisbrook, Dunedin	lost 7-19
22.	v.	Counties-Thames Valley	at The Pukekohe Stadium, Pukekohe	won 35-10
23.	v.	North Auckland	at Okara Park, Whangarei	won 18-7
24.	v.	Bay of Plenty	at Rotorua International Stadium	won 23-15
25.	v.	NEW ZEALAND (FOURTH TEST)	at Eden Park, Auckland	lost 9-10
26.	v.	Fiji	at Buckhurst Park, Suva	lost 21-25

Record: Played 26, won 21, lost 5, for 607, against 320.

SCORING:

	Tries	Convs.	Pens.	Drop Goals	Total
British Isles	83	43	63	0	607
Opposition teams	34	14	46	6	320

SCORING IN THE TEST MATCHES

	Tries	Convs.	Pens.	Drop Goals	Total
British Isles	3	1	9	0	41
New Zealand	6	3	7	1	54

TEAM INFORMATION

Position	Club and Country	Age	Height	Weight	Occupation
Fullbacks:					
Andy Irvine	Heriot's F.P. and Scotland	25	5.10	12. 8	Chartered Surveyor
Bruce Hay	Boroughmuir and Scotland	27	5.10	13. 5	Electrician
Wingers:					
Peter Squires	Harrogate and England	25	5. 9	11. 9	Schoolmaster
John J. Williams	Llanelli and Wales	29	5. 9	11. 7	Marketing Manager
*Elgan Rees	Neath	23	5. 8	12. 7	Schoolmaster
Gareth Evans	Newport and Wales	23	5.11	13.11	Banking Representative
Centres:					
Steve Fenwick	Bridgend and Wales	25	5.10	13. 2	Schoolmaster
David Burcher	Newport and Wales	25	5.10	13. 5	Schoolmaster
Mike Gibson	North of Ireland and Ireland	34	5.10	12. 7	Solicitor
Ian McGeechan	Headingly and Scotland	30	5. 9	11. 3	Schoolmaster
Fly-halves:					
Phil Bennett	Llanelli and Wales	28	5. 7	11. 4	Sales Representative
John Bevan	Aberavon and Wales	29	5. 8	12. 8	Schoolmaster
Halfbacks:					
Douglas Morgan	Stewarts-Melville and Scotland	30	5. 9	11.10	Chiropodist
*Brynmor Williams	Cardiff	25	5.9½	12. 7	Schoolmaster
*Alun Lewis	London Scottish	23	5.10	13. 0	Schoolmaster
Number 8 forwards:					
Willie Duggan	Blackrock College and Ireland	27	6.3½	15.12	Electrical Contractor
Derek Quinnell	Llanelli and Wales	28	6.3½	16. 7	Sales Representative

Flankers:

Name	Club and country				Occupation
Tony Neary	Broughton Park and England	28	6. 1	14. 7	Lawyer
Trevor Evans	Swansea and Wales	29	6. 1	14. 4	Real Estate Agent
Terry Cobner	Pontypool and Wales	30	6. 0	14. 4	Schoolmaster
Jeff Squire	Newport and Wales	25	6. 3	15. 7	Schoolmaster

Locks:

Name	Club and country				Occupation
Gordon Brown	West of Scotland and Scotland	29	6. 5	16.12	Building Society Manager
Allan Martin	Aberavon and Wales	28	6. 5	16. 8	Schoolmaster
Nigel Horton	Moseley and England	29	6. 5	16. 8	Policeman
Moss Keane	Lansdowne and Ireland	28	6.4½	16.13	Agricultural Inspector
Bill Beaumont	Fylde and England	25	6.3½	16. 4	Textile Salesman

Props:

Name	Club and country				Occupation
Phil Orr	Old Wesley and Ireland	26	5.11	15. 7	Clothing Manufacturer
Clive Williams	Aberavon and Wales	28	6. 0	15. 8	Plasterer
Graham Price	Pontypool and Wales	25	6. 0	15. 4	Student
Fran Cotton	Sale and England	29	6. 2	16. 7	Schoolmaster
Charlie Faulkner	Pontypool and Wales	33	6. 0	15. 8	Steelworker

Hookers:

Name	Club and country				Occupation
Bobby Windsor	Pontypool and Wales	28	5. 9	14. 9	Steelworker
Peter Wheeler	Leicester and England	28	5.11	14. 0	Insurance Broker

*An uncapped International player before the tour.

Of the original team Roger Uttley (Gosforth and England) and Geoff Wheel (Swansea and Wales) were unable to tour, being replaced by Jeff Squire and Moss Keane.

Once on tour three replacements needed to be made. Bill Beaumont replaced Nigel Horton; Charlie Faulkner replaced Clive Williams and Alun Lewis replaced Brynmor Williams.

British Isles: Appearances on tour	Wair-Bush	Hawkes Bay	Pov.Bay-E.C.	Taranaki	Wang.-K.C.	Mana-Horo	Otago	Southland	NZ Unis	FIRST TEST	S.C-M.C-N.Otago	Canterbury
	1	2	3	4	5	6	7	8	9	10	11	12
Irvine	R	1	R	1	1	—	1	R	—	1	1	1
Hay	1*	—	1*	—	—	1	—	1*	1	—	—	—
J. J. Williams	W	W	—	W	W	—	W	—	—	W	W	W
Rees	—	—	—	—	—	—	W	W	W	—	W	—
Squires	W	—	W	—	W	W	—	—	W	W	—	—
Gareth Evans	—	W	W	W	R	W	—	W	—	—	C	W
McGeechan	C	—	C	—	C*	—	—	C	C	C	FH	—
Gibson	—	C	C	—	—	—	C	C	—	—	C	—
Burcher	C	—	—	C	—	C	C	—	C	—	—	C
Fenwick	—	C	—	C	C	C	—	—	—	C	—	C
Bennett	FH	—	—	FH	FH	—	FH	FH	—	FH	—	—
Bevan	—	FH	FH	—	—	FH	—	—	FH	—	—	FH
Morgan	—	½	½	—	½*	—	—	—	½	—	½	½
Bryn. Williams	½	—	—	½	R	½	½	½	—	½	—	—
Lewis	—	—	—	—	—	—	—	—	—	—	—	—
Duggan	R	8	8	—	—	8	8	8	—	8	—	8
Quinnell	8	F	—	8	8	R	—	—	8	—	8	—
Trevor Evans	F	—	F	F	—	—	F	F	—	F	—	F*
Cobner	F	—	—	F	—	F*	—	—	—	F	F	F
Neary	—	F	F	—	F	—	—	—	F	—	F	—
Squire	—	—	—	—	F	F	F	F	F	—	—	R
Brown	—	L	—	L	—	—	—	L	L*	—	—	L
Beaumont	—	—	—	—	—	—	—	—	—	—	L	—
Martin	—	L	L	—	L	—	L	L	R	L	L	L
Keane	L	—	L	—	L	L	R	—	L*	L	—	—
Horton	L*	—	—	L	—	L	L*	—	—	—	—	—
Orr	P	—	—	P	P	—	—	P	R	P	—	—
Cotton	—	P	P	—	P	—	P	—	P	—	P	P
Clive Williams	—	P	P	—	—	· P	—	—	P	—	P	—
Faulkner	—	—	—	—	—	—	—	—	—	—	—	—
Price	P	—	—	P	—	P	P	P	—	P	—	—
Wheeler	H	—	—	H	H	—	H	—	H	—	H	—
Windsor	—	H	H	—	—	H	—	H	—	H	—	H

Key: 1-fullback. W-Winger. C-Centre. FH-Fly-half. ½-Halfback.
8-Number 8 forward. F-Flanker. L-Lock. P-Prop. H-Hooker.
*-Retired hurt. R-Replacement during a match.

W.C.-Buller	Wellington	Marlb-Nelson	SECOND TEST	NZ Maoris	Waikato	NZ Juniors	Auckland	THIRD TEST	Counties-TV	Nth Auckland	Bay of Plenty	FOURTH TEST	Fiji	Total
13	14	15	16	17	18	19	20	21	22	23	24	25	26	
—	1	—	1	—	1	—	1	1	—	1	R	1	1	19
1	—	1	—	1	—	1	—	—	1	—	1*	—	—	11
—	W	—	W	W	—	R	W	W*	—	—	—	—	—	14
W	—	W	—	—	W	W	—	—	W	W	W	W	—	12
W	—	W	—	W	—	—	—	—	—	—	—	—	—	9
—	W	—	W	—	W	W	W	W	W	W	—	W	W	18
—	C	—	C	—	C	C	—	R	—	C	R	C	C	16
C	—	C	—	C	—	C*	—	—	C	—	C*	—	—	11
C	—	C	—	C	C	—	C	C	C	—	C	—	C	15
—	C	—	C	—	—	—	C	C	—	C	—	C	—	12
—	FH	—	FH	—	FH	—	FH	FH	—	FH	W	FH	W	15
FH	—	FH	—	FH	—	FH	—	—	FH	—	FH	—	FH	12
½	—	½*	—	½	R	½	½	R	½	—	—	½	—	15
—	½	R	½	½	½*	—	—	½*	—	—	—	—	—	12
—	—	—	—	—	—	—	—	—	—	½	½	—	½	3
—	—	—	8	8*	—	—	8	8	—	8	8	8	—	15
—	8	F	F	—	8	—	F	F	—	F	—	—	—	14
F	—	F	—	F	—	F	—	—	F	—	F	—	F*	14
—	F	—	F	—	F	—	—	F	—	F*	—	—	—	11
F	F	—	—	F	—	F	F	—	F	R	—	F	F	14
8	—	8	—	R	F	8	—	—	8	—	F	F	8	15
—	L	L	L	—	L	—	L	L	—	L	L	L	R	15
L	—	L	L	—	L	—	L	L	—	L	—	L	L	10
—	L	—	—	L	—	L	—	—	L	—	—	—	L	14
L	—	—	—	L	—	L	—	—	L	—	L	—	—	12
—	—	—	—	—	—	—	—	—	—	—	—	—	—	4
—	—	R	—	P	R	P	—	—	—	P	—	—	—	12
P	P	—	P	P*	—	P	P	P	—	P	—	P	—	16
P	—	P	—	R	P*	—	—	—	—	—	—	—	—	9
—	—	—	—	—	—	—	—	—	P	—	P	—	P	3
—	P	P*	P	—	—	—	P	P	P	—	P	P	P	15
—	H	—	H	—	H	—	H	H	—	H	—	H	—	13
H	—	H	—	H	P	H	—	—	H	—	H	—	H	14

NEW ZEALAND:
APPEARANCES IN THE TESTS v. BRITISH ISLES 1977

	First	Second	Third	Fourth	Series Total	All Tests for N.Z.	All games for N.Z.
C. P. Farrell	1	1	—	—	2	2	2
B. W. Wilson	—	—	1	1	2	2	2
B. G. Williams	W	W	W	W	4	30	90
G. B. Batty	W	—	—	—	1	15	56
N. M. Taylor	—	W	—	R	2	2	7
B. R. Ford	—	—	W	W*	2	2	2
B. J. Robertson	C	—	C	C	3	18	60
W. M. Osborne	2⅝	C	2⅝	2⅝	4	7	19
J. L. Jaffray	—	2⅝	—	—	1	5	15
D. J. Robertson	1⅝	—	—	—	1	9	30
O. D. Bruce	—	1⅝	1⅝	1⅝	3	6	24
S. M. Going	½	½	—	—	2	29	86
L. J. Davis	—	—	½	½	2	3	16
L. G. Knight	8	8	8	8	4	4	27
I. A. Kirkpatrick	F	F	F	F	4	39	113
K. Eveleigh	F	F	—	—	2	4	25
G. N. K. Mourie	—	—	F	F	2	2	10
A. M. Haden	L	L	L	L	4	4	30
F. J. Oliver	L	L	L	L	4	5	18
B. R. Johnstone	P	P	—	—	2	3	10
W. K. Bush	—	P	P	R	3	9	28
K. K. Lambert	P	—	—	P	2	11	40
J. T. McEldowney	—	—	P	P*	2	2	8
R. W. Norton	H	H	H	H	4	27	61

BRITISH ISLES:
MOST TEST APPEARANCES IN ALL TOURS 1924-77

W. J. McBride (1962-66-68-71-74)	17
R. E. G. Jeeps (1955-59-62)	13
C. M. H. Gibson (1966-68-71-74-77)	12
G. O. Edwards (1968-71-74)	10
A. J. F. O'Reilly (1955-59)	10
R. H. Williams (1955-59)	10
S. Millar (1959-62-68)	9
D. I. E. Bebb (1962-66)	8
P. Bennett (1974-77)	8
G. L. Brown (1971-74-77)	8
M. J. Campbell-Lamerton (1962-66)	8
T. M. Davies (1971-74)	8
I. R. McGeechan (1974-77)	8
J. McLauchlan (1971-74)	8
B. V. Meredith (1955-59-62)	8
A. E. I. Pask (1962-66)	8
J. W. Telfer (1966-68)	8
J. P. R. Williams (1971-74)	8

N.B. It is widely accepted that British Isles tours, with selection representation from the Four Home Unions, date from the 1924 tour of South Africa.

NEW ZEALAND:
INDIVIDUAL SCORING: TEST MATCHES

	Tries	Convs	Pens	DG	Total
B. Wilson	—	1	4	—	14
B. Williams	—	2	3	—	13
G. Batty	1	—	—	—	4
S. Going	1	—	—	—	4
B. Johnstone	1	—	—	—	4
I. Kirkpatrick	1	—	—	—	4
A. Haden	1	—	—	—	4
L. Knight	1	—	—	—	4
B. Robertson	—	—	—	1	3
Totals	6	3	7	1	54

BRITISH ISLES:
INDIVIDUAL SCORING: TEST MATCHES

	Tries	Convs	Pens	DG	Total
P. Bennett	—	—	6	—	18
D. Morgan	1	1	1	—	9
A. Irvine	—	—	2	—	6
J. J. Williams	1	—	—	—	4
W. Duggan	1	—	—	—	4
Totals	3	1	9	—	41

BRITISH ISLES:
MOST POINTS IN NEW ZEALAND 1930-77

B. John	1971	180
P. Bennett	1977	112
R. Hiller	1971	102
D. W. Morgan	1977	98
A. R. Irvine	1977	87
M. C. Thomas	1950	73
T. J. Davies	1959	72
B. H. Black	1930	65
D. Hewitt	1959	65
B. Lewis-Jones	1950	63
S. Wilson	1966	62

BRITISH ISLES:
MOST TRIES IN ONE MATCH IN NEW ZEALAND

D. J. Duckham v. West Coast-Buller	1971	6 tries
A. R. Irvine v. King Country-Wanganui	1977	5 tries
J. C. Bevan v. Waikato	1971	4 tries
J. C. Bevan v. Manawatu-Horowhenua	1971	4 tries
T. G. R. Davies v. Hawkes Bay	1971	4 tries
D. Hewitt v. Hawkes Bay	1959	4 tries
P. Jackson v. West Coast-Buller	1959	4 tries
P. Jackson v. Nelson-Marlb.-Golden Bay	1959	4 tries
J. R. C. Young v. West Coast-Buller	1959	4 tries

N.B. The record number of tries in one match for the British Lions in any tour match is 6 shared by Duckham (see above) and J. J. Williams who also scored 6 for the Lions against South West Districts in Mossel Bay, South Africa 1974.

BRITISH ISLES:
MOST POINTS IN ONE MATCH IN NEW ZEALAND

A. R. Irvine v. King Country-Wanganui 1977   Points
(1 try, 6 convs., 3 pens.) 25
M. C. Thomas v. Nelson-Marlb.-Golden Bay-Mout. 1959
(8 convs., 3 pens.) 25
T. J. Davies v. North Auckland 1959 (4 convs. 5 pens.) 23
D. Hewitt v. Hawkes Bay 1959 (4 tries, 3 convs., 1 pen.) 21
M. C. Thomas v. Nelson-Marlb.-Golden Bay-Mout. (1950)
(1 try, 6 pens.) 21
D. W. Morgan v. West Coast-Buller 1977
(1 try, 4 convs., 3 pens.) 21
B. John v. New Zealand Universities 1971
(1 try, 3 convs., 3 pens., 1 d.goal) 21
A. R. Irvine v. King Country-Wanganui 1977 (5 tries) 20
D. Hewitt v. Hawkes Bay 1959 (2 tries, 4 convs., 2 pens.) 20
P. Bennett v. King Country-Wanganui (1 try, 8 convs.) 20
B. John v. New Zealand Maoris 1971 (1 convs., 6 pens.) 20

BRITISH ISLES:
INDIVIDUAL SCORING: ALL TOUR MATCHES

	Tries	Convs	Pens	DG	Total
P. Bennett (1st, 2nd, 3rd, 4th)	3	16	27	—	125
D. Morgan (3, 4)	3	16	18	—	98
A. Irvine (1, 2, 3, 4)	11	8	9	—	87
J. J. Williams (1, 2, 3)	10	—	—	—	40
E. Rees (4)	8	—	—	—	32
M. Gibson	2	2	4	—	24
G. Evans (2, 3, 4)	6	—	—	—	24
P. Squires (1)	5	—	—	—	20
B. Hay	5	—	—	—	20
D. Burcher (3)	5	—	—	—	20
S. Fenwick (1, 2, 3, 4)	1	1	3	—	15
I. McGeechan (1, 2, 3, 4)	3	—	—	—	12
B. Williams (1, 2, 3)	3	—	—	—	12
J. Squire (4)	3	—	—	—	12
T. Cobner (1, 2, 3)	3	—	—	—	12
W. Duggan (1, 2, 3, 4)	2	—	—	—	8
D. Quinnell (2, 3)	2	—	—	—	8
W. Beaumont (2, 3, 4)	2	—	—	—	8
A. Martin (1)	—	—	2	—	6
J. Bevan	1	—	—	—	4
G. Brown (2, 3, 4)	1	—	—	—	4
P. Orr (1)	1	—	—	—	4
C. Williams	1	—	—	—	4
P. Wheeler (2, 3, 4)	1	—	—	—	4
R. Windsor (1)	1	—	—	—	4
Lions total	83	43	63	—	607
Opposition teams scored	34	14	46	6	320

The following players did not score on tour: T. Evans (1); A. Neary (4); N. Horton, M. Keane (1); F. Cotton (2, 3, 4); G. Price (1, 2, 3, 4); C. Faulkner, A. Lewis.

The figures in parenthesis following a player's name represent the actual tests played on tour by that player.

CAPTAINCY
Phil Bennett led the team in each of his 15 tour appearances. In his absence Trevor Evans (in 4 matches); Terry Cobner (3); Ian McGeechan (2); Fran Cotton (1); and Tony Neary (1) were the captains.

NEW ZEALAND:
TEST MATCH RESERVES 1977

	First	Second	Third	Fourth
N. M. Taylor	x	—	x	x*
T. M. Twigden	—	x	—	—
O. D. Bruce	x	—	—	—
D. J. Robertson	—	x	x	x
L. J. Davis	x	x	—	—
M. W. Donaldson	—	—	x	x
P. H. Sloane	x	x	x	x
G. A. Seear	x	x	x	x
W. K. Bush	x	—	—	x*
B. R. Johnstone	—	—	x	—
J. McEldowney	—	x	—	—

*Required to go on field of play as replacement.

BRITISH ISLES:
TEST MATCH RESERVES 1977

	First	Second	Third	Fourth
B. H. Hay	x	x	x	—
G. L. Evans	x	—	—	—
D. W. Morgan	x	x	x*	—
F. E. Cotton	x	—	—	—
P. J. Wheeler	x	—	—	—
D. Quinnell	x	—	—	—
P. J. Squires	—	x	—	—
P. Orr	—	x	x	x
R. W. Windsor	—	x	x	x
J. Squire	—	x	x	—
I. R. McGeechan	—	—	x*	—
D. H. Burcher	—	—	—	x
A. R. Lewis	—	—	—	x
J. D. Bevan	—	—	—	x
T. P. Evans	—	—	—	x

*Required to go on field of play as replacement.